FOR THE SAKE OF THE WORLD

FOR THE SAKE OF THE WORLD

Karl Barth and the Future of Ecclesial Theology

Edited by

George Hunsinger

WILLIAM B. EERDMANS PUBLISHING COMPANY
GRAND RAPIDS, MICHIGAN / CAMBRIDGE, U.K.

Wm. B. Eerdmans Publishing Co.
255 Jefferson Ave. S.E., Grand Rapids, Michigan 49503 /
P.O. Box 163, Cambridge CB3 9PU U.K.

Printed in the United States of America

09 08 07 06 05 04   7 6 5 4 3 2 1

Library of Congress Cataloging-in-Publication Data

For the sake of the world: Karl Barth and the future of ecclesial theology /
    edited by George Hunsinger.
            p.   cm.
    Includes bibliographical references.
    ISBN 0-8028-2699-7 (pbk.: alk. paper)
        1. Barth, Karl, 1886-1968 — Congresses.   I. Hunsinger, George.

    BX4827.B3F67   2004
    230'.044'092— dc22

                                                    2004044121

www.eerdmans.com

Contents

CONTENTS

Introduction

GEORGE HUNSINGER

In June 1999 a standing-room-only crowd turned out for a conference that kicked off the new Center for Barth Studies at Princeton Theological Seminary. Its theme — "For the Sake of the World: Karl Barth and the Future of Ecclesial Theology" — attracted participants from across the United States as well as from the United Kingdom, Canada, Europe, and Korea. Forty percent were pastors and 10 percent were laypeople, with students and professors making up the rest. Among the events were a reception at the Center of Theological Inquiry, a worship service led by Dr. William Sloane Coffin, Jr., and a banquet whose program featured Mozart string quartets along with Prof. John Godsey's reminiscences of Barth as a teacher. This volume contains the conference papers.

The Barth/Brunner Correspondence

The first presenter was John W. Hart. Currently serving as a Presbyterian minister, he summarized his doctoral dissertation at Oxford University on the Barth/Brunner correspondence.[1] This important exchange, spanning four decades, has recently appeared in the Karl Barth *Gesamtausgabe* (the

---

1. See now John W. Hart, *Karl Barth vs. Emil Brunner: The Formation and Dissolution of a Theological Alliance, 1916-1936* (New York: Peter Lang, 2001).

1

posthumous series of Barth's complete works).[2] It is hoped that an English translation will appear in the not too distant future.

Barth published his famous No to Brunner in 1934. Less well known is that a rift had been brewing between them for nearly twenty years. Although commonly linked in people's minds, the two had serious disputes that would prove to be long-lived. An attempted reconciliation in 1960 did not work out.[3] As Brunner lay dying in 1966, Barth was moved to communicate through a mutual friend. "If he is still alive and it is possible, tell him again, 'Commended to *our* God,' even by me. And tell him, *Yes,* that the time when I thought that I had to say 'No' to him is now long past, since we all live only by virtue of the fact that a great and merciful God says his gracious Yes to all of us." These were the last words Brunner heard before he died.[4]

Hart brings out the background to the controversy, beginning with letters from 1916. This initial exchange affords, among other things, a rare glimpse into Barth's understanding of pastoral care. The empathy offered to Brunner, who had confessed feelings of spiritual inadequacy, was drawn directly from the Reformation, being God-oriented rather than self-referential. Later on, as a Word of God theologian, Barth found it impossible to agree with his friend on theological method. As early as 1925 (i.e., well before 1934), Brunner was already searching for a neutral "point of contact," while in principle Barth rejected any such possibility. Eventually Barth would come to see that the only meaningful "point of contact" was the incarnation of the Word of God. By the operation of grace in our lives, Barth would argue, not through the exercise of any neutral human capacity, we are drawn, through faith, into union with Christ. Only in this way — by union with Christ on the basis of his incarnate "point of contact" with us — are we given a share in the truth of God's own self-knowledge. The same focus on Christ alone, by grace alone, through faith alone, also prevented Barth from embracing Brunner's idea of a systematically prior apologetics (or "eristics"). By contrast, Barth's approach to apologetics was a posteriori and ad hoc. Behind the scenes Brunner persistently sought to change Barth's mind on these matters — to no avail. When in 1934 Brun-

2. *Karl Barth–Emil Brunner Briefwechsel, 1916-1966,* ed. Eberhard Busch, Karl Barth Gesamtausgabe 33 (Zürich: Theologischer Verlag, 2000).

3. Eberhard Busch, *Karl Barth: His Life from Letters and Autobiographical Texts* (Philadelphia: Fortress, 1976), p. 449.

4. Busch, *Karl Barth,* pp. 476-77.

ner finally threw down the gauntlet in public, an exasperated Barth responded with anger and dismay.

Daniel L. Migliore of Princeton Seminary, as Hart's respondent, introduces some important distinctions. Although Barth saw God as other than the world, Migliore observes, he also saw God as intimately related to it. How clear was Barth in the 1920s, however, and with Brunner in particular, that the ontological otherness of God must not be separated from his worldly immanence? Moreover, Migliore cautions, it would be best not to draw too sharp a contrast between "dialectic" and "dialogue." For just as Barth's dialectic is dialogical in its own way, so Brunner's emphasis on dialogue is also dialectical. Yet another question concerns the way Brunner related philosophy to theology according to a law/gospel pattern. The former supposedly establishes a foundation that can be built upon by the latter. The early Barth, by contrast, already seems on the way to a "nonfoundationalist" reversal of this idea. For him, doesn't a gospel/law pattern already implicitly govern theology's relation to philosophy? Migliore concludes by suggesting that differing views of the Holy Spirit led the two theologians to differing ecclesiologies.

Barth on Christian/Jewish Solidarity

After the immeasurable horrors of the Holocaust and the emergence of the modern Israeli state, Christians have begun to confront, belatedly, the disturbing legacy of anti-Semitism in the church. For Christian theology the discussion has focused in particular on the question of "supersessionism" — a term at once descriptive and pejorative. Any theology that sees the church's relationship to the Jews as "supersessionist" is tainted by the implication of anti-Semitism and its terrible consequences. "Antisupersessionism" is thus widely affirmed as indispensable to Christian repentance. It is not without relevance, however, that different meanings can attach to the term.

Supersessionism is the idea that Israel has been replaced as God's people by the church. By rejecting Jesus as the Messiah, Israel allegedly forfeited its divine election. Along with certain corollaries (e.g., that the old covenant is nullified by the new), this notion has played a tragic role in the church's historic persecution of Jews.

Though Barth is sometimes accused of being supersessionist, he is clearly not so in this sense. His repudiation of the belief that Israel has for-feited its election could not be stronger. Nor does he subscribe to the be-lief, still more virulent, that God has disavowed Israel in order to punish it for (supposedly) crucifying Christ. Barth is as responsible as anyone in re-cent theology for recovering the normative apostolic teaching that God has not rejected his people, that God's gifts and promises are irrevocable, and that all Israel will be saved (Rom. 11:1-2, 26, 29).

To understand why some have seen Barth as wanting, a distinction needs to be made between divine election and human faithfulness within the covenant. One alternative to supersessionism, popular in academic cir-cles, is the idea that divine election takes place on two different tracks, one for Christians, the other for Jews. If Jews have perhaps been unfaithful to the covenant in one way, Christians will have been so in another. Since di-vine faithfulness overrides all human disobedience (Rom. 3:3-7), the elec-tion of the Jews is ultimately assured, as is the subsequent extension of election to the Gentile church. Because both are covenant partners of the one electing God, neither can be more or less legitimate than the other. Anyone rejecting the idea of two parallel covenants, or of one covenant on two tracks with two different peoples of God, is thought to be super-sessionist.

As Eberhard Busch shows in his essay, Barth rejects the two-track view. He simply cannot make it square with the New Testament. In partic-ular he cannot make it square with Romans 9–11, which he expounds, and Busch summarizes, at length. According to the New Testament, as Barth sees it, the rightful heirs of the covenant (i.e., those who participate in its fulfillment) are to be found in the particular community of Gentiles *and* Jews who have accepted Jesus as the Messiah. From a Christian point of view, the Jewish community that rejects Jesus as the Messiah cannot be re-garded, in the strict and proper sense, as the covenant's rightful heirs (which is not the same as saying that they cease to be heirs at all). Paul de-scribes himself as living with great "sorrow" (λύπη) and unceasing "an-guish" (ὀδύνη) in his heart (Rom. 9:2) because of this rejection. (Paul's sense of anguish, by the way, would seem to be as conspicuously absent in contemporary "antisupersessionism" as in Barth, not to mention the larger history of the church.)

Paul does not validate the rejection of Jesus by the Jews. Nor does he see it as invalidating their election. He sees it as serving God's purposes in spite of itself. It brings down a divine judgment that ultimately serves the divine mercy — first for Gentiles, but finally also for the Jews themselves. If divine election and human covenant faithfulness are two very different things, and if in various ways Jesus is logically indispensable to both, then one can indeed reject supersessionism as pernicious while still believing that the only rightful heirs of the covenant (in the strict and proper sense) are those who accept Jesus as the Messiah, and as the world's Lord and Savior. This is Barth's position, as it is arguably that of the New Testament, when canonically read.

The unavoidable dispute between Christians and Jews — which would be irresolvable *either way* without a drastic reframing of identity by one side or the other — can therefore not be narrowed (as many "antisupersessionists" suppose) only to the question of whether Jesus is accepted as the promised Messiah. It also includes the vexed question of which community is, strictly speaking, the rightful heir of the covenant.

The question of "rightful inheritance" would seem to be a fairer, and more precise, way of framing the issue than resorting to a loaded term like "supersessionism." In other words, each community can claim "rightful-inheritance status" for itself, and dispute the other's claim to it, without recourse to derogatory terms. The Christian community of Gentiles and Jews that accepts Jesus as the Messiah does not "supersede" the Jewish community that does not. But it does offer the proper human response to the ultimate fulfillment of the covenant as divinely appointed in Jesus (despite various forms of faithlessness, like anti-Semitism, by which the Christian community disfigures itself). The community that fails to accept Jesus as the Messiah does not lose its election (as in "supersessionism"), but by definition it does exclude itself here and now — however provisionally — from *participating*, by Word and sacrament, in the divinely appointed fulfillment.

Because the resulting disorder would seem to be irresolvable from the human side (especially after centuries of anti-Semitism), though not from the divine, the community that already participates in the covenantal fulfillment does not *replace*, but actually *anticipates* the full inclusion of that segment of the *one* covenantal community which, for the time being, has excluded itself. According to the testimony of Romans 9–11, the participating segment stands in *a real yet still painfully imperfect unity* with that portion of the elect people of God that does not yet include itself in the covenant's fulfillment. To this complex eschatological situation, a term like "supersessionism" is irrelevant.

5

Since Christians need not, and ought not, doubt the abiding election of the Jews, eradicating the persistence of "supersessionism" in the church — as urgent as that is — actually touches neither of the two questions that remain: "messiahship" and "participation." Disavowing supersessionism, however, does make possible, as Busch rightly points out, Barth's view that Christians stand with Jews in an indissoluble solidarity. Indeed, one might wonder whether the term "solidarity" is strong enough, since the bond between the church and Israel that Paul posits in Romans 9–11 is profoundly covenantal. In any case, Busch shows that Barth not only taught this solidarity but also lived it out — not least when it really counted, during the Nazi reign of terror.[5]

Busch does not suppose that Barth never said anything regrettable about the Jews. At the same time, he does reject the criticism that Barth's typology of Israel and the church is overly schematic. One might at least ask, however (as Busch does not), whether Barth's typology is sufficiently *dialectical,* whether its inner logic (apart from Busch's ingenious reconstruction) is sufficiently *clear,* and whether Barth's use of it is suitably *flexible.*

Barth, on exegetical grounds, constructs two "types" — one representing the judgment that accompanies grace, while the other represents the grace that obtains in judgment. Whereas for Barth "Israel" names the first type ("no grace without judgment"), "the church" designates the second ("no judgment without grace"). Arguably, however, Barth becomes insufficiently dialectical whenever his typology flattens out into a simple contrast between "judgment" (Israel) and "grace" (the church). Moreover, why the first type (*judgment* in grace) should not sometimes apply to the church at least as properly as the second type might apply to the (elect) Jewish people (*grace* in judgment) never seems adequately explained.

Emendations would still be possible, perhaps, within the logic of Barth's position as Busch sets it forth.[6] In any case, the dialectic in this typology is not "supersessionist," especially if Busch is right that it applies primarily to Gentiles and Jews *within* the Christian community. Busch concedes that he is trying to understand Barth better than he understood

---

5. See also Eberhard Busch, *Unter dem Bogen des einen Bundes: Karl Barth und die Juden, 1933-1945* (Neukirchen-Vluyn: Neukirchener Verlag, 1996).

6. For an interesting passage where, in a different context, Barth allows for flexibility, see Karl Barth, *Church Dogmatics* IV/2 (Edinburgh: T. & T. Clark, 1958), p. 631.

himself. He proposes to retrieve the inner meaning of Barth's thought. He also suggests that a church faithful to the apostles and the prophets will find Barth's proposal of "indissoluble solidarity" more pertinent than either a rightly discredited "supersessionism" or a well-intended though insupportable "two-track covenant."

In her beautifully constructed response, Katherine Sonderegger dissents, gently but firmly, from Barth as interpreted by Busch. She opts instead for a version of the twofold covenant. Although Christians and Jews profoundly disagree, and will do so until history's consummation, about the Christ of Israel, they are united, says Sonderegger, by "a deeper agreement." For both await the coming of the Messiah, while each affirms that the time of revelation is closed. Each remains obedient in its own way to the God of the covenant. The intractable disagreement about Jesus as the *but Jesus* Christ is secondary, she proposes, to these deeper agreements. *is the covenant*

For Sonderegger the issue of rightful inheritance does not seem to be strongly affected by whether Jesus is accepted or rejected as the Messiah. She supports her position with an important distinction. The Judaism known by Paul, she suggests, is categorically different from the latter-day Judaism that persists without the temple. Rabbinic Judaism as we know it today is a completely different religious system. It does not fall within the scope of the argument in Romans 9–11. Christians therefore need to confront this Judaism on its own terms, according to its own self-definition.

The Jewish decision not to rebuild the temple should be seen as an affirmation of its hope in the long-awaited Messiah's future advent. Sonderegger invites Christians to join with Jews in a common hope. Avoiding the term "supersessionism," she allows exactly the right questions to be raised. How important is accepting Jesus as Lord and Savior (and just so, as Israel's Messiah) in determining true obedience and rightful inheritance of the covenant? Are the areas of agreement between Christianity and rabbinic Judaism deeper than those of disagreement? Can the church afford to make Christology secondary to eschatology for the sake of post-Holocaust Jewish/Christian rapprochement? *can't be prior to*

Karl Barth and the Politics of the New World Order

Karl Barth, unlike some of his adherents, was involved in political controversy throughout his life. In his early ministry he was known as the "red pastor" for his labor-organizing efforts to improve wages and working conditions among local industrial workers. Then, in opposition to his teachers' support for the "pre-emptive" German aggression against Belgium that helped to spark World War I, he broke with modern academic theology. In midcareer, as the principal author of the Barmen Declaration, he became the intellectual leader of the evangelical resistance to Hitler. During the cold war he emerged as an outspoken critic of anticommunism, urging the church to a neutralist stance "between East and West." Having backed military action against the Nazis at a time of indecision, he later opposed postwar German rearmament and the deployment of nuclear weapons in Europe. During his final years he was increasingly antiimperialist, antimilitarist, and antinuclear, as the pacifist tendencies of his early career resurfaced. For those drawn to Barth, in part, by his exemplary combining of progressive politics with traditional faith — the "impossible possibility" he embodied throughout his life — it is a matter of some irony that currently in U.S. theological circles (and just how "progressive" are they?) he has come to be seen as a symbol of reaction.

Barth's commitments to social justice and nonviolence were grounded in the gospel — as two examples will serve to make clear. First, in discussing how God's righteousness is related to God's mercy, he wrote: "To establish justice for the innocent who are threatened and the poor, the widows, the orphans, and the strangers who are oppressed . . . God stands at every time unconditionally and passionately on this side: always against the exalted and for the lowly, always against those who already have rights and for those from whom they have been robbed and taken away" (II/1, p. 386 revised).[7] Here Barth had passages from the Old Testament prophets in mind. He later extended this line of thought into a fundamental critique of modern capitalism (III/4, pp. 531-45).

Barth wanted his social criticism to be evangelical rather than ideological. He took his bearings from the biblical narratives rather than any external system of ideas. These narratives, he felt, gave him a fixed orientation that could be flexibly applied in concrete decisions. His case for "practical pacifism," as the second example of his evangelical approach, displays this anti-ideological sensibility:

7. This and subsequent parenthetical references in the text are to Karl Barth, *Church Dogmatics*. The Roman numeral signifies the volume, the number following that the part, and the final number(s) the page(s).

The direction of Jesus must have embedded itself particularly deeply in the disciples. . . . They were neither to use force nor to fear it. . . . What the disciples are enjoined is that they should love their enemies (Matt. 5:44). This destroys the whole friend-foe relationship, for when we love our enemy he ceases to be our enemy. It thus abolishes the whole exercise of force, which presupposes this relationship, and has no meaning apart from it. . . . There is a concrete and incontestable direction which has to be carried out exactly as given. According to the sense [*Sinn*] of the New Testament we cannot be pacifists in principle, only in practice. But we have to consider very closely whether, if we are called to discipleship, we can avoid being practical pacifists, or fail to be so. (IV/2, pp. 549-50)

Like the orientation Barth discerned in Scripture toward justice for the oppressed, the presumption in favor of nonviolence was patterned on the prior activity of God. The pattern of this activity was particularly embodied in Christ's passion as it led him to the cross. This was the pattern to which faithful obedience was meant to conform.

Barth's observation about the *sense* of the New Testament — i.e., that Christ's followers cannot be pacifists in principle but only in practice — is something like what Wittgenstein meant by a *grammatical* remark. It attempts to make explicit the norms that are embedded in certain practices. In this case it makes explicit the "direction" of Jesus — the narrative pattern of his life and death as attested in the New Testament, and especially the Gospels. Any claim to follow him that did not involve a practical commitment to nonviolence would be *nonsense*.

In discussing Barth's political convictions, Clifford Green focuses on three concerns: economic justice, peace, and ecological ethics. The triumph of the capitalist market, as sketched by Green in contemporary form, echoes themes in Barth about worthy or valuable work. Work that really possesses dignity, Barth observed with disarming simplicity, will need to serve the cause of humanity. He then asked:

What are we to think of all the work which is thought worthwhile, and which is therefore done by those involved, only because they can definitely count on the stupidity and superficiality, the vanity and bad taste, the errors and vices of numerous other people? What are we to think of all the work to which people are drawn only because there are others who are prepared to ruin themselves either physically or morally? What are we to think of the work which flourishes in one place only because human beings elsewhere are afflicted with unemployment and therefore with want? What are we to think — as we must ask in relation to the problem of war — of direct or indirect participation in the work of an armaments factory, the achievements of which in so-called peace have often proved to be one of the most potent causes of war? Finally, what are we to think of work which, while it is intrinsically neither useful nor harmful, presents so unworthy an aspect just because it is directed neither to good nor evil, nor indeed to human beings at all, but past them to such an illusory dynamism, which, in its conjunction with sheer nothingness, conspires to generate an almost unequivocally demonic process — a process that consists in the amassing and multiplying of possessions expressed in financial calculations (or miscalculations), i.e., the "capital" which in the hands of the relatively few, who pull all the strings, may equally well, in a way wholly outside the control of the vast majority and therefore quite arbitrarily or accidentally, be a source of salvation or perdition for entire nations or generations? (III/4, pp. 531-32 revised)

Green spells out in detail the particular positions Barth took during his lifetime on matters of economic justice and peace. He goes on to question Barth's suitability for developing an ecological ethic today. Drawing on a study by H. Paul Santmire, Green suggests that Barth's understanding of the world of nature was "purely instrumental." Creation, for Barth, was supposedly nothing more than a means for the fulfillment of the covenant. It had no value in and of itself. Only if a theology can conceive of creation or the natural world as possessing value in and of itself can it serve as a suitable basis for ecological responsibility.

This criticism deserves comment. As Aristotle has pointed out, it is logically possible for something to function as an end in itself while also serving as the means to a greater end. Santmire seems to suppose, however, that ascribing an instrumental function to the natural world eliminates its being an intrinsic good in its own right. He claims, as cited by Green, that for Barth the natural world "has no evident permanent meaning in the greater scheme of things." This critique overlooks passages in Barth where the natural world is taken as an intrinsic good.

Barth believed that the created order as a whole — along with every particular being within it — had eternal value and significance for God. Discussing the immense diversity within the unity of all God's dealings with the world, Barth wrote that God not only values, but also exists in communion *(Gemeinschaft)* with, every created being. "[God's] communion with the angels is certainly different from his communion with the rest of the world. His communion with human beings is different from his communion with other spiritual creatures. His dealings with the faithful differ from his dealings with people in general. . . . And finally he is always infinitely diverse in his communion with each individual angel, thing, human being or believer, as compared with all the rest" (II/1, p. 316 revised). "God is he who in his Son Jesus Christ loves all his people [Israel and the church], in his people all human beings, and in human beings the whole creation" (II/1, p. 351 revised).

For Barth no individual creature, nor any portion of the created order — ranging all the way from inanimate objects to angels — can be conceived as devoid of communion with the God who made it and continually cares for it. The whole creation, and every creature within it, is an intrinsic good in and of itself. No aspect of the whole, as loved by God, will be excluded from the final redemption — not even "the wing-beat of the day-fly in far-flung depths of geological time" (III/3, p. 90). Of course, much more than this would be needed for an ecological ethic. Barth has not anticipated and solved all our problems. But he does make a positive contribution on which one might build, even for the ecological crisis. (See also his remarks on "reverence for life" in III/4, pp. 348-57; cf. III/2, p. 137.)

David Hollenbach expands upon Clifford Green's paper by developing three points: (1) Barth's theology of freedom in community, (2) its relationship to social justice on the international scene, and (3) its relationship to humanitarian intervention by military means. Barth's theology, as Hollenbach notes, sees human freedom as essentially relational. Freedom can be realized only in community, that is, only as human beings exist in connection with one another and with God. The God who lives eternally as Father, Son, and Holy Spirit is relational to the core. Through the incarnate Son, this relational deity negates all community-destroying sin and death so that true community might be restored on earth. Nation, race, world markets — three "pseudosovereignties" singled out by Hollenbach — can all become false gods. They can violate community by elevating the narrow self-interest of the few over the social misery of the many.

The God of the prophets and the apostles, Barth might say, expects the church to unmask such idols for what they are by espousing the cause of those in need. When it does so, what the church is doing theologically is enacting parables of grace. It is bearing witness to the theological ultimacy, established by the gospel, of community-creating and community-restoring love. Barth is thus perhaps more inclined to ground Christian social ethics in the doctrine of reconciliation than in the doctrine of creation. It is the latter that Hollenbach rightly sees at the heart of recent U.S. Catholic social teaching. Limits on national sovereignty, in any case, as well as concern for human rights in the global community, are both mandated, in various ways, by Christian ethics. Military intervention by the international community for the purpose of preventing genocide, Hollenbach argues, can be justified when these points are understood.

Barth on the Providence of God

The providence of God, according to Barth, is necessarily an article of faith. Whether this faith amounts to a form of arrogance is discussed in the contributions by Caroline Schröder and Randall Zachman. Schröder contends, provocatively, that for Barth faith assumes an unseemly stance of "superiority" over unbelievers who fail to discern that the world is governed by divine providence. Zachman counters that, on the contrary, faith in providence, for Barth, is a matter of "humble astonishment" in the face of a mystery that cannot be known in any other way (III/3, p. 266). Whether Barth's view of faith manifests arrogance or humility may be safely left to the reader.

God's providence, as explained by Barth, is the doctrine that God preserves and protects, accompanies and rules over all that God has created. It means that God is the Lord who is ceaselessly active in the world, and whose action orders all things to himself as their final goal. It means that God "[directs] all creatures to this one goal, and [subordinates] all other goals to this one." It means that God follows "a unified plan which is in the process of execution," and that "there is no creature which this plan does not embrace, and which does not in its own place and its own way help forward this plan." Providence therefore means that God preserves his creatures "from the wretchedness of a pointless existence," while he "wills and accomplishes one thing — his own glory as Creator" (III/3, p. 168).

It seems that for Barth at least three factors conspire to make God's providence hidden to ordinary modes of perception: the otherness of grace, the immensity of its scope, and the obscurity of evil. In virtue of these factors, he suggests, divine providence is either known by faith or not at all.

The otherness of grace is such that grace is absolutely sovereign in its activity, and yet nontyrannical in relation to the creature. It operates continuously as the total relevant context, the inner motor and the final goal of all things. Grace is in but not of the world, being the source of all creaturely freedom, integrity, and hope, even as it retains its unconditional sovereignty at every point. This supreme, providential grace not only accompanies our activity but also determines it, "even to its most intimate depths," yet without violating our creaturely freedom (p. 132). In this mysterious conjunction of two freedoms — the one superior without being oppressive, the other subordinate without being compromised (though not without being chastened) — a profound asymmetry manifests itself. The two subjects, divine and human, are incomparable in their interconnection (p. 135). They belong to "two different, two totally different orders" (p. 133), even as they cooperate so closely as to form "a single action" (p. 132). The otherness of providential grace, Barth affirms, is a mystery known only to faith.

Moreover, the scope of grace in its providential activity is immense. It rules over all things by ruling in particular over each, even as it rules over each in particular by coordinating the complexity of all things. Nothing is outside its reach, direction, and control. Yet the pattern that governs the whole cannot be inferred from general observation. By our own lights, what we see is little more than "multiplicity and confusion" (p. 44). We have no inherent ability to perceive the general workings of providence in all its immensity and detail. Faith in providence, Barth argues, must always move from the particular to the general. It is only because faith sees how providence operates at the center — in the history of the covenant as fulfilled in Jesus Christ — that it can affirm the workings of providence throughout the whole which that center governs. Faith in providence is also like the gathering of manna. It moves from the partial and provisional insights that were given as sufficient for yesterday to the equally partial and provisional insights that are given as sufficient for today.

Finally, divine providence is obscured by the destructive forces of evil. A huge topic in itself, Barth's views at this point can barely be sketched. They are distinctive for affirming at one and the same time that evil is really evil, that evil is invalidated by divine love (not the reverse), and that divine sovereignty over evil is absolute. The origin of evil in the good creation remains obscure while its outcome is certain. Its reality is confirmed by Christ's cross even as its defeat is attested by his resurrection. Yet the destructive power of evil is "intrinsically evil," and it remains "altogether inexplicable" (p. 354). "We have here," writes Barth, "an extraordinarily clear demonstration of the necessary brokenness of all theological thought and utterance" (p. 293).

Therefore providence is an article of faith. And while this faith does not become sight, that does not mean it remains blind. Faith in providence would not be faith if it were not "relative, provisional and modest knowledge in need of correction, yet true, thankful and courageous knowledge." Being no more than faith, but no less, it continually sees something — "hints and signs, . . . threats and judgments, gracious preservations and assistances" — that indicates God's providential hand (p. 23).

Barth on Christian Love

Two models of love are presented in Caroline J. Simon's stimulating paper, one associated with Karl Barth, the other with André Trocmé. The Barth model assigns primacy to the love of Christians for one another within the household of faith, while the Trocmé model emphasizes the love Christians should have for outsiders. Simon acknowledges that these models need not be mutually exclusive. She insists, however, that where the emphasis falls can make a significant difference. At the same time, she suggests that the Barth model might not have served well in the situation faced by Trocmé and his congregation when they set out to save the lives of hundreds of Jewish children during the Nazi occupation of France.

Simon seems to make a telling point. Consider this statement from Barth:

> As the community exists for the sake of the world loved by God, so the mutual love practiced within it is practiced for all, for the world, in a provisional and representative manifestation of the action for which all are determined. Yet it is practiced here, between these human beings. It is based on the love of God and of Jesus, and as the fulfillment of the second commandment ordered in relation to the first commandment of love for God and for Jesus. It can flourish only on this soil. As such it cannot be practiced by all, it cannot be meaningfully addressed to all. (IV/2, p. 805)

Neighbor love is defined here as the love practiced among believers in the Christian community. It is different from a universal love of humanity, because it is practiced by those who know that the horizontal is governed by the vertical — i.e., that neighbor love is governed by God's love for us, and just so by our love for God.

What we would like to hear a little more about from Barth at this point is just how he thinks the love practiced within the community is related to his explicit affirmation that the community exists "for the sake of the world loved by God." It is one thing to say that the mutual love practiced within the community is neighbor love in the strict and proper sense, but quite another to say that neighbor love can have no application to those outside it.

Barth's view would be undialectical if that were actually his point. Despite the misleading form his argument takes in "The Act of Love" (IV/2, pp. 783-824), his view is not likely to be so one-sided. What he wants to stress is that, theologically speaking, "the neighbor" is not defined primarily as "the one in need," but rather as "the one who attests God's love" — for me, for the community, and for the world. It is God's love which defines what my needs really are, not the reverse. Nevertheless, the principle of analogy that we would expect to find remains curiously underdeveloped in Barth's argument.

We would expect Barth to argue that mutual love within the community is paradigmatic but not exhaustive. We would expect him to draw an explicit analogy from mutual love within the community to love for those outside — for others, for strangers, for enemies. We would not expect him to stress the distinction, in other words, without also pointing to the unity. We would not expect him to restrict the objects of neighbor love to those who are in a position to practice it. Neighbor love in the strict and proper sense of "mutual love" would not rule out looser, less definitive forms. On the contrary, it would actually govern those forms and orient them. The distinction between love within the community and love for those outside it would be as significant as Barth urges yet also graded and finally relative. Where the emphasis should fall in any particular situation would be entirely flexible. A careful reading of Barth with these questions in mind would show that such expectations are not entirely unmet. But we are in Prof. Simon's and Prof. Webster's debt for forcing a rereading upon us.

Barth on Eternity

Barth's conception of eternity is, as I argue in my contribution to this volume, governed by his understanding of the Trinity. If the doctrine of the Trinity is difficult, and the idea of eternity no less difficult, then a trinitarian doctrine of eternity will be doubly difficult. Perhaps it will not be amiss, therefore, if I try just a bit to simplify the terms of my argument.

The doctrine of the Trinity, as Barth understands it, is built up of three traditional elements, whose names in Greek are: *ousia, hypostasis,* and *perichoresis.* (It is helpful to start with the Greek, since the terms are notoriously difficult to translate.)

1. The divine being *(ousia),* which is one, concrete, and indivisible, pertains for Barth to God's essential otherness, lordship, and deity. It means that God is self-identical in all his forms and relations. Barth associates it with the biblical God's statement "I am the Lord."

2. The three divine modes of being *(hypostases)* indicate that though the divine *ousia* is simple, indivisible, and noncomposite, it is nonetheless internally differentiated. The concrete divine *ousia* is intrinsically relational, because intrinsically trinitarian. The divine *ousia* subsists in three *hypostases* simultaneously: the Father, the Son, and the Holy Spirit. Each of these is an irreducible mode of the one divine *ousia.* Their mutual subsistence implies that a dynamism exists within the divine *ousia* of beginning, middle, and end, or of the Father (the one begetting), the Son (the one begotten), and the Holy Spirit (the one proceeding mutually between the two). Barth associates this dynamic mutuality with the biblical statement "God is love."

3. To the ideas of self-identity and self-differentiation is added the idea of self-unification *(perichoresis).* The three *hypostases* subsist in a form of eternal becoming in which they dwell dynamically within one another. This dynamic indwelling is the trinitarian divine life. It involves a mysterious conjunction of simultaneity and teleology. Barth associates the idea of *perichoresis* with the biblical affirmation that God is "the living God."

The triune God exists eternally in and for himself, Barth believes, only as he also exists in and for the world, and in and for the world only as he exists primarily and essentially in and for himself. God's trinitarian being is eternally necessary while his being in relation to the world is eternally contingent. Creation and election — God's decision to create the world, and God's pretemporal decision of election which grounds the creation, and which destines the creation for a share in God's eternal life despite its fall into the chaos of sin and death — are both eternal in this contingent as opposed to necessary sense.

The doctrine of the Trinity, as Brian Leftow indicates in his response, gives Barth's conception of eternity a uniquely dynamic and teleological aspect. As an expression of the divine freedom, love, and life, eternity is at once self-sufficient and yet also the ground of the created order that depends on it. Eternity is in some sense the archetype and prototype in relation to which created time is the imperfect ectype. But the tragic separations endemic to created time will be preserved, negated, and overcome in Christ when the destiny of all temporal things is effectually manifested in his final, universal revelation.

Barth as Teacher

The volume ends with John Godsey's wonderful tribute to Barth as a teacher, presented in rich detail and based on personal experience. In a way unsurpassed in modern theology, Barth has been a teacher to the teachers of the church. This volume is perhaps a small token of why that has already been the case, and why it promises to continue as we move into the twenty-first century.

The Barth-Brunner Correspondence

JOHN W. HART

The 1934 natural theology debate between Karl Barth and Emil Brunner has become a classic text in theological study, as well as one of the easy hooks upon which to hang a description of Barth's theological intentions. The premise of this paper is that what happened between Barth and Brunner in 1934 was the culmination of several long-running theological arguments between them. This paper will explore the beginnings, development, and breakdown of Barth and Brunner's theological alliance through the lens of their twenty-year personal correspondence.[1]

Let me make two preliminary observations about the Barth-Brunner correspondence. First — it is simply fascinating. Other than Barth's correspondence with Eduard Thurneysen, no other source is both so theologically substantial and so personally revealing. This paper in no way claims that Brunner was Barth's primary conversation partner. Nonetheless, as he corresponds with Brunner, much light is shed on the development — particularly the consistency of the development — of Barth's theological intentions. If Barth felt it necessary to cut himself off angrily from Brunner, a theologian so close to his own position when viewed in the context of theological history, it must point to certain vital commitments held by

1. The Barth-Brunner correspondence, edited by Eberhard Busch, was published by Theologischer Verlag Zürich in 2000 as a volume in the Barth *Gesamtausgabe*. Quotations in this paper are from a partially annotated typescript prepared by Dr. Busch's assistant, Frau Astrid Rönchen. The author would like to thank the Barth Nachlasskommission and the Emil Brunner-Stiftung for permission to quote from this correspondence.

Barth which he would not compromise. In fact, the Barth-Brunner correspondence demonstrates how radically and consistently Barth works out
his fundamental insight from 1916 — that "*God* is God and God is *God*,"
and that thinking about this God can be faithfully accomplished only if it
is, in Barth's words in a letter to Brunner in 1930, "a theology which, like a
spinning top, supports itself on only one point."[2]

The bulk of the correspondence falls between the years 1916 and 1936.
In this period there are over 110 letters between the two men. The pattern
of the correspondence reveals the unequal relationship between them. Almost without exception, Brunner initiates a topic of conversation. Usually
Barth replies, and frequently Brunner follows up with a final comment.
There is probably some truth that the Barth-Brunner relationship was like
an "older brother/younger brother" relationship, since the correspondence
is marked by increasing competition and insecurity on Brunner's part and
increasing frustration and dismissiveness on Barth's part. Throughout the
correspondence Brunner seeks Barth's approval of his work. And yet, as
Brunner's own son would later write, "When all is said and done, Emil
Brunner's activities were of little importance for [Barth's] activities."[3]

Obviously a correspondence covering twenty years deals with a host
of topics. This paper will focus on five interactions between Barth and
Brunner that illuminate the shaky beginning and steady deterioration of
their theological alliance.

The Object of Theology (1916)

Barth and Brunner first meet in the early 1910s through their common involvement in Swiss religious socialism. The person who introduces them,
and the man who serves as the indispensable middleman throughout the
ups and downs of their relationship, is Eduard Thurneysen.[4]

---

2. Barth to Brunner, October 24, 1930.

3. Hans Heinrich Brunner, *Mein Vater und Sein Ältester* (Zürich: Theologischer
Verlag, 1986), p. 136.

4. Thurneysen met Brunner when Thurneysen served the YMCA in Zürich while
Brunner was a doctoral candidate at the university. They were both very involved in the religious socialism movement in Zürich. Brunner and Thurneysen's friendship was cemented
when Thurneysen became the pastor at the church in Leutwil (Canton Aargau), following
Brunner's service there for nine months as interim pastor (letter from Frau Lilo Brunner-

In July 1916 Brunner, serving as pastor of the Reformed church in Obstalden, first writes Barth in response to a sermon Barth had preached at the 1916 Aarau Christian Student Conference, entitled "The One Thing Necessary." The key line of Barth's sermon is that instead of doing all kinds of possible things, we should do the one thing necessary, that is, "we should begin at the beginning and recognize that God is God." Barth goes on: "As academics, we obstruct the way to God by, first of all, requiring definitions and concepts: 'Who is God' 'What is faith?' Let us respect our logical needs, but let us not let them fuel our fatal natural instinct to persist in our questions about the definition of God rather than making our decision for God. We will always walk around the circumference and never arrive at the center so long as we refuse to begin at the beginning before our definitions are set."[5]

Brunner begins his letter: "I cannot argue with you about it — it has simply delighted me, grasped me, and also tormented me."[6] Brunner's torment concerns his own Christian life. He confesses: "As often as I have attempted 'to let God matter, to let Him speak,' it has not helped me forwards. Naturally, I am to blame for this, and I know that . . . you are nevertheless right. . . . I probably preach the same way as you . . . — but often only with a half-clear conscience." Brunner confesses his struggles with the ups and downs of his personal faith:

> This is my experience: Either I will completely be at the center . . . : God lives, let God matter. But then I soon find that all I have in my hands are four letters [G-o-t-t] . . . , an abstract thought, with which I can neither understand nor master my life. I can say, Let God matter. But, in reality, what matters is not God but my thought that "God should matter." . . . Or, on the other hand, depressed from this experience, I . . . fall into the

---

Gutekunst, Brunner's daughter-in-law, to J. W. Hart, January 10, 1993). There is no evidence that Barth and Brunner met during this year. For information on Thurneysen's life, see Busch and Rudolf Bohren, *Prophetie und Seelsorge: Eduard Thurneysen* (Vluyn: Neukirchener Verlag, 1982). For Brunner's early life see "Intellectual Autobiography of Emil Brunner," trans. Keith Chamberlain, in *The Theology of Emil Brunner*, ed. Charles W. Kegley (New York: Macmillan, 1962), pp. 3-20, and H. H. Brunner, pp. 61-62, 121, 389. Shortly after beginning his ministry in Leutwil, Thurneysen renewed his friendship with Barth — now serving as pastor of the church in the neighboring town of Safenwil — a relationship that had begun when they were fellow theological students both in Bern and Marburg.

5. Quoted in annotation of typescript of Brunner's letter to Barth, July 3, 1916.

6. Brunner to Barth, July 3, 1916.

other extreme: "God should matter" [becomes] "The Good should matter," [faith mixed up with] a moral-cultural lifestyle, a system of ethics, that, up to a certain point, shines through one's life, but naturally (as little as "the law" in Paul) has no power. . . . I've always had the feeling — and my moral experiences confirm it — that I have still not yet penetrated to God, that my faith has produced nothing.[7]

This leaves Brunner experiencing the Christian life as a "vicious circle": "In order to have . . . faith, one must become a completely different person. Again and again I find myself to be lazy and unfaithful; my faith is so weak that it often does not make headway over-against the robust old Adam. Therefore, I need first to become a different person in order to have faith; but I have to have faith in order to become a different person!" Poignantly Brunner ends with the salutation: "With kind regards, your still somewhat-fallen-short companion on the way."

Barth responds immediately and with great pastoral care: "I understand you very well. It is exactly the same for me as it is for you, at every point. . . . You really don't mean, with this sense of utter lack, that you are in some sense a special case? I *really* experience the same things — you are in no way a 'fallen-short companion on the way.' This you must *believe*." Barth goes on to repeat the point of his lecture:

It really becomes clearer and clearer to me that this religious labyrinth has no exit. . . . It is a question of God, and why do we marvel if He is not found in the psychological labyrinth of our religious experience? "Why do you seek the living among the dead?" (Luke 24:5). . . . We are not Pietists; we can know and really *know* that faith in no way consists (neither positively nor negatively, neither optimistically nor pessimistically illuminated) in taking this whole psychological reality as serious and important. Rather, with our eyes closed as it were, we hold on to God.

For Barth the key to Christian living (as well as Christian thinking) is to turn one's focus from human subjectivity to divine objectivity: "Does not

---

7. Brunner's daughter-in-law remarks that Brunner always questioned the vitality of his Christian life: "'My prayers are not long enough, I don't live out love. I am not faithful enough. I am not humble enough. I do not live enough what I preach.' There was always, always this self-questioning." J. W. Hart interview with Lilo Brunner-Gutekunst, January 13, 1992.

the entire misery of our situation exist simply in that, again and again, we turn back to ourselves instead of stretching out to the Objective? Don't we fail — due to some kind of pride . . . — to give our obedience and trust to God as *God,* God above all in his objectivity?" Barth's specific counsel to Brunner is to do what Barth does: "I *cut off* these thoughts the moment I notice the trap being laid. . . . Then I wait until joyfulness, faith, enthusiasm, etc. returns (sometimes they don't return for a long time). And this objective hold on God as God is always more important to me compared to the previous unfortunately unavoidable variations of the inner life. I believe that here unfolds the constant which I (as well as you) have sought in vain in my subjective faithfulness." Barth concludes his letter with a phrase that will remain characteristic throughout his life: "For my part, I do *not* believe in your unbelief."[8]

This early exchange of letters reveals what will become an ongoing difference between Barth and Brunner. Brunner's attention will always focus on the human side of the divine/human relationship: understanding the dynamics of the believer's life, seeking how to reach the unbeliever with the gospel, making the connections between God and humanity. Barth's letter, on the other hand, illustrates a fundamental motif in Barth's theology, what George Hunsinger calls his "soteriological objectivism."[9] In other letters from these early years, Brunner complains about Barth's "one-sidedness,"[10] that is, Barth's constant focus on the revealed God alone, and use of such dubious doctrines (in Brunner's view) as predestination. From the very beginning of their relationship, Barth and Brunner are divided by the object of theology. For Barth the proper object of theology is God in his revelation. For Brunner theology must not only speak about God, but must also speak decisively about the believing subject.[11]

---

8. Barth to Brunner, July 9, 1916.

9. George Hunsinger, *How to Read Karl Barth: The Shape of His Theology* (New York: Oxford University Press, 1991), pp. 37-39, 103-51.

10. January 30, 1918; November 28, 1918.

11. Brunner's "objectivistic" critique of Barth intensifies after their 1934 natural theology debate, when "theological objectivism" becomes Brunner's constant critique of Barth. See Brunner, *Vom Werk des Heiligen Geistes* (Tübingen: J. C. B. Mohr, 1935), pp. 14-15, 30-31; Brunner, *Truth as Encounter,* trans. Amandus W. Loos and David Cairns (London: SCM Press, 1964), pp. 41-46, 81-83; Brunner, *Revelation and Reason,* trans. Olive Wyon (Philadelphia: Westminster, 1946), pp. 39-40.

The Method of Theology (1920)

During the 1919-20 academic year, Brunner takes a sabbatical from his pastorate to study at Union Theological Seminary in New York. Thus he is out of touch with Barth during the year in which Barth absorbs Overbeck's *Christianity and Culture*[12] and begins preparing his second edition of *Romans*.[13]

A month after Brunner returns to Switzerland, he receives a Sunday visit from Barth and Thurneysen in Obstalden. It is not a pleasant visit, at least not for Brunner.[14] After attending worship and then joining Brunner for lunch afterward, Barth and Thurneysen launch into a severe critique of Brunner's sermon, charging that Brunner had preached "cheaply, psychologically, boringly, churchly, without distance, etc." This disastrous visit prompts Brunner to read *The Inner Situation of Christianity* — Barth and Thurneysen's reaction to Overbeck — in order to understand how Barth's thinking is developing.[15] In a letter following up on their visit, Brunner takes issue with Barth and Thurneysen's radically dialectical expressions. Brunner poses the problem in a parable: "[You have confused] the dialectical No with the critical No. Dialectics is, as is well-known, Hegelian, not Kantian philosophy. For Kant, the No is critical, like the watch-dog who barks at everyone except for the owner of the house. But the dialectical watch-dog barks at everything in principle." While Brunner grants a place for a no, he feels that Barth's radical emphasis on the divine/human dis-

---

12. Franz Overbeck, *Christentum und Kultur*, ed. Carl Albrecht Bernoulli (Basel: Benno Schwabe, 1919).

13. Brunner was one of the earliest fans of Barth's first edition of *Romans* (1919). (See Barth, *Der Römerbrief*, ed. Hermann Schmidt, 1st ed. [Zürich: Theologischer Verlag, 1985].) He wrote a glowing review of it for the journal of the Swiss Reformed Church. (See Brunner, "The Epistle to the Romans by Karl Barth: An Up-to-Date, Unmodern Paraphrase," in *The Beginnings of Dialectical Theology*, ed. James M. Robinson, trans. Keith Crim and others [Richmond: John Knox, 1968], pp. 63-71.) For Brunner's comments on the first edition of *Romans*, see Brunner, "Toward a Missionary Theology: How I Changed My Mind," *Christian Century* 66 (1949): 816-18, on p. 816; Brunner, "A Spiritual Autobiography," *Japan Christian Quarterly* 21 (1955): 238-44; and Brunner, "Intellectual Autobiography," p. 8.

14. Brunner to Barth, September 2, 1920.

15. *Zur inneren Lage des Christentums* (Munich: Chr. Kaiser, 1920). This pamphlet contained a sermon by Thurneysen and an essay by Barth. Barth's essay is translated as "Unsettled Questions for Theology Today," in *Theology and Church*, trans. Louis Pettibone Smith (London: SCM Press, 1962), pp. 55-73.

tance is the wrong approach: "You maintain the distance as a dynamic — and thus an unlimited — principle; there is no stopping it, as little as with the Law. The dialectical watch-dog will tear apart anyone who dares to approach God." In contrast, Brunner argues that "the Gospel ultimately means something positive": "The question is not *whether* something positive appears (the dialectical No), but *where* it appears (the critical No): Christ appears *in* time, the kingdom of God grows *in* time together with the weeds, we *have* this treasure in earthen vessels, faith *justifies* proleptically and forensically." Brunner argues that, historically, the institutional church has always been tempted to construct "complicated dialectical tricks" in order to oppose the prophets' message of God's nearness and simplicity.

Brunner concludes his comments on Barth's article by saying, "You have strayed into a very dubious neighborhood." He suggests that Barth would have more success stressing Johann Blumhardt's yes[16] (which places the emphasis on the content of faith) rather than Overbeck's no (which stresses the dynamic principle of preserving the divine-human distance). Brunner concludes: "For me, this entire development is an excellent proof that I am correct when I maintain that . . . knowledge *and* experience, the objective-material *and* the subjective-personal . . . form an insurmountable polarity."

Barth does not reply to Brunner's letter. But by the time Barth's second edition of *Romans* is published at the end of 1921, Brunner has begun to grasp what Barth is driving at.[17] With an astonishing humility, Brunner confesses that Barth has won him over to the "dialectical No":

> I was glad that I was not completely unprepared to be assailed by this colossal thought. This scandal was already powerfully indicated to me for the first time on that always memorable (for me) Sunday in Obstalden in August 1920. For more than half a year I kicked against the pricks without breaking through. Then your first proofs arrived (chapters 2-5). . . . Understand me when I say that after studying these proofs, the entire letter to the Romans has brought liberation for me. Instead of offering me scandals, it offers me *the* scandal. Now I see for

16. For Barth on Blumhardt, see Barth, *Protestant Theology in the Nineteenth Century,* trans. Brian Cozens and John Bowden (London: SCM Press, 1972), pp. 643-53.

17. Barth, *The Epistle to the Romans,* trans. Edwyn C. Hoskyns, 6th ed. (London: Oxford University Press, 1933).

the first time the logic of the scandal, its entirety, its encompassing significance for *everything.*

In August 1920 Brunner neither understood nor accepted Barth's radically dialectical method. But after reading the second edition of *Romans,* Brunner claims he finally understands "the encompassing significance of *the* scandal," that is, the radical distance between Creator and creation and its accompanying comprehensive judgment on humanity and humanism in all its expressions. But while Barth's second edition of *Romans* catches Brunner's imagination, he will not continue in Barth's direction. For at the same moment he is reading *Romans,* Brunner is also absorbing Ferdinand Ebner's *The Word and Spiritual Realities.*[18] Brunner's subsequent embrace of Ebner's "I-Thou," "divine summons/human response" philosophy blunts his adoption of Barth's "dialectical No."[19] Instead, Ebner's influence moves Brunner back to searching for divine/human continuities under the concept of "dialogue" rather than "dialectic."[20]

The Foundation of Theology (1925)

By 1925 Barth and Brunner are no longer pastors, but professors — Barth at Göttingen and Brunner at Zürich — writing their first systematic works. Barth, in his lectures in dogmatics at Göttingen, begins to develop a dogmatic theology built on theology's self-grounded axiom: the actuality that God has addressed humanity in revelation. The two most noticeable developments in Barth's theology in his Göttingen lectures are that he anchors his dialectical theology dogmatically in the doctrine of the Trinity, and that he draws on the insights of the Protestant scholastics.[21]

18. Ebner, *Das Wort und die geistigen Realitäten,* in *Schriften,* ed. Franz Seyr, 3 vols. (Munich: Kösel, 1963-65), 1:75-342.

19. Barth expressed his suspicions about Ebner's philosophy as early as October 1922, in reference to Friedrich Gogarten. See Barth, *Revolutionary Theology in the Making,* trans. James D. Smart (Richmond: John Knox, 1964), p. 110.

20. For the earliest evidence of Ebner's influence on Brunner, see Brunner, *Erlebnis, Erkenntnis und Glaube,* 2nd rev. ed. (Tübingen: J. C. B. Mohr, 1923), pp. v, 119; Brunner, "Das Grundproblem der Philosophie bei Kant und Kierkegaard," *Zwischen den Zeiten* 6 (1924): 31-46; and Brunner, *Die Mystik und das Wort* (Tübingen: J. C. B. Mohr, 1924), pp. 89-94, 395 n. 1.

21. "The problem of the doctrine of the Trinity is the recognition of the inexhaustible

At the same time, Brunner's first systematic statements reveal that he is moving in a different direction than Barth. In 1925 he publishes an essay entitled "Law and Revelation: A Theological Foundation."[22] In this article Brunner attempts to explain the relationship of philosophy and theology in terms of the Law as the "border" or "limit" of human knowledge. Brunner writes that in the relationship between theology and philosophy, "there is a border where both touch each other, thus where they . . . touch like two army spearheads *over-against* each other. This *common* point, which is precisely the point where there is a collision, is the Law." Thus, for Brunner, there is a double significance for the Law. In the positive sense the Law is the way in which God encounters humanity as humanity proceeds on its own way to God. Negatively the Law, as that which uncovers humanity's sin, separates God and humanity. The Law is "the stage prior to the 'face of God' . . . : It is God and yet not God, God as he wants to be *for* us but as he maintains himself *against* us." Therefore the Law brings a crisis: it brings knowledge of sin and judgment, which points to the need for the revelation of grace. Revelation alone makes possible the "full" knowledge of sin; nevertheless, since the Law is the touching point between revelation and philosophy, philosophy knows "something of the Law."

Barth writes to Brunner soon after "Law and Revelation" appears.[23] He is not content with what he has read:

> Now that I see more clearly where you're headed, I have nothing to say *against* you. Except that a demon (whose voice I still cannot translate into a scientific formula) prevents me from *following* you, (1) in your *undertaking as such,* which seems to me (as you usually conduct your undertakings) to be "somehow" too grandly designed (I still don't know clearly enough what theology is, so I can hardly venture to think about its relationship to philosophy . . .); and (2) in the *execution* of your undertaking, which appears to me to be "somehow" too simple, too unambiguous. (It's the same here as with your other works. . . . I

vitality or the indestructible subjectivity of God in his revelation" (Brunner, *Die Mystik und das Wort,* p. 98). For the influence of Protestant scholasticism on Barth, see Barth, *Revolutionary Theology,* p. 154, and Barth's foreword in *Reformed Dogmatics,* trans. G. T. Thomson (Grand Rapids: Baker, 1978), pp. v-vii.

22. Brunner, "Gesetz und Offenbarung: Eine theologische Grundlegung," *Theologische Blätter* 4 (1925): 53-58.

23. Barth to Brunner, March 13, 1925.

see you giving answers where I am really first stirred up at discovering questions.)

As for Brunner's undertaking:

> I have absolutely *no desire whatever* to get involved in the hand-to-hand combat of philosophers with one another (1) because I don't have what it takes, (2) because it's not my office, and (3) because nothing would be more unpleasant for me than the realization that my theology stands or falls with a *particular* philosophy. You must understand how strange it makes me feel to look at you with your "foundation" — where one must first be converted from being an Aristotelian into a Kantian, and then from a Kantian into a Christian, and also that as a Christian one *must* necessarily be a Kantian (which I will concede is the most desirable and helpful position).

Regarding the execution of Brunner's argument, Barth objects that Brunner's opposition between law and gospel is too harshly Kantian: "Is not the Law *also* revelation, [or is it] only punishment and opposition? Or does the praise of the Law in Psalm 119 count only as a 'limit . . .'?" Second, while "philosophy *as such* can 'sense' something of the 'Law' in the theological sense, it can *say* nothing, and that is a matter of importance. For then one must consider whether philosophy can 'sense' the 'Gospel' just as much as the 'Law.'" Barth asks why Brunner calls his article a "theological foundation" if he builds upon an understanding of the Law which is common to Kantian philosophy. Barth concludes by remarking on the fact that people are reading Barth's and Brunner's works side by side: "While I am grateful that by the means of your clearer formulations many people better understand my 'abracadabras,' you must certainly take account of the fact that in my work there remains an 'X' of which you have not laid hold."

Brunner writes back with four observations.[24] First, he thanks Barth for reprimanding him about his "certainty": "It was not my intention . . . to lay a theological foundation. . . . Nothing was intended other than a preliminary attempt to define the borders of philosophy and theology. But now, I think, it sits there, condemned: 'foundation.'" But Brunner's second point is less conciliatory: "We cannot avoid this task" of engaging with philosophy,

24. Brunner to Barth, March ??, 1925 (date not specified in the typescript).

because poor theological conclusions often result from the appropriation of bad philosophy. Third, Brunner argues that he is simply reformulating what Paul and Calvin teach: the law is the tutor for the gospel. "This point of connection *(Beziehungspunkt)* [between revelation and reason cannot be] surrendered." (It is not until 1929 that he coins his more famous term, the "point of contact" [*Anknüpfungspunkt*].) Brunner continues:

> I am not capable of speaking of revelation in the Christian sense without marking out the border of revelation against that which is not revelation, i.e., reason. Perhaps this comes in my genes, being the son of a teacher; but clarity as such appears to you to be somewhat pedantic and dangerously certain. But how do you answer your students when they ask about your doctrine of revelation: "Yes, revelation is necessary — one does not know Christ through reason. But doesn't the person who knows nothing of Christ know the Law just as well as the person who does?"

With a dig at Barth's dogmatics lectures, Brunner concludes by arguing that Barth cannot escape the question of revelation and reason in the long run: "It is more important that we clarify the relationship of reason and revelation — which is identical to saying that we must clarify the concept of revelation — than that we be instructed in all the subtleties of the doctrine of the Trinity."[25]

The Barth-Brunner correspondence demonstrates that by 1925 the basic disagreement between Barth and Brunner is firmly set in place. Despite their shared emphases on the Word of God in revelation, the christocentric nature of that revealed Word, and their vital appropriation of Luther and Calvin, Barth and Brunner still demonstrate two fundamen-

---

25. In a handwritten marginal note, Brunner writes: "It is not for nothing that Reformed theology begins with the chapter: De theologia naturale et revelata. What is left without right, what is revelation without its opposite: reason?" In the next issue of *Zwischen den Zeiten* (3 [1925]), Barth takes a glancing shot at Brunner. In "Menschenwort und Gotteswort in der christlichen Predigt" (pp. 119-40), Barth argues that the statement "the Bible is the Word of God because it is" does not "mean the proclamation of a credo, quia absurdum, but rather of a credo, ut intelligam, of the irreversibility of this sequence. No intelligere can precede the credo, not even an ethical intelligere. The credo is primary or it is not credo at all" (p. 124). That this sentence is aimed at Brunner is confirmed by Thurneysen (Barth, *Revolutionary Theology*, p. 219).

tally different ways of doing theology. As Barth makes clear in his first lectures in dogmatics, theology is *Nachdenken,* a "thinking after" the living Word of God as he has revealed himself to humanity. Theology focuses relentlessly on Scripture and on the God who has revealed himself to be triune, because God is the first and proper object of theology.

Brunner, on the other hand, is and will remain a philosophical theologian, a theologian whose interest lies at the intersection of the Word of God and the mind of humanity. This gives his theology two foci. Like Barth, he is concerned with exploring and explaining the God who has revealed himself in Jesus Christ through Scripture. But Brunner also argues for the necessity of understanding the human conditions for reception of this Word. As early as 1925, Brunner is concerned with finding a *Beziehungspunkt* — a "point of connection" — between the Word of God in revelation and nonbelieving, sinful humanity.[26]

The Task of Theology (1930)

In 1929 Brunner publishes an article entitled "The Other Task of Theology."[27] This article crystallizes the development of Brunner's thinking since 1925, as well staking out his position in contrast to Barth. Brunner grants that theology's "first and essential task" is "reflective interpretation" on the Word of God. But he maintains that theology has another task: a polemical engagement with human reason, which he terms "eristics," from the Greek word *erizein* (to debate). Brunner posits two fronts against which eristic theology fights. First, it engages rational thinking *outside* the church, challenging nonbelievers' false philosophical assumptions. Second, eristics engages thinking *within* the church, championing an existential theology of the Word over against a theoretical, objectivistic dogmatics — an explicit jab at Barth.

That summer Brunner visits Barth, and there ensues an extremely heated argument over Brunner's article.[28] Brunner is clearly upset by their

26. In the next two years, Brunner coins other terms for this "point of connection": the "point of attachment" *(Berührungspunkt)* and "the point of contact" *(Anknüpfungspunkt).* See Brunner, *The Philosophy of Religion from the Standpoint of Protestant Theology,* trans. A. J. D. Farrer and Bertram Lee Woolf (New York: Scribner, 1937), pp. 20, 98.

27. *Zwischen den Zeiten* 7 (1929): 255-76.

28. Brunner to Barth, June 8, 1929.

meeting because it reveals the depth of Barth's disagreement with him. As Brunner puts it: "We have reached a critical point."

In fact, by this time the entire "dialectical theology" movement has reached a critical point. In addition to his disagreements with Brunner, Barth has been harboring even deeper suspicions of his colleagues Friedrich Gogarten, Rudolf Bultmann, and Paul Tillich. In early 1930 Barth writes to Thurneysen, laying out his concerns:

> The whole line is entirely not a good thing; under no circumstances do I want to be associated with it. Is it not the case that all of us, who apparently stand close to each other, have gradually come to want exactly what we . . . did not want and struggled against from the beginning — standing in the nearest relationship to . . . a grounding not in actuality, but in laying the *possibility* of faith and revelation on the table? . . . What is all this . . . if it is not the renewal of *the* relationship between theology and philosophy, just like Kant, Hegel, Schleiermacher, De Wette, etc. — only that now, for a change, philosophy has become something negative, existential, etc. . . . Is it just a question of a harmless difference, while the rest of our theologies are "fundamentally" at one? I don't know, . . . but I simply oppose with all the hairs on my head the entire state of affairs . . . , and I don't know whether I should bunch together one great article of resistance and bid farewell to Emil, Paul, Friedrich, and Rudolf.[29]

In fact, Barth does write such an article by dusting off an unpublished lecture from 1927 entitled "Theology and Modern Man," and publishing it in *Zwischen den Zeiten*.[30] In the article Barth argues that theology raises three scandals for the modern person: (1) God's freedom in revelation forces modern people to deal with predestination; (2) theology scandalizes modern free thinkers by being a science which is bound to the church; and (3) faith — rather than history, psychology, or philosophy — is the tool for discovering truth. This third scandal is particularly challenging to the modern mind, because it means that theology does not offer any

---

29. *Karl Barth–Eduard Thurneysen Briefwechsel,* ed. Eduard Thurneysen, 2 vols. (Zürich: Theologischer Verlag, 1973, 1974), 2:700-701.

30. Barth, "Die Theologie und der heutige Mensch," *Zwischen den Zeiten* 8 (1930): 374-96. The parenthetical page numbers in the text that follows are to this work.

proof for its statements, but demands "pure unsecured obedience, a trust stripped of all guarantees" (p. 384).

Barth then analyzes the modern responses to these three scandals. First, there is the response of "brutal atheism," which rebels against the proper work of theology. Then there is the response of "sentimental Liberalism," which attempts to "domesticate" theology. Finally, there is the Roman Catholic response, which attempts to "control" theology. Barth uses a vivid image to describe these three responses: "If you see a wild and threatening horse galloping straight at you, you could either jump out of the way [atheism] or try to soothe it with friendly words [Liberalism]. Or, if you had enough self-confidence, you could jump on its back and become its rider and master [Roman Catholicism]" (p. 393). Barth then, pointedly yet without explicit attribution, inserts into this three-year-old lecture the positions of his dialectical colleagues as another illustration of this third response of trying to "control" the Word of God:

> Perhaps it might be a negative metaphysics, an apparently very non-Thomistic metaphysics, not the zenith but the nadir of human knowledge, an ontology of the "hollow space," to whose dimensions faith and theology correspond exactly, and . . . are clearly indicated [Bultmann]? Perhaps an "eristic" theology, which would have the task of making it clear to the modern person, with paternal wisdom, that he, without recourse to Christian faith, necessarily must become entangled in an evil self-contradiction [Brunner]? Or perhaps a doctrine of history, whose truth would correspond exactly to what the biblical presentation describes as the reality of the relationship of God and humanity [Gogarten]? (p. 394)

The error of his three colleagues is only slight, but it is disastrous:

> It is more dangerous [than Roman Catholicism] because unbelievably good theology loses its way at one small point: it no longer says that human thinking reckons with the Word of God only through faith. But isn't it precisely on this one little point that everything hinges? Is there any secure place which we can give to theology? Is not theology precisely theology only in the uncertainty of the real science of faith, . . . only as a stranger in the areas of the other sciences, without its own area? . . . Perhaps this is the fatal question which our generation is

asked, whether theologians are in the position to recognize this last and dangerous temptation for what it is. (pp. 395-96)

The appearance of "Theology and Modern Man" prompts Brunner to write to Barth.[31] He is completely baffled by the essay's proposition that theology can proceed only from the doctrine of predestination: "A theology constructed out of predestination is an impossibility. . . . Not merely my eristics or Gogarten's anthropology or Bultmann's doctrine of 'pre-understanding,' but every doctrinal certainty becomes completely out of the question." Brunner attempts to show, through citations from Barth's *Christian Dogmatics*, that Barth's theology as well requires "guarantees" and eristics.[32] Specifically, Brunner maintains that Barth's increasing use of Anselm means that he is unwittingly moving in Brunner's direction: "Anselm is a powerful Eristician. '*Why* did God become man?' — that is entirely and completely an eristic way of asking the question, just as the way he conducts his proof is eristic. Eristics . . . is the demonstration of the gap which God's revelation or God's grace covers." Brunner argues that *Christian Dogmatics* also demonstrates eristic thinking when, in paragraph 17, it speaks of the *conditions* of the *possibility* of grace: "Whoever says possibility says eristics. Whoever sets up conditions of grace, guarantees it."

Brunner concludes that "Theology and Modern Man" is an unhelpful contribution to their debate, since its polemic against a theology seeking "guarantees" is a polemic against all theology, including Barth's. All theologians, especially Barth, guarantee their theological work if nowhere else than in their confidence in the ability of human logic:

[Just look at] your unsubdued faith in the power of (theological) logic, with which you trust yourself to examine thoroughly the depths of the Trinity. How solid you must consider the human capacity for thought, that you trust your conclusions so unconditionally based on a concept of revelation. . . . How does it happen that humanity, which has nothing left of the image of God, has such a phenomenally trustworthy logic? . . . In reality you trust humanity in its fallen condition no less

31. Brunner to Barth, October 20, 1930.
32. Barth, *Die Christliche Dogmatik im Entwurf,* Erster Band, *Die Lehre vom Worte Gottes, Prolegomena zur christlichen Dogmatik,* ed. Gerhard Sauter (Zürich: Theologischer Verlag, 1982).

than I (your proof is not by virtue of *regenerated* logic, but is a result of *purely natural* logic), but you do not want to bring it into relationship with the original possession of a knowledge of God through creation.

Barth responds immediately to Brunner's letter.[33] He states bluntly that he can no longer view their "increasingly visible fundamental differences [as] merely accidental, [which] can be rectified by me through further clarifications." If Brunner had read Barth's earlier work more carefully, he would have seen that it "does not run so parallel to yours." Barth feels that Brunner's letter leaves him with only one way to express their differences, "something completely catastrophic":

> Accept the fact . . . that you completely misunderstand not only my prolegomena, . . . but also my *Romans,* since you have obviously not noticed that since 1920 (not *1930,* but 1920) it has been for me a question of "constructing theology from predestination." . . . What have I said to you in this lecture that I have not always maintained as my presupposition, and which I have often expressed to you? And which of my "constructions" in all their forms do not spring from the ground of this presupposition, bound to it and conditioned through it, up to the last little proposition? That is true of the *Prolegomena* as well.

Barth asserts that they are doing theology differently, and the dividing issue is anthropology: "You have not let it be pointed out to you . . . that this anthropological background is lacking in me. Thus, my entire work, despite all the manifold similarities, is to be explained differently from yours. Thus, if not from the very beginning, then for a goodly time, you should have made the most fundamental stand against my work." Barth continues: "Why do you interpret me thus now . . . as if I indeed work with 'guarantees,' when you used to be in the habit of reproaching me in other discussions that I lacked such guarantees and that you must, so to speak, supply them with your eristics? . . . Have you ever heard from me . . . anything other than that I consider all theology to be nonsense which does not absolutely begin 'formally' with obedience?"

Barth ends the letter by suggesting that there exist only two possibilities. Either Brunner converts Barth to "predestination *and* eristics," or

33. Barth to Brunner, October 24, 1930.

Barth converts Brunner to — in the correspondence's most intriguing statement — "a theology which, like a spinning top, supports itself on only one point."

By the end of 1930 Barth concludes that the "dialectical theology" movement has come to an end, torn apart over the issues of revelation's relationship to anthropology and philosophy. It is Brunner's "The Other Task of Theology" which makes this conclusion inevitable in Barth's mind. But neither Brunner, Gogarten, nor Bultmann agrees that the differences are as fundamental as Barth perceives them to be.[34] Thus the "breakup," particularly between Barth and Brunner, drags on for another six years. But in Barth's perspective, only Thurneysen remains committed to what Barth considers his original and controlling insight: the attempt to construct "a theology which, like a spinning top, supports itself on only one point," that is, a theology which respects the absolute freedom of God in his revelation, a reality which creates its own possibility, a reality which is both received and thought out only within the realm of church and faith. As a theology of the living God, it relies upon no external preconditions or possibilities or supports, but only upon grace, revelation, and faith.

Natural Theology (1932-34)

In 1932 both Barth and Brunner publish works, which escalates the division between them. Barth's revised *Church Dogmatics* appears first, containing a ten-page excursus against Brunner's "eristics."[35] Brunner responds with an article entitled "The Question of the 'Point-of-Contact' as a Problem for Theology," in which he further develops his emphasis that a faithful and relevant theology needs a clearly worked-out anthropology.[36] At the end of the year, Brunner writes Barth to thank Barth for sending

34. Throughout 1930 Bultmann attempted to arrange a "summit of the pillars" (i.e., Barth, Bultmann, Brunner, Gogarten, Thurneysen) in order to talk through their differences. But Barth successfully resisted Bultmann's efforts. See *Karl Barth–Rudolf Bultmann: Letters, 1922-1966,* trans. Geoffrey W. Bromiley (Grand Rapids: Eerdmans, 1981), pp. 49-59.

35. Barth, *Church Dogmatics* I/1, trans. G. W. Bromiley, 2nd ed. (Edinburgh: T. & T. Clark, 1975). See §2.1, "The Necessity of Dogmatic Prolegomena," pp. 26-35.

36. Brunner, "Die Frage nach dem 'Anknüpfungspunkt' als Problem der Theologie," *Zwischen den Zeiten* 10 (1932): 505-32.

him a copy of the first volume of the *Church Dogmatics*.[37] He observes that *Church Dogmatics* confirms what they both have come to realize, "that we are . . . proceeding in opposite directions." Brunner attributes their disagreement to Barth's retrograde developments: "You are heading in the direction of a 'perennial theology,' which rejects the special feature of human questions for every time; you believe that, in the twentieth century, you must also answer the questions of the sixteenth century. I, on the other hand, have turned in the direction of the kind of dogmatics which sees its service as answering the questions asked by the modern person." This, Brunner claims, is "where all of our differences have their ultimate ground": "For me, theological work, . . . in the end, is nothing other than a particular type of evangelism, namely the battle against pagan thinking. . . . Perhaps (this is still always my hope), when your great work is brought to completion, you will turn yourself again to the work for which you are so specially equipped, and — if God grants it — you will be allowed really to ring the great bell which the whole world can hear." Instead, Barth responds with a formal renunciation of Brunner as a theological colleague:[38]

> Yes, it is as you write: we continue in opposite directions, only for me it has been, for a long time now, a question not only of an opposition of method and style of writing, but even more a material opposition occurring right down the line. . . . I can understand as a theological friend only one in whom I have trust that he will not make a pact with the ancient serpent, neither with respect to nature nor with respect to grace. I no longer have this trust in you. You have made this pact on both sides as solemnly as possible. . . . It grieves you to hear that from me. But it has first grieved me to see gradually over the years and now completely clearly that we . . . want and intend something completely different materially, so that nothing now remains but for us to renounce the fictitious picture that there is a special solidarity in our work. . . . This renunciation is my answer to the point-of-contact. . . . All you need to do is to understand . . . your letter as radically as possible . . . in order to get the story of the gulf which divides us. All [its] points are non-debatable for me. . . . Here, here at the level of these . . .

37. Brunner to Barth, December 12, 1932.
38. Barth to Brunner, January 2, 1933.

points it must be shown whether we are united in Christology, justification, the Scripture-principle, etc. If we can still be surprised with one another here, how then can it not be that we also intend completely different things in these other doctrines . . . ? . . . The hyphen which has bound your name and mine . . . was a fictitious alliance.

Brunner's response is to lay the blame for their separation at Barth's feet:[39]

There is truth in the saying: as much unity as is possible in some way. You have always been the strong one; you have perceived yourself to be the mightiest alone. You could accomplish it all by yourself. But also consider what it means for Christian people if you throw off everyone — *everyone* — from yourself, and will have fellowship with no one else who comes to the fore theologically. And what will happen if it comes to the point where you have the theological tradition of the entire Church against you! Do what you must, but we will always ask ourselves whether this separation belongs to the necessary issues, or to the uncertain issues, where there is freedom.

One year passes. Then, in May 1934, Brunner writes a short note to Barth, alerting him of the impending publication of his latest monograph, *Nature and Grace: A Conversation with Karl Barth.*[40] Brunner explains the intention behind the pamphlet:

I ask you to accept this booklet as graciously as possible. I have tried as far as I am able to understand what unites and divides us, and I express our opposition as falling within a Reformation-Biblical co-partnership. And thus my wish for fellowship is as clear as my wish for theological specificity. For that reason, I maintain that your teaching on natural theology is not entirely biblical and is not entirely Reformed. But I know that, despite this, you are united with me that it is important to struggle in our Church and in the world for the value of the biblical message in its Reformation interpretation until the end. I believe in this co-partnership.

39. Brunner to Barth, January 16, 1933.
40. Brunner to Barth, May 8, 1934. Brunner, "Nature and Grace," in *Natural Theology,* trans. Peter Fraenkel (London: Centenary, 1946), pp. 15-64.

But, against Brunner's hopes, Barth does not recognize a "co-partnership" in *Nature and Grace*. On the back inside cover of his copy of Brunner's pamphlet, Barth sketches his negative review:

> When B[runner] speaks of God, it becomes and remains dark to my eyes.
> – He does not know the mystery of God, predestination, freedom, the miracle of grace. . . .
> – He does not know how tiresome his struggle against my "one-sidedness" is. . . .
> – He has also certainly not understood Calvin.
> – He makes a caricature of Roman Catholic natural theology so that he can differentiate himself from it. . . .
> – He has still not fully seen how fundamental our opposition is.
> – He writes like a "school-master."
> – It would have been better if he had not written this article.[41]

On September 30 Brunner, clearly worried, writes to Barth.[42] This is caused by the fact that "you have yet to acknowledge either my article or my letter" and that "I constantly see people who rely on your theological leadership who completely cannot grasp the point of disagreement between us." Brunner's anxiety shines through at the close to the letter:

> That we quarrel in our lecture halls . . . doesn't matter at all. . . . But in front of the world? — No. Today? — No. We are one in *the* matter which must really be fought for today in public opinion. You think your position is the best weapon against the German-Christians, etc.; I think mine is better. . . . But most people, who are neither your nor my students, think about it differently. They think, "This shouldn't matter to both of them. What we understand from them is that they both intend the same thing: one Church, which stands on God's Word alone, and they mean Christ alone, and therefore they think that no peace can be concluded with the German-Christians and the like." Is not this the case? Whoever is finally right, Barth or Brunner — what do the people of the world care about that? You can write calmly against me

41. Barth's copy of *Natur und Gnade* is located in the Karl Barth-Archiv, Basel.
42. Brunner to Barth, September 30, 1934.

— that is in order. But not as an enemy, not as against one who stands "on the other side." That should be avoided by all means. . . .

I will maintain, as before — despite everything that divides us — our fellowship in the main things, unless you disavow it.

Barth does disavow it, by return post, in a letter which is summed up in its opening line: "It is too late now."[43] Barth writes:

I regret the existence of your article in the highest, and I reject its contents most definitely and completely. . . .

I wish you had not written that article! But I must go further: I wish you had not begun the whole campaign which you have led against me since 1929, or at least that you knew exactly what you wanted to say and could and would say it without misunderstanding! But that is a completely idle wish, because now that you must develop your position in this direction I may say . . . , on the contrary, that your article has created a fact.

As Barth sees it, Brunner has issued a severe challenge to Barth's theological resistance to the German Christians, and so Barth must answer it in that vein: "All the world points to [*Nature and Grace*] and asks me what I have to say. Now I *will* say what I have to say, and that will be a plain No. Although I have for so long kept silent, now I will no longer be impeded. . . . This soup finally must be eaten. I wish nothing more than that you had not served it to us! 'I would give anything for him to keep quiet!' one could hear me groan more than once [this summer]. But now it has happened, and now on both sides everything must be taken up as it lies in the moment." Barth ends his letter: "Humanly speaking as before, with sincere greetings, but theologically speaking with the deepest concerns imaginable."

Brunner replies by return post in a state of high agitation.[44] He is baffled by the inability of the "Barthians" to interpret *Nature and Grace* according to its plain meaning. The problem, Brunner states, is Barth's "sectarian spirit," "that you consider your peculiar doctrine, which goes way beyond anything the Church has ever taught, to be the only legitimate,

43. Barth to Brunner, October 1, 1934.
44. Brunner to Barth, October 2, 1934.

Christian and Church position; that you maintain it in spite of all documentary evidence to the contrary; that you alone teach Reformation doctrine. That is the psychology of the major sects, and it is completely and utterly non-churchly. . . . Since Barth teaches something one way, everybody is a heretic who teaches it some other way." Brunner is unable to end the letter. He adds a postscript the next morning before mailing the letter:

> You have carried out a year-long theological terror. And yet you have been spared, because your hangers-on no longer let even friendly criticism get near to you. Thus, otherwise completely different people were glad if, for once, someone woke you up in some way, who had something to say against you. . . . There are very many righteous ones who have fallen in with you in the Church struggle, but who theologically place themselves on my side, and it is exclusively the Barthians who are annoyed. You obviously have no idea how isolated a theologian you are, not because you represent a peculiar opinion — who doesn't? — but because you identify this peculiar opinion with the article on which the Church stands or falls. Thus stands the issue objectively. And outside the Barthian circle — which is almost a magical circle — everybody knows this, whether they are otherwise orthodox, liberal, Calvinist, Lutheran, Pietist or whatever. In this matter, the entire Church stands against: Barthianism.

In his "No! Answer to Emil Brunner," Barth delivers a devastating final response to their ten-year debate. He completely rejects Brunner's theological program, arguing that theology must "turn away from all 'true' or 'false' natural theology" so that the church can "learn again to understand revelation as *grace* and grace as *revelation*."[45]

Conclusion

The Barth-Brunner correspondence clearly demonstrates that their "natural theology debate" was the climax of a long-running disagreement over many issues: the nature of "dialectical" method, the relationship of theol-

45. Barth, "No! Answer to Emil Brunner," in *Natural Theology,* pp. 65-128, quotes on p. 71.

ogy and philosophy, the place of anthropology in theology, and the task of theology. Let me close by making four observations about the correspondence's contribution to Barth scholarship.

First, an examination of the correspondence supports Bruce McCormack's thesis of "continuity" over von Balthasar's thesis of "stages" in understanding Barth's theological development.[46] Though it takes several years for Barth to clarify and express the severity of his disagreements with Brunner, Barth's consistent objections to the direction of Brunner's theology begin early and continue to escalate.

Second, the correspondence demonstrates that Barth's rejection of natural theology is grounded in theological, not political, reasons. The issues raised by Friedrich-Wilhelm Marquardt's political reading of Barth have led some scholars to ground Barth's opposition to natural theology in his political resistance to Nazism.[47] While the political and church struggles of the early 1930s increase the intensity of the Barth-Brunner debate, Barth's outright and uncompromising opposition to Brunner's experiments with natural theology are expressed as early as 1929, with strong reservations registered as early as 1925.

Third, the Barth-Brunner correspondence reveals an ongoing difference in these two theologians' material commitments. In particular, Barth and Brunner continually emphasize different poles of the divine-human action. Barth understands "God is God" to be the first and most demanding word of theology. Thus he gives prominence to the doctrine of election, and radically and objectively develops the Reformation *sola* slogans: grace alone, Scripture alone, faith alone, Christ alone. In contrast, Brunner has a nonnegotiable commitment to human freedom and responsibility. Thus, in Brunner's thinking, the great disturbance in life — the "crisis" — is the fact of human sin, whereas for Barth the "crisis" is the disturbance caused by God's grace. Thus for Barth the key decision is the one made by

---

46. Bruce L. McCormack, *Karl Barth's Critically Realistic Dialectical Theology* (Oxford: Clarendon, 1995), and Hans Urs von Balthasar, *Theology of Karl Barth*, trans. John Drury (New York: Holt, Rinehart and Winston, 1971). Other scholars who stress continuity in Barth's development include Michael Beintker and Ingrid Spieckermann. See Beintker, *Die Dialektik in der "dialektischen Theologie" Karl Barths* (Munich: Chr. Kaiser, 1987); Spieckermann, *Gotteserkenntnis: Ein Beitrag zur Grundfrage der neuen Theologie Karl Barths*, Beiträge zur evangelischen Theologie 97 (Munich: Chr. Kaiser, 1985).

47. Friedrich-Wilhelm Marquardt, *Theologie und Sozialismus* (Munich: Chr. Kaiser, 1972). See also Peter Winzeler, *Widerstehende Theologie* (Stuttgart: Alektor Verlag, 1982).

God in the eternal election of humanity in Jesus Christ; for Brunner the key decision is the responsible decision of the individual for faith. This material distinction is seen as early as 1918, when Brunner first notes what will become his ongoing criticism of what he terms Barth's "one-sidedness."

Finally, the correspondence also reveals the distinctive theological methods of these two theologians, particularly their different understandings of "dialectic." Barth's dialectical method acknowledges that humanity cannot speak directly of God, even of the self-revealing God, who remains concealed even in his self-revelation. From his earliest days, Barth understands this fundamental ontological and noetic gap between God and humanity in its most radical sense. There is no human possibility of theology — theology is possible only as the church's thoughtful obedience of faith, "following after" the revelation as witnessed to in Scripture, always standing in need of God's justifying grace. Extending Barth's metaphor from "Theology and Modern Man": God's revelation is a galloping horse on the loose — wild, powerful, and solely in charge of where it is going. For Barth dialectical theology respects revelation's sovereign freedom and its inability to be controlled. Therefore the theologian's task is to "follow after" the horse by clinging for dear life to the horse's tail.[48]

Conversely, Brunner's philosophical commitment to Kantianism makes it difficult for him to accept such a radically discontinuous understanding of dialectic. The most revealing evidence here is Brunner's September 2, 1920, letter to Barth: Barth's "dialectical watch-dog" is too indiscriminate for Brunner, who prefers a "critical (i.e., Kantian) watch-dog." For a brief period immediately following the publication of the second edition of *Romans*, Brunner seems to understand and embrace Barth's more radically dialectical theology. But since the radicalism of Barth's dialectic is not easy to assimilate with Brunner's other commitments — Kantian critical idealism, Kierkegaardian existentialism, and Ebnerian personalism — as early as 1925 Brunner begins to slough it off, allowing his other commitments to come to the fore. Thus, while Barth develops a *dialectical* theology, Brunner constructs a *dialogical* theology.[49]

The Barth-Brunner correspondence demonstrates that these men

---

48. Barth, "Die Theologie und der heutige Mensch," p. 393.

49. Stefan Scheld, *Die Christologie Emil Brunners* (Wiesbaden: Franz Steiner Verlag, 1981), p. 98.

represent two fundamentally different ways of doing theology. This is the case despite the fact that, viewed within the context of the history of theology, it would be difficult to find many theologians closer to Barth than Brunner. In the end, the breakup of the Barth-Brunner alliance tells us less about Brunner's theology than it does about Barth's. For what separates Brunner from Barth is what separates Barth from every theologian — he builds his theology on a dialectical, actualist, and christocentric radicalizing of the Reformation *solas*. Though the gulf is narrow between Barth and Brunner, this is the gulf which completely surrounds Barth in the history of theology.[50]

---

50. For an extensive examination of the entire Barth-Brunner relationship, see the author's *Karl Barth vs. Emil Brunner: The Formation and Dissolution of a Theological Alliance, 1916-1936* (New York: Peter Lang, 2001).

The Barth-Brunner Correspondence

DANIEL L. MIGLIORE

The first word in response to this paper must be a sincere word of thanks. Not only has John Hart provided us with a generous sampling of excerpts from the recently published correspondence between Barth and Brunner, he has also tracked the exchange in a remarkably deft and clear manner. We are taken step-by-step on a journey that seems to move inexorably to its conclusion in Barth's decisive No! Carefully researched and balanced in its conclusions, Hart's paper has whetted our appetite for his soon-to-be-published book as well as for the actual texts of the Barth-Brunner correspondence edited by Eberhard Busch for the *Gesamtausgabe.*

Since I did not have access to the correspondence on which the paper is based, my response must be limited to the excerpts provided by Hart and to the already available literature. I will first make a few comments about each of the five epistolary "interactions" of Brunner and Barth identified in Hart's paper. Then I will conclude with a few words about some of the larger issues raised by this remarkable correspondence for the theme of this first session of our conference, "Karl Barth and the Future of Dialogue."

In the first section of his paper Hart shows that Barth and Brunner are divided from the very beginning regarding the object of theology. When Brunner writes about his personal struggles of faith in the summer of 1916, Barth is sympathetic but warns Brunner that the "religious labyrinth has no exit." "We are not Pietists," Barth reminds his friend. Summarizing this early exchange, Hart comments: "For Barth the proper object of theology is

God in his revelation. For Brunner theology must not only speak about God, but must also speak decisively about the believing subject."

While I think Hart's conclusion is sound, I wonder whether it could easily leave a mistaken impression. Isn't Barth's idea of the "object of theology" more complex, even in 1916, than is captured by a contrast between "God in his revelation" on the one hand and "God and the believing subject" on the other? Although Brunner is eager to tell Barth that he too has been grasped by the summons to recognize that "God is God," it is fairly clear that the two theologians understand this theme rather differently.

I suggest there is a dimension of the theme "God is God" that for Barth in 1916 is only germinating and for Brunner is apparently completely missing. In the autumn of that same year Barth gave his lecture on "the new world of the Bible." Even at this very early stage of his break from liberal theology, Barth knows that a theology that attends to the biblical witness that "God is God" cannot talk about God as simply separate from the world. In his lecture Barth explicitly parses the theme "God is God" in a trinitarian manner. The affirmation "God is God" refers not to a God in isolation from the world but to the Father who purposes the establishment of a new world, to the Son who is the glorious beginning of a new world, and to the Holy Spirit who is in the world and in us making for "a new heaven and a new earth and, therefore, new persons, new families, new relationships, new politics." In other words, for Barth the theme "God is God" means more than that God is infinite and transcendent. The God who is really God is related to and active in the world and in men and women of faith.

My first question, then, is whether there is any indication in the early correspondence with Brunner that Barth wants to be understood this way. If not, it may not be surprising that the seeds of misunderstanding are present from the very beginning of the conversation. As Hart's excerpts show, Brunner evidently has no clue how the emphasis on the "objectivity of God" has anything to do with his concern that theology must also speak of the real human subject. Eventually, as we know, Barth will make it luminously clear that he does not intend to speak of God alone but of God *and* humanity. He will insist on doing this, however, on a christological and trinitarian basis and in the proper order. It seems clear from the correspondence, however, that Brunner has no idea how Barth's call to "stretch out" to "God in his objectivity" touches Brunner's own concern, and he feels he has to scold Barth's "one-sidedness." Then, some years later, he will think he has discovered a "new Barth" with the publication of Barth's anthropology in the *Church Dogmatics.*

Moving to the section on the method of theology, Hart draws our attention to Brunner's distinction in the correspondence of 1920 between the "dialectical No" and the "critical No." Favoring the Kantian critical no, Brunner rejects Barth's dialectical no as undiscriminating. Hart suggests that Brunner's commitment to dialectical theology — which reached its peak with his work on Schleiermacher in 1924 and his book *The Mediator* in 1927 — was blunted by his growing interest in Ferdinand Ebner's I-Thou philosophy. It was Ebner's philosophy, says Hart, that eventually moved Brunner toward a theology of "dialogue" rather than "dialectic." While Hart may well be right in this judgment, I think further clarification of the different meanings the terms "dialectic" and "dialogue" may have had for Brunner and Barth is needed.

On Barth's side, a so-called dialectical method was no fail-safe answer to the question of responsible thinking and speaking of God. In his lectures in dogmatics given in Göttingen in the early 1920s, Barth advises his students neither to be intimidated by the word "dialectic" nor to use it too frequently lest it become a mere slogan. The living reality of God in revelation determines Barth's use of dialectic rather than his being wedded formally to a method called dialectic.

On Brunner's side, despite his distinction between an undiscriminating dialectical no and a critical no in theology, I do not think he would have had difficulty owning the term "dialectical." What Brunner calls critical philosophy is also for him a form of dialectical thinking, albeit a dialectic different from what Brunner early on calls Barth's undiscriminating dialectic. As far as I can tell, in the mid-1920s Brunner uses the term "dialectic" not as an alternative to but in conjunction with the theme of critical thinking. Brunner identifies Plato, Kant, and Kierkegaard as among the eminent critical philosophers. Each could be described as a dialectical thinker. In his inaugural lecture at Zürich in 1924, for example, Brunner cites Socrates' relentless method of questioning (Do you really know what you think you know?) as exemplary of critical (I think we must also read, dialectical) thinking. For Brunner Kant's critical philosophy reaches its greatest height in the transcendental dialectic. Then too, Brunner can speak of Kierkegaard as the greatest Protestant apologist or eristic thinker, and unquestionably viewed him as a model of the truly critical, dialectical thinker.

My point is that Brunner too would probably stake a claim on the term "dialectical." Indeed, in *Nature and Grace* Brunner charges that Barth "kills the dialectic" of the knowledge of sin by failing to concede that if knowledge of sin comes only by the grace of God, it is equally true that the grace of God is comprehensible only to someone who already knows about sin. But while Brunner would no doubt also claim to be a dialectical theologian, Barth differs from Brunner, first in refusing to canonize any particular philosophical uses of dialectic, and second in grounding his use of dialectic in the dialectic of revelation, which is decisively the dialectic of God's grace and judgment, of God's forgiveness of the sinner, and above all, of the revelation and hiddenness of God's presence and activity in Jesus Christ.

In sum, the difference between Barth and Brunner regarding dialectical thinking in theology is not simply that Barth chooses the path of dialectic while Brunner chooses the path of dialogue. As Barth will later explain, dialectic in theology is not "any sort of dialectic" but "the very special dialectic of the revelation and being of God" in the person and work of Jesus Christ. I see no reason why Barth could not have said the same thing of dialogical thinking in theology: it is not just "any sort of dialogue" but "the very special dialogue" of the revelation and being of God with us in Jesus Christ.

In his section on the foundation of theology, Hart explains that a key issue between Barth and Brunner revolves around Brunner's effort to "explain the relationship of philosophy and theology in terms of the Law as the 'border' or 'limit' of human knowledge." I think this section of Hart's paper may well bring us to the crux of the divergence between Brunner and Barth, viz., their different understandings of the relation between law and gospel.

For Brunner there is a critical and propaedeutic function of the law that is always presupposed by the gospel. According to Brunner, the law of God is present not only in the Old Testament but also in the created order and in human conscience. Brunner describes the law as a kind of back side of God in distinction from the gospel that shows the "face of God." In the law God confronts us in the strange form of being against us, that is, by exposing our guilt before the law, rather than being for us as the one who forgives our sins, as announced in the gospel. All this sounds very much like Luther sans Calvin. Barth for his part shows his Reformed colors by asking Brunner whether the law of God is not more than limit and opposition.

But Barth's emerging position is no mere repristination of Calvin on law and gospel. In refusing to base theology on any particular philosophy or philosophical ethic, even one purporting to be based on the law of God, Barth is already on a path that will lead to his explicit reversal of the order of law and gospel in his famous lecture on this topic in 1935.

(A parenthetical comment. Since both Brunner and Bultmann speak of encounter with the law as the necessary presupposition of understanding the gospel, I am intrigued by the rather different tone of the correspondence between Barth and Brunner on the one hand and between Barth and Bultmann on the other. Am I right that in dealing with Bultmann, Barth is — while certainly as firm as with Brunner — nevertheless rather more ready to have the conversation continue? What is to be made of this in view of the fact that Bultmann's systematic use of Heidegger in the interpretation of the New Testament message is surely no less, and perhaps even more, invasive of the dogmatic task than is Brunner's adoption of Kantian and Kierkegaardian critical philosophy in his eristics? If Barth could say of his Marburg friend, that whoever takes a swing at Bultmann had better be careful not to hit Luther, could not Barth also have said of his fellow Reformed theologian, that whoever takes a swing at Brunner had better be careful not to hit Luther and/or Calvin?)

However that may be, Brunner thinks Barth pays no attention to the necessary presupposition of the law in apprehending the revelation in Christ. Barth for his part thinks Brunner postulates a knowledge of the law as something inherent in human nature and available outside of the revelation in Christ. My question is this: At least in the excerpts of the correspondence Hart provides, does either theologian linger long on the point that it is God the Holy Spirit who goes ahead of the preaching of Christ and prepares human sinners and unbelievers to receive the gospel? The doctrine of the Holy Spirit and particularly how the Spirit's work is to be discerned is unquestionably a deep issue between Barth and Brunner from the beginning.

In the next section of Hart's paper, on the task of theology, he notes that Brunner's talk about the "other task of theology" calls forth from Barth the striking image of "a theology which, like a spinning top, supports itself on only one point." Barth and Brunner's exchange on the topic of the task of theology often seems to lack clarity because it fails to make important distinctions, as for example, between the basis of theology and the tasks of theology. In the second edition of *Nature and Grace*, Brunner admits he made a terrible mistake in speaking of the development of a true *theologia naturalis* as *the* task of our theological generation. Brunner does not deny that discussion with non-Christian thought cannot be the basis of theology or its primary task. (Cf. the title of Brunner's inaugural lecture at Zürich in 1925: "Offenbarung als Grund und Gegenstand der Theologie.")

As usual, however, Barth is far more precise in describing the nature and task of theology. Already in the Göttingen dogmatics, he insists that Christian preaching and dogmatics must think and speak about God by strictly following the event of revelation, i.e., by describing God and humanity as they are depicted in this event. That said, must we not assume that Barth would concede that there are other theological disciplines besides dogmatics that have their own distinctive tasks?

In 1934 Barth says No! all along the line to Brunner's argument of a necessary "point of contact" and his program of eristics. Barth now sees a "material opposition" between them, and not only with regard to matters like revelation and the image of God but "right down the line." He asks, how can it not be that we also intend "completely different things" in other central doctrines (Christology, justification, the Scripture principle, etc.)? I am not sure whether Hart wants to follow Barth to the point of seeing the two theologians as intending "completely different things" in all the central doctrines of the faith. His conclusion is more modest: "These men represent two fundamentally different ways of doing theology." That leaves open the question whether Barth and Brunner teach "completely different" Christologies and doctrines of justification, a question that could be decided only by close study of their principal doctrinal writings.

My guess is that a major material difference between Barth and Brunner — not mentioned by Hart in his paper but considered at some length in his forthcoming book — is in the area of ecclesiology. My check of the *Church Dogmatics* shows that there are five areas where Barth engages Brunner in debate after the breakdown of their relationship: regarding the issue of eristics in I/1, the doctrine of the virgin birth in I/2, issues in anthropology in III/2, differences in ethics in III/4, and issues in ecclesiology in IV/2. Of these, the ecclesiological divergence may finally be the deepest. Which prompts one to wonder whether Barth really did misjudge Brunner early on when he wrote to him: "We are not Pietists." While Barth was far more "catholic" than "pietistic" in his ecclesiology, the reverse was true of Brunner. But this important ecclesiological difference is a topic in itself, and one that Hart is well prepared to address.

In conclusion I would like to make a few comments on the theme of our session this afternoon, "Karl Barth and the Future of Dialogue."

First, Hart says that "while Barth develops a dialectical theology, Brunner constructs a dialogical theology." I would like to ask whether that is intended to be an either/or choice, and if so, in what sense? If one has to choose between dialectical and dialogical theology, what is the future of dialogue on the soil of Barth's dialectical theology? Or can there be a dialectical theology in dialogue that is not a dialogical theology? If so, what would be the assumptions of a dialectical theology in dialogue?

Second, Hart's paper helps us see how emphatically Barth rejects any "foundationalism" in theology in the sense of positing a particular philosophy (whether Aristotle in the case of Thomas, Kant in the case of Brunner, or Heidegger in the case of Bultmann) as the necessary starting point and basis of Christian theology. As we know, however, Barth does not intend that his position be construed as isolating Christian theology from other disciplines or even from other faiths. For example, in the correspondence Barth tells Brunner that he agrees that Kant's philosophy is "the most desirable and helpful" to Christian theology. What did Brunner make of that statement? What do we make of it as it bears on the theme "Karl Barth and the Future of Dialogue"?

Third, Brunner describes himself as a preacher, an apologist, and a missionary, and his theology is obviously shaped by these contexts. Brunner's talk of the "other task" of theology is surely related to the question today about the possibility of a public theology. Are an ecclesial theology and a public theology mutually exclusive categories? I doubt that Barth thought so, although it would depend, of course, on how "public theology" is defined. I find it telling that one of Barth's criticisms of Brunner's ecclesiology in *Church Dogmatics* IV/2 is that it undercuts the responsible *public* expression of Christian faith. Brunner was obviously concerned that Barth's conception of theology would result in an ecclesiastical ghetto. While that is no doubt a danger, I think today we can appreciate Barth's emphasis on theology as an ecclesial discipline far better than Brunner did. In a radically pluralistic society, it makes increasing sense to undertake what David Tracy calls "the journey into the particularity" of one's tradition as offering as good a hope as any of both doing responsible theology and making a contribution to the common good.

Fourth, while the Barth-Brunner correspondence can act as a stimulus for the theme of "Karl Barth and the Future of Dialogue," the deep issues are surely far from resolved in this fascinating correspondence. In a sense, Barth is making a clean sweep in his debate with Brunner. He makes crystal clear what he doesn't want. To grasp the sense in which his theology is an open ecclesial theology, one must turn to such passages of the *Church Dogmatics* as his wrestling with the Enlightenment conception of human selfhood in III/2 or his reflections on the light of life and the other lights in IV/3.

I raise these questions in gratitude to John Hart for his very informative and stimulating paper.

Indissoluble Unity:
Barth's Position on the Jews
during the Hitler Era

EBERHARD BUSCH

If we wish to rethink how the church is related to Judaism, how might Karl Barth's struggle with that question during the Nazi era be of help to us? It is obvious that we cannot simply repeat his statements today. Yet turning to Barth would be pointless were we curiously to conclude, as have some commentators, that his protest against anti-Semitism was actually in league with his adversaries. (These commentators, it seems, imagine the Nazi era as a proverbial night in which all cats are gray.) It would, moreover, be of little use to find in Barth some interesting preliminary ideas, to the extent that they agree with our own, in order then, where we differ from him, to magnify all the supposed problems in his position that we believe ourselves to have successfully overcome. In neither case would we learn anything, but only confirm our own position. If our encounter with a teacher of the church is to be fruitful, we must enter into a conversation in which we are not only the questioners, but also those who are questioned. Admittedly, such a teacher, whom we may critically question, is only an authority subject to the Word of God. But a proper teacher of the church is indeed an authority under the Word, and his or her question to us, therefore, is whether in our desire to move forward we are following God's Word as attested in the Bible or only our own authority. Certainly there can also be futile en-

This essay was translated by James Seyler and Arnold Neufeldt-Fast, Ph.D., and edited by Darrell L. Guder and George Hunsinger.

counters. Could it be that the light Barth believed he glimpsed was merely a flickering ember, too weak to have been instructive even then, let alone worthwhile for today? According to the currently predominant interpretation, not only Barth's doctrine in those sorry times but also his conduct must be regarded as deficient. It is this matter that I wish to explore.

The Contemporary Historical Context

To begin with, in this interpretation a glaring weakness is perceived in Barth's practical conduct, a weakness also supposedly reflected in his theological teachings. Klaus Scholder interprets the situation as follows.[1]

In 1933, with his strong emphasis on the first commandment and on the binding force of God's Word, Barth took a stand that, though well intentioned, should have been expressed with less intolerance. While he concentrated upon keeping doctrine pure in the church's pulpits, he saw no problems in the Nazi state itself. Inevitably he glossed over the significance of "the Jewish question." Because he managed to implant his views during the German church struggle into the emerging Confessing Church, he himself was principally to blame that this church ignored the Jewish crisis so completely. This is a picture that has been painted with many variations, enriched by two further elements. Some claim that even after returning to Switzerland (one researcher ascribes this to his desire for a higher salary),[2] he was still uninterested in taking a stand for the Jews. He worked quietly in his study on his *Dogmatics* as if Hitler did not exist.[3] Others suggest that he was hindered by the Christocentrism of his stance from seeing the Jews as concrete human beings. He regarded them partly as God's chosen people, but also partly as divinely rejected.[4] That Barth alone, not Gogarten,

1. Klaus Scholder, *Die Kirchen und das Dritte Reich,* vol. 1 (Frankfurt et al., 1977), pp. 546-59.

2. Wolfgang Gerlach, "Theologische Höhenluft über der Wupper," *Deutsches Allgemeines Sonntagsblatt,* November 3, 1985, p. 16. The slander that twists Barth's expulsion from Germany into a retreat for dishonorable reasons has its parallels in the Nazi propaganda of that time.

3. Gerlach, *Als die Zeugen schwiegen: Bekennende Kirche und die Juden* (Berlin: Institut Kirche und Judentum, 1987), p. 408.

4. F. W. Marquardt, *Die Entdeckung des Judentums für die christliche Theologie: Israel im Denken Karl Barths* (Munich: Chr. Kaiser, 1967), pp. 266ff.

Hirsch, or Althaus, finally drafted a confession of guilt and repentance toward the Jews[5] has been interpreted as an admission of his own failure.

In light of the sources, however, we can see that such appraisals involve a web of misrepresentations. Let me give some examples. The Civil Service Act of April 1933 contained more than simply a section on the protection of Aryan culture, though that is what we usually read about it. It was especially effective for eliminating critics of the Nazi state. After the act was instituted Barth asked Rust, the minister for cultural affairs, whether he could continue to teach in Bonn, even if he were to exercise the same loyalty to Hitler's regime that the nationalists had shown toward the Weimar Republic (i.e., none whatsoever).[6] Clever interpretation turns this into Barth's approval of the state, so that he might continue to indulge in his theology undisturbed.[7] Again, to take another example, if Barth, in his widely distributed sermon of December 1933 (which he even sent to Hitler), interpreted the Jewishness of Jesus as a nonnegotiable item of faith, and emphasized that he regarded both Jews and Gentiles as children of the living God,[8] then the commentators conclude that Barth would have remained silent on the Jewish question had the text not compelled him to do otherwise.[9] Scholder supports his allegation that Barth was silent about the Jews in 1933 by citing from a letter,[10] without revealing that it asserts: "The solution to the Jewish question that is currently being sought in Germany is an impossibility — humanly, politically, christianly. . . . It is necessary that the Evangelical Church make itself heard with a resounding 'no'" and "enter the fray in diligent support of the members of the synagogue." The trouble was, however, that such a church "as things stand simply does not exist."[11] Similarly, another commentator, Krumwiede, seeks to document Barth's lack of interest in the Jews with a letter dated September 1,

---

5. Cf. Eberhard Busch, *Unter dem Bogen des einen Bundes: Karl Barth und die Juden, 1933-1945* (Neukirchen-Vluyn: Neukirchener Verlag, 1996), pp. 523-37.

6. According to Hans Prolingheuer, *Der Fall Karl Barth: Chronographie einer Vertreibung, 1934-1935*, 2nd ed. (Neukirchen-Vluyn: Neukirchener Verlag, 1984), p. 233.

7. For one example out of many, see Busch, *Unter dem Bogen*, p. 41.

8. Karl Barth, "Die Kirche Jesus Christi," in *Theologische Existenz heute*, 5 (Munich, 1933). A copy of Barth's letter to Hitler is in Scholder, *Die Kirchen und das Dritte Reich*, vol. 2 (Berlin, 1985), p. 77.

9. For references see Busch, *Unter dem Bogen*, pp. 165f.

10. Scholder, *Die Kirchen und das Dritte Reich*, 1:558 n. 101.

11. Barth to Frau Schmidt, January 1, 1934, in Barth-Archiv, Basel.

1933, while leaving out its content.[12] The letter states: "The Jewish question is certainly, seen theologically, the key to all that is happening in our time. . . . Here, especially, I could not participate, even in the smallest fashion, in National Socialism. Here, if anywhere, one must draw the line which, if crossed, can only be seen as a betrayal of the Gospel."[13] What kind of scholarship is this whereby Germans, in dealing with someone who was a victim of the Nazi regime, now claim in retrospect that he was wrongly brought to trial and then expelled from the country because in truth he was a child of that same diabolic spirit!

It is indeed true that during the months of his direct involvement in the German church struggle he fought for the principle that God's Word is exclusively binding. Why was Barth's central concern not to repudiate the German Christians — who were completely unacceptable to him — but rather to criticize those within the church who rejected the German Christians? Recent commentators dismiss Barth's opposition to the more intermediate group as exaggerated and harsh, although its significance at that time was clearly understood not only in the church and among theologians, but also by Thomas Mann, by the Social Democratic Party in exile, and even by some synagogues.[14] I repeat Barth's statement: "Such a church as things stand simply does not exist" — not even among those who rejected the German Christians. A church failed to exist, in other words, which, as an expression of its very being, would speak out in support of the Jews. The really existing church was distorted to the core because it did not support the Jews as the most obvious thing it had to do. How so?

In April 1933 Barth wrote about the intermediate group: "The assumption that one could be in agreement with the German Christians' Preamble (in their affirmation of the Nazi state), yet still be a pure church in opposition to them, . . . will prove to be one of the most deceptive illusions of an era replete with such illusions. Let us leave out the Preamble, totally and forthrightly, and then we will speak further about that which follows."[15] Unlike the mix of Christendom and Nazi doctrine promulgated

12. H.-W. Krumwiede, "Göttinger Theologie im Hitler-Staat," *Jahrbuch der Gesellschaft für niedersächsische Kirchengeschichte* 85 (1987): 160.

13. Barth to Frau Dalmann, September 1, 1933, in Barth-Archiv, Basel.

14. References in Busch, *Unter dem Bogen*, pp. 87-95, 179-80.

15. Barth to Georg Merz, cited in W. Koch, "Barths erste Auseinandersetzungen mit dem Dritten Reich," in *Richte unsere Füße auf den Weg des Friedens* (Munich: Chr. Kaiser, 1979), p. 501.

by the German Christians, a type of "two kingdoms" doctrine prevailed among the intermediate group opposed to them. Politically, it was supposed, one could be a brownshirt or a German nationalist, and therefore support the state's policy toward the Jews, as long as it proceeded "lawfully." Ecclesiastically, on the other hand, one wished to uphold the church's confessional stance. Therefore one would not separate oneself from baptized Jews, even though one viewed them as an alien race. It was completely pointless, in Barth's judgment, to exit a German Christian church that segregated itself from baptized Jews, as recommended by Bonhoeffer, in order to set up a free church based on such a two-kingdoms doctrine.[16] As long as that doctrine (in its prevailing version) was not repudiated, this church would be founded on a colossal mistake. It would be unable to speak out for any Jews outside the church, since it abandoned them to the devices of the state.

That Barth's stance should indicate a "lack of interest" in the Jews, as commentators constantly repeat, does not seem to rest on sound logic. By attacking this two-kingdoms doctrine head-on — by insisting on the first commandment and on Matthew 6:24 ("You cannot serve God and mammon")[17] — Barth attacked the roots of the church's political miscarriage of justice. He insisted that the church's positions toward the Nazi state, its ideology and its racism, should be defined strictly according to the Word of God, not according to state ideology. It was well understood at the time that this was Barth's concern. In October 1933 in Berlin, in his first encounter with the newly organized church resistance of the Pastor's Emergency League *(Pfarrernotbund)*, Barth articulated the crux of his stance: "What does the church have to say about what is happening in the concentration camps? Or about the treatment of the Jews?" The church, he urged, must not remain silent on these questions. For "the one whose duty it is to proclaim the Word of God must address such events with what the Word of God declares."[18] That sums up, in a single sentence, the practical thrust of

16. See Dietrich Bonhoeffer, *Gesammelte Schriften*, vol. 2 (Munich: Chr. Kaiser, 1965), pp. 165-70. Cf. Barth, "Lutherfeier 1933," in *Theologische Existenz heute*, 4 (Munich: Chr. Kaiser, 1933), pp. 4-5.

17. See Barth, "Reformation als Entscheidung," in *Theologische Existenz heute*, 3 (Munich: Chr. Kaiser, 1933), pp. 12-14; Barth, "Gottes Wille und unsere Wünsche," *Theologische Existenz heute*, 7 (Munich: Chr. Kaiser, 1934), p. 6.

18. *Reformationstag 1933: Dokumente der Begegnung Karl Barths mit dem Pfarrernotbund in Berlin*, ed. Busch (Zürich: Theologischer Verlag, 1998), pp. 69-70, 106.

his quarrel with the two-kingdoms doctrine. Again, this was understood at the time. It was not merely his refusal to swear the oath of unconditional allegiance to Hitler — in which his concern was certainly to take seriously God's Word as exclusively binding — it was those Berlin statements about the treatment of the Jews that led politically to his dismissal from the university, to the Confessing Church's movement away from him, and finally to his expulsion from Germany.[19]

From his life in Switzerland between 1935 and 1945, two further episodes may be mentioned. The first took place after the *Kristallnacht* of 1938. At that time Barth gave a lecture to the Swiss Protestant Relief Agency, which from then on, and with his assistance, gave support to the racially persecuted. Its motto was John 4:22, "Salvation is from the Jews." In his remarks Barth stated: In the German "plague of anti-Semitism," in the destruction of Jewish synagogues and Torah scrolls, in the willful "physical extermination" of the Jews, a profound struggle exists against the God of the Jews. Moreover, because the God of the Jews is also the God of Christians, the church is also under "fundamental attack." Therefore the church must now urge, "even if no one else does," that military resistance to the German state "is unconditionally necessary."[20] In the years that followed, Barth persisted with this appeal so outspokenly that the Nazi Foreign Ministry, together with the Swiss government, tried to do everything to silence him.[21] Rabbi Geis explained in retrospect: "Who, other than Karl Barth, could have demonstrated more clearly the struggle and courageous resistance that develops from grace?"[22]

The second episode dates from July 1944. After the failed attempt to assassinate Hitler, and after Rabbi Taubes had informed him about the extermination of the Hungarian Jews, Barth pleaded with his government to act.[23] In a lecture, his voice quavering, he spoke of a new Golgotha and asked about the presence of God with his suffering servant. We must cling, he said, to the promise of Jeremiah 31. As surely as the fixed order of the

---

19. *Reformationstag 1933*, pp. 20-26.

20. Barth, *Eine Schweizer Stimme, 1938-1945* (Zürich-Zollikon, 1945), pp. 69-107.

21. See Busch, "Der Theologe Karl Barth und die Politik des Schweizer Bundesrats: Eine Darstellung anhand von unveröffentlichten Akten der Schweizer Behörden," *Evangelische Theologie* 59 (1999): 172-86.

22. R. R. Geis, *Leiden an der Unerlöstheit der Welt: Briefe, Reden, Aufsätze*, ed. D. Goldschmidt and I. Überschär (Munich, 1984), p. 240.

23. For more, see the citation in Busch, *Unter dem Bogen*, pp. 515-17.

heavens will not pass away, so surely will "the offspring of Israel" never "cease to be a nation before me forever" (Jer. 31:36). It was a "proof for the existence of God," he stated, that any nation murdering the Jews as Pharaoh and his army had done, must "inevitably" meet a horrific end.[24] A statement as blunt as this is still painful for Germans today. The unambiguous clarity of Barth's position at that time has convinced me, at least, that the difficult passage from volume II/2 of his *Dogmatics* on Israel and the church (written in approximately 1940) must be interpreted in a different light than has commonly been the case. It should be read in such a way that, in agreement with his critique of the two-kingdoms doctrine, it lays out the theological basis for his political action. In fact, we must examine this passage all the more carefully because an allegation exists that although Barth fought against political anti-Semitism, he did so as an anti-Judaic theologian.[25]

The One Elected Community in God's One Covenant of Grace

While drafting that passage, Barth wrote: "Though everything is very difficult and deep, I think I have nevertheless seen a certain light."[26] His text itself is certainly "very difficult." That is also a function of its subject matter. Even when the enigmatic relationship between Israel and the church becomes somewhat clearer to us, even when we have left behind every form of anti-Judaism and have traveled a long road as Paul did in Romans 9–11, we will still stand before the ultimate mystery of God's election and confess: "How unsearchable are his judgments and how inscrutable his ways!" (Rom. 11:33). The difficulty also lies in the fact that Barth attempted to say something new on this question, while he was also apparently influenced by dubious traditions and tenacious patterns of thought. Frequently taken up and reworked in modernity, these old thought forms have in some ways influenced his attempt and clouded it as well. One must note, however, how he dealt with them. One difficulty lies in Barth's manner of expres-

---

24. Barth, *Eine Schweizer Stimme, 1938-1945*, pp. 307-33.

25. Cf. Katherine A. Sonderegger, *That Jesus Christ Was Born a Jew: Karl Barth's "Doctrine of Israel"* (University Park: Pennsylvania State University Press, 1992).

26. Busch, *Unter dem Bogen*, p. 441.

sion. The meaning of his statements — complicated, spiraling, and often compressed as they are — becomes evident only when one grasps the precise intellectual structures in which he develops his thought. They force us to understand the author, against some of his own statements, better, in Schleiermacher's phrase, than he understood himself. This passage, however, remains opaque if one draws only a few quotations from it, whether in the interest of pro- or anti-Jewish sounding statements, or for the sake of showing the contradiction between the two, wanting to improve them by omitting one side or the other.

What is the "certain light" here that Barth believed he had seen? It involves three basic principles, the neglect of which renders his text incomprehensible. The first principle is this: We can arrive at a new theological outlook on the relationship between Israel and the church only if we recognize that God's Word as attested in Holy Scripture is exclusively binding. At that time this principle was asserted against the German Christians, against the two-kingdoms doctrine of moderates in the church, and also against more long-standing traditions. It also meant breaking with a concept widely ingrained among German Lutherans, who saw this relationship within a larger abstract "orders of creation" scheme, grounded in the law, and into which every human being is born. These theologians sometimes wished to soften the harshness of the disparity between Jews and Christians, supposedly based in the created order, by referring to the love of one's neighbor, or of one's enemy, or to baptismal waters. Nevertheless, this disparity remained effective as the law of God, namely, the disparity between Germans and Jews, i.e., between one's own race and a race of aliens.[27] Barth's first principle categorically rejects this entire conceptual framework.

It also breaks with Schleiermacher's liberal view, according to which Judaism's relationship to Christianity is no different from that of any pagan religion.[28] Under the condition, then, that the Old Testament is to be removed from the Christian Bible,[29] this view permits a wide latitude of practices and attitudes. These include evangelism of the Jews as a form of mission to the heathen; the thesis of a historical supersession of the dead

27. For much greater detail, see Busch, *Unter dem Bogen*, pp. 97-124.
28. Friedrich Schleiermacher, *Christlicher Glaube nach den Grundsätzen der evangelischen Kirche* (Berlin, 1835), 1:77-80.
29. Schleiermacher, *Kurze Darstellung des theologischen Studiums* (Leipzig, 1910), par. 115.

Jewish religion by the living Christian one; even a religious dialogue such as one might have, for example, with Buddhism; and a tolerance according to which one must treat those of different faiths at least as human beings. Against these conceptions, it must be said that from Barth's point of view they are not formulated according to the exclusively binding character of God's Word as attested in Scripture. Here as elsewhere, Barth believed he had learned from Paul that "scriptural proof is everything, so to speak."[30] And therefore, he wrote in 1967, he did not much engage with the voices of modern Judaism (though in fact he did so much more than he let on), because the witness of Scripture gave him "so much to think about and to take in."[31]

In short, the criterion — the norm the church needs to assess itself as well as its relation to Judaism — can be found only in the biblical witness. The result of Barth's "scriptural proof" is basically to recognize that the church stands with Israel in an indissoluble solidarity. This solidarity means that the New Testament is inseparable from the Old Testament, which can never be abandoned. Although Christians cannot understand the Old Testament without the New, neither can they understand the New Testament without the Old. A few quotations will illustrate.[32]

The church can only be the church, Barth wrote, "in its unity with Israel." "By its fellowship and solidarity" with Israel, the church indeed "stands or falls." It is the very One who stands at the center of the church's faith who binds it to Israel. For "those who believe in Jesus cannot fail to accept the Jews. They must accept them as the ancestors and relatives of Je-

---

30. Barth, *Die kirchliche Dogmatik* (Zollikon-Zurich, 1936-68), II/2, p. 284.

31. Barth, *Briefe 1961-1968* (Zürich: Theologischer Verlag, 1975), pp. 420-21. It is important to understand Barth here correctly. He is not contending that one's hearing of the Scripture replaces hearing the Jewish testimonies from the past and today. This would be as unacceptable as saying that the church's necessary attending to the biblical witness rendered its attending to the church's own utterances over time superfluous. Barth demonstrates his commitment to *sola Scriptura* here by emphasizing that it is even less possible that such hearing of Jewish and churchly voices should ever replace our listening to Scripture as it speaks to us about the Jewish people and the Christian church. Rather, in our listening to Scripture we perceive the illumining and normative light in which both Jewish and ecclesial statements are to be seen, understood, discussed, and judged. The assumption Barth makes is that there is a continuity not only between the church and the New Testament community, but also between Judaism and biblical Israel, so that their illumination with this light is entirely appropriate and does not alienate them from their calling and identity.

32. *KD* II/2, pp. 223, 318.

sus. Otherwise, they cannot accept Jesus the Jew. Otherwise, along with the Jews they reject Jesus himself." The anti-Jewish reproach that the Jews had rejected Christ was then turned against the church. The church, Barth argued, dare not say: "The Jews crucified Jesus Christ. Therefore, this people has ceased to be the holy people of God. The Christian people has now taken its place. The church is the historical replacement for Israel. With the existence of the church, Israel as such has become a chapter in history. Of this disobedient people it can only be said that God has abandoned it."[33] For Barth, all Christian anti-Judaism is rooted in the idea that Israel is superseded by the church, an idea he completely rejected.

Of course, the so-called anti-Judaism of the New Testament seems to pose many difficulties for any argument resting its case on "scriptural proof." Whether these difficulties placed his position in doubt was something Barth grappled with intensively. He has been reproached for having adopted the New Testament's anti-Judaism instead of just dropping the appeal to Scripture for substantive and critical reasons.[34] However, the German Christian abridgment of the Bible in pursuit of a scripture free of Judaism must not be forgotten. What the reproach overlooks is that abandoning the appeal to Scripture would have validated the German Christian insinuation that anti-Judaism was legitimated by the "second" Testament. Such substantive criticism is defenseless against the possibility that the excised portions can continually be reclaimed and used to counter its Jewish-friendly outcome. Moreover, even if such a "cleansing" of the New Testament occurs, a host of passages even more harshly critical of Israel can be found in the "first" Testament. Indeed, Christian anti-Judaism had focused precisely on those texts, because in them God announces the end, the extermination and the destruction of his obstinate people.

Continuity exists between both Testaments, Barth observes, in the passages that are critical of Israel. But when taken in continuity, he continues, they can be understood as the nonrevocation of Israel's covenant.[35] The procedure of critical cleansing, by contrast, would always eliminate those sections of the first Testament as well. For Barth this is a liberal procedure that projects images of another god onto the biblical witness. In the

33. *KD* II/2, pp. 319f.

34. L. Steiger, "Die Theologie vor der 'Judenfrage' — Karl Barth als Beispiel," in *Auschwitz — Krise der christlichen Theologie*, ed. R. Rendtorff and E. Stegemann (Munich: Chr. Kaiser, 1980), pp. 82-98.

35. See as early as *KD* I/2, pp. 566-68.

modern period, in fact, this procedure has mostly been used against the Jews. Barth sees no point in standing it on its head. For him there is only one way. All the difficult texts must be read in the total context of God's actions toward his people in judgment and grace,[36] as attested in the biblical account. The bold thesis thus took shape in Barth's mind that the offensive passages are actually indispensable for establishing the twin propositions that God's covenant with Israel is irrevocable and the church's connection with Israel is indissoluble.

Barth's second principle is this: The church's connection with Israel can be indissoluble only if grounded in the core of the Christian faith — namely, in the belief that Jesus is the Christ — but then the connection is secure. If the connection were only historical, then it would also be only external and always dissoluble. Yet how can Christ connect Christians with Jews, since belief in Christ is precisely what divides them? Barth looks more closely at the matter. Christ divides Christians from Jews only if he is interpreted as the founder of a new covenant or a new religion. In that case the birth of Jesus among the Jews is merely accidental, if not indeed the dark background against which he shines forth in radiant light (E. Hirsch). Israel is then of no consequence for the church (R. Bultmann).[37] If, furthermore, the church's confession of Christ is defined as essentially anti-Jewish, then the entire sweep of church history must be accused of being anti-Jewish from the New Testament onward. This allegation leads to the zeal with which christocentric theologians in our day are castigated as anti-Jewish even when they are the ones who emphasize solidarity with Israel. Disreputable theologians of the last two hundred years are meanwhile left unscathed, who based their rejection of the Jews not on the Jewish refusal to believe in Christ, but on their alien religion or race. The unavoid-

---

36. See *KD* I/2, p. 567. According to Barth, God's grace cannot be understood when separated from God's judgment. Nor can God's judgment be understood to mean expulsion from the covenant. It is rather an event within the covenant. God exercises "grace in judgment" and "judgment in grace." According to Barth, anti-Judaism does not understand that God's judgment, bound to grace, takes place on the basis of the covenant. It does not cut one off from the covenant. For Barth this misunderstanding is precisely how external criticism of the supposed New Testament (or rather, biblical) "anti-Judaism" thinks. In effect, it disputes that the gracious God of the covenant is also the uncompromising judge of his community.

37. Rudolf Bultmann, "Glauben und Verstehen," in *Gesammelte Aufsätze*, vol. 1 (Tübingen: J. C. B. Mohr, 1958), p. 333.

able consequence is that, for the sake of peace, the church's confession of Christ is watered down. The answer to the question, "Are you he who is to come?" (Matt. 11:3), is quietly pushed off into the future. At the end of it all, Christians no longer know why they are Christians, nor why those Christians who are Gentiles are accounted as members of the covenant people without having to become Jews.

The proposition that the church's connection with Israel is decisive derives from a new understanding of the core Christian confession, which excludes its being used for anti-Jewish purposes. Barth does not ask how the Jews relate to Jesus Christ but how he relates to them. Although Jews may say no to Christ, Christ says yes to them; and it is the latter, not the former, that is determinative. Barth urges us "to see each other as Christ sees us: as Jews struggling with the true God, and Gentiles at peace with false gods, yet both united as 'children of the living God.'"[38] From this perspective, two points immediately become clear. First, the Christ was necessarily a Jew, for otherwise he could not have opened up the covenant to the Gentiles. Second, Israel's election was definitively confirmed, for in Christ the only salvation that ever reaches Gentiles is that which comes "from the Jews" (John 4:22). The church can only repudiate the idea that it supersedes Israel, Barth argues, when it sees that Jews and Gentiles both stand together through their common foundation in Christ. This connection can be validated, however, only if confessing Christ is taken with new seriousness, not by watering it down.

At this point Barth takes up an insight that he highly valued in Calvin.[39] Biblical discourse about the old and new covenant, Calvin taught, does not mean two covenants, but a single covenant of grace in two "dis-

---

38. Barth, "Die Kirche Jesu Christi," in *Theologische Existenz heute,* 5 (Munich: Chr. Kaiser, 1933), p. 17.

39. John Calvin, *Institutio christianae religionis* 2.9-11, and esp. 2.10.2. See also Barth, *Unterricht in der christlichen Religion (1924-1925),* vol. 2 (Zürich: Theologischer Verlag, 1990), pp. 381-98. At the beginning of 1933 Barth entered into conversation with the Jewish theologian H. J. Schoeps, but one can understand why Barth did not find his thesis helpful. Schoeps wanted to transfer the concept of the Christ revelation, which he had learned from Barth, to the Sinai revelation. (See Schoeps, *Jüdischer Glaube in dieser Zeit: Prolegomena zu einer systematischen Theologie des Judentums* [Berlin, 1932].) This move would have departed from Barth's concern, namely, that the church lives with the synagogue "in a fellowship that is not possible between any two other 'religions.'" For that very reason, "What more could the church desire than to be confronted constantly by all that it inherits from the synagogue in all its distinctiveness?" See Busch, *Unter dem Bogen,* pp. 174-79, esp. 179.

pensations." When Barth interprets God's reconciling action in Christ as the fulfillment of the covenant, Calvin's insight is enlarged. Israel belongs *within* the covenantal fulfillment, Barth submits, bringing a new accent to Calvin's orientation. Although the two "dispensations" are different, they are inseparable aspects of a single covenant because of the reconciliation accomplished in Christ. The primary content of *Church Dogmatics*, volume II/2, is the working out of this proposal.[40] The covenantal fulfillment, God's eternal election as embodied and revealed in Jesus Christ, is an event with two aspects. The first is God's free decision of grace. In Jesus Christ God elects himself for fellowship with a particular people, thereby humbling himself to dealings with sinners. The second is God's election of these very sinners to be lifted up to fellowship with himself. In the process he executes judgment. He declares an uncompromising no to the sinfulness of his elected partner. He negates the essential reason why fellowship with him is blocked. At the same time, God shows mercy to this partner. He counteracts the partner's culpable lack of readiness with a powerful "nevertheless." By electing in Christ to be in fellowship with sinners, God takes the judicial condemnation, the offense of the sinner, to himself alone and no one else.[41] He takes this burden upon himself in the cross of Jesus Christ, who in this way is both the "Messiah of Israel" and the "hidden Lord of the church." With that very step God mercifully elects sinners to salvation and to life in fellowship with himself.

The risen one of Easter demonstrates this merciful judgment. He is at once the "Lord of the church" and the "revealed Messiah" of Israel.[42] With the covenantal fulfillment in Christ, Israel's election is made so definitive that it cannot be revoked even by a breach of covenant on its part. The church must therefore bear witness, "in defiance of all Gentile arrogance, to the eternal election of Israel."[43] Because the covenant is fulfilled precisely through divine grace to sinners, furthermore, the Gentiles, who are all the more sinners, and who previously stood outside God's just and gracious activity, are no longer excluded from the covenant. This covenantal fulfillment means — and it is fundamental to see this — that for Jews and Christians alike, both sides of God's reconciliation in Christ — namely, the

---

40. *KD* II/2, pp. 101-214.
41. *KD* II/2, pp. 177-90; e.g., p. 177: "God wills to lose that man might gain."
42. *KD* II/2, p. 218.
43. *KD* II/2, p. 225.

divine judgment and grace — are valid across the board and without any basic difference. The only difference is that Israel is elected first. Precisely because Israel remains elect in Christ, the Gentiles have only one possibility, namely, their calling to be joined to the one covenant. Therefore, anyone who would reject the Jews also rejects Christ. Therefore, only by trusting precisely that God's covenant with Israel is indeed unbroken — as seen through the world's reconciliation with God in Christ — can Gentile Christians be assured that they too are elected by grace. Therefore, only as the Messiah of Israel is Christ also the Savior of the world.

The third principle follows. What attests God's election of himself for communion with sinners and of sinners for communion with himself is the existence of a community. It exists in two "dispensations" — not simply in temporal succession, as Calvin maintained, but rather in a differentiated unity. Joined together by the arc of the one covenant that spans over them both, they are, despite their difference, the one "community of God,"[44] says Barth, the one "body"[45] of Jesus Christ, who fulfills the covenant of grace through reconciliation. The overarching covenant that binds them together into one community of grace is, however, "no neutral vantage point of observation."[46] The church, therefore, may not stray from its appointed place under this arc. Rather, its thinking must always begin and proceed from the place assigned to it. Otherwise, the church would no longer know why it is called into Israel's covenant, nor why, from a Christian perspective, the covenant with Israel is not terminated, and why the church is inseparable from the Jews in one community.

The search for Barth's "doctrine of Israel" leads to a dead end. His single-minded concern is to recognize the "election of the community." The covenantal community exists, as he defines it, "according to God's eternal decree, in two forms: as the people of Israel (in all its vast history, both past and future — ante- and post-*Christum natum!*) and likewise also as the church of Jews and Gentiles (from its revelation at Pentecost to its fulfillment at the return of Christ)."[47] Accordingly, Israel is the primary form of God's community, because it retains its chosen status even after the birth of Christ. Therefore, states Barth, one may not call "the Jewish

---

44. Note the title of the section in which Barth treats Israel and the church: "The Election of the Community."

45. *KD* II/2, pp. 220, 286.

46. *KD* II/2, p. 221.

47. *KD* II/2, p. 218.

nation the 'rejected' and the church the 'chosen community.'"[48] The one community elected by God takes two definitive forms, so that the church cannot exist by repressing Israel.

One difference between the two forms is that Israel is a "people," of which one usually becomes a member through birth, whereas one becomes a member of the church by being called.[49] Furthermore, although the church may well have been revealed at Pentecost, it did not originate there. It already "preexisted" in a hidden form in the Israel of the Old Testament.[50] Therefore, as long as Judaism is rooted in this Israel, it cannot seriously be a foreign body to the church, nor the church to Judaism. Judaism is essential to the church, because the church, as the second form of the one community, has been engrafted into God's people. It is essential for the church to have Jews not only around it but also in it. The presence of Jews in the church was represented by the first apostles, particularly by Paul, who were simultaneously Jewish and Christian. They did not abandon Judaism because of their faith in Christ, but remained Jews, loyal and obedient members of Israel, the eternally elect people.

Though hidden except to faith in Christ, the reality of this twofold community is not entirely imperceptible. It can be recognized, according to Barth, by its witness to the fulfilled covenant of grace. The covenantal community is represented not only by the church, as classical dogmatics would have it, but first of all by Israel — and then along with Israel by the church as well. Both attest the election of grace, says Barth, by their very "existence."[51] This idea has not always been well understood. What Barth means is that the significance of their witness is not to be distilled from an abstract phenomenology of Judaism and Christianity, nor from an abstract prescription of what they ought to be. Rather, both offer their witness by their relative positions, which they receive and actually possess through the fulfillment of the covenant by Christ's accomplishment of reconciliation. Israel's position is that of the first-chosen, while the church's position is that of being called into the covenant from among the Gentiles. The communal

48. *KD* II/2, pp. 219-20.

49. Terminologically Barth reserves the term "people" *(Volk)* for Israel, while he uses "assembly" *(ecclesia)* as a synonym for the church. The two together he calls "community." This agrees with the definitions in Franz Rosenzweig, *Der Stern der Erlösung* (1921) (Frankfurt, 1993), p. 381.

50. E.g., *KD* II/2, pp. 234-35.

51. See on this Busch, *Unter dem Bogen*, pp. 457-58.

witness takes on a double form, corresponding to the twofold election of grace. God chooses to be himself in communion with sinners — that is what Israel attests as the first-chosen. God chooses sinners to be in communion with himself — that is what Gentile Christians attest as those who were called later. Each therefore bears witness to a distinctive aspect of the covenant. Both aspects are to be respected in their uniqueness. Under the arc of the one covenant, each complements the other.[52] Both bear witness to God's gracious election and covenant in significantly different ways, but only so that their testimonies need and complete each other.

At the same time, each one attests to the other precisely what the other tends to forget. The church, therefore, cannot be a witness to the covenant of grace all alone, but only together with Israel. With their twofold witness they manifest the community's unity from different vantage points. Mission to the Jews is thereby excluded as making no sense, since both together are already witnesses to the electing God. They bear witness concurrently vis-à-vis the lost masses who do not belong to the community. In *Church Dogmatics* II/2 Barth illustrates this lostness by referring to the nationalistic führer state.[53] They bear their respective witness in particular ways. Since the first-chosen are the people *(Volk)* defined by birth, whereas the church is defined by being called into the one community, the essential task for the church is to carry out its mission precisely among the Gentiles, for they are the ones who are now called to enter the covenantal community.[54] Barth concurs with Franz Rosenzweig, that in its mission to Gentiles the church's most immediate task is to convert the heathen in Christendom.[55] "Salvation is from the Jews" (John 4:22) thus takes on a specific meaning. It means that salvation now comes from the Jews to the Gentiles so that the latter, through the church's mission, can enter the one community.[56] Jews who believe in Christ, with Paul as their prototype, form the special link from Jews to Gentiles and from Gentiles to Jews.

52. Barth says "resonates together" *(zusammenklingt), KD* II/2, p. 288.

53. *KD* II/2, pp. 341-44.

54. *KD* II/2, p. 312.

55. Rosenzweig, pp. 309ff., esp. 317 and 379. In 1928 K. H. Miskotte referred Barth to this "great book," which brings to light "signs of the unity of God's one community (in Israel and in the church)." See Karl Barth and K. H. Miskotte, *Briefwechsel 1924-1968*, ed. H. Stoevesandt (Zürich: Theologischer Verlag, 1991), p. 79. Barth asked Miskotte to help him read this book, which seemed to him difficult to understand (p. 104).

56. *KD* II/2, p. 289.

The Difference between Jews and Christians
in the One Community of God

The Jewish and Christian forms of testimony are so diverse, however, that one might doubt whether they can really make one community. Aren't they so disparate as to make two disconnected religious entities? Can the one covenantal community really come into being without bringing on at least one of two calamities: either the Jewish testimony being suppressed by the Christian testimony or the Christian testimony being absorbed by the Jewish testimony? Barth's thinking runs very much in another direction. Crucial to the community's differentiated unity, he argues, is that the two forms render the very same testimony in two different ways. What links them together is precisely the reason for their difference. Without this division of labor the church would not necessarily need Israel's testimony. Israel, however, expresses something unique that the Gentile church cannot attest, so that the church would be deficient were Israel not to represent it. Israel's testimony represents something, however, that cannot put the gospel of Christ into question, and that cannot alienate the Gentile church from the gospel, because the difference is rooted in that which binds both testimonies into one.[57] The two forms of witness display the covenant's twofold fulfillment in Christ. As a result, neither form is neutralized, and in their distinction they enhance one another.

Recognizing this complementarity is difficult, however, because, according to Barth, a "nonnecessary" fact overlays the necessary difference. For the most part, Israel does not recognize that the covenant first made with it has now been fulfilled in Christ. Israel "abstracts" itself from this fulfillment,[58] and therefore also from its membership in the one commu-

---

57. "The Jew keeps the question of Christ open." This is the much quoted statement of Bonhoeffer, often taken out of context (*Ethik* [Munich: Chr. Kaiser, 1985], p. 31). Barth would agree that "Christ" is not a possession that the church can brandish without and against "the Jew." When the church does that, it fails to perceive the "sign" of the divine goodness and seriousness that "the Jew" signifies for Christianity (Bonhoeffer). For Barth the statement would be unacceptable in the sense often ascribed to it, however, that the Jewish testimony can help Christianity deal with the question, "Are you the one who is to come?" as if unanswered, in order then to regard the question as quite irrelevant and to seek common ground with Jews at all kinds of other points, e.g., in the hope for a decisive event yet to come in which the question could be revealed as totally nonessential.

58. *KD* II/2, p. 289.

nity. According to Barth, however, Christ does not abstract himself from Israel. He is "above all, theirs," since he has elected to "make his abode in the flesh and blood of Judah and Israel." "Because the irrevocable promise which was made to them remains in effect, their chosenness and their membership in the one fellowship is confirmed and proven. It is confirmed . . . with regard to their service, which they cannot escape," as well as "with regard to God's mercy toward them," which they "cannot make unreal."[59] This promise gives the church hope that at the conclusion of God's ways the nonnecessary divide will be overcome. Then, as Barth's wonderful statement puts it, "the difference within the community will confirm its unity."[60] The church hopes for the advent of this fullness, because it is already a reality in Christ, even if not now manifest in the community on earth. But the church cannot properly hope that the difference will be set aside. For the church lives forever "on nothing else than God's faithfulness to Israel."[61] As long as the Jews do not realize that they are inseparably linked in one covenantal community by the same divine faithfulness that calls and adds others to them, then the church "must take the lead, confessing the unity of the fellowship of God," but with the desire "that Israel's particular service to the one fellowship not cease, but continue in faithfulness."[62]

For Barth the indispensable function of Jewish Christians — precisely in the church, as represented by the original apostles — is to open the eyes of Gentile Christians. The former enable the latter to see that the distinctiveness of Israel's witness is confirmed by Jewish Christian obedience to Israel's being chosen first, before the calling of the Gentiles. When the larger part of Israel rejects the messiahship of Jesus, that invalidates neither its election nor the necessity of its distinctive witness. The larger part of Israel, despite its refusal of Christ, also gives this witness in its own way. By no means, moreover, does belief in Christ relieve Jewish Christians from offering the very witness to Gentiles that is proper to Israel as the first-chosen people. Just what do the two forms of the one community attest? According to Barth, Israel *bears witness* to the divine judgment, to the promise as heard, and to the humanity that is passing away. The church

---

59. *KD* II/2, p. 231.
60. *KD* II/2, p. 228.
61. *KD* II/2, p. 294.
62. *KD* II/2, p. 257.

bears witness to God's mercy, to the promise as believed, and to the humanity that is yet to come.[63]

These concepts have caused much offense. Many thought that here, once again, Israel was regarded as accursed. Israel's present suffering was thus supposedly fitting. It could be delivered from its straits only by casting off its Judaism and coming into the church. However, this reading is clearly a mistake. Otherwise how could Barth also see Jewish Christians as providing the distinctive witness of Israel? It is very important to see that Barth seeks to read the old texts in a new way. He is seeking to unravel the special scriptural character of the two witnesses, especially as expounded in Romans 9–11. The exposition of this text takes up fully three-quarters of his section on the relationship of the church and Israel. And yet, it is in Paul's text itself that one can discover anti-Jewish-sounding thoughts that run counter to the preceding thesis of Romans 9. For Paul's central thesis is that the covenant with Israel is unbroken, and that Israel and the church cannot be extricated from one another. With regard to this thesis the anti-Jewish-sounding statements pose at least three difficult problems for Barth.[64]

---

63. See *KD* II/2, pp. 226-336 (ET: 195-305). Note the titles of the three sections which lay out the difference in the togetherness of "Israel and the Church."

64. Note that the three divisions which follow are not derived solely from Rom. 9–11. In reflecting theologically on the general relationship between the two biblical Testaments, Barth follows an analogous threefold division (*KD* I/2, pp. 77-133). In dialogue and dispute with contemporary Jewish theologians (p. 87), he develops his position as follows: Both Testaments say the same thing, but in different ways. The Old Testament speaks (1) of the covenant of God, (2) of the revelation of the hidden God, and (3) of the eschatological coming of God. By saying the same thing, the New Testament connects the church "indivisibly" with the people of the Old Testament (p. 111). "It can only have to do with their [the church's] incorporation into the one covenant" (p. 115). At the same time, moving beyond the Old Testament, the New Testament attests (1) the fulfillment of the covenant in the incarnation of God; (2) the perfecting of the hiddenness of God in the passion of Christ, which is revealed at Easter as the good news; and (3) the One who has come as the One who is to come. Note further that when presenting God's gracious election in Christ in II/2, Barth again adopts a threefold pattern: (1) God determines himself to be the covenant partner, (2) God confirms himself as witness to the covenant, (3) God elects humanity to be his covenant partner. At the same time, he presents his doctrine of election in yet another threefold pattern: (1) as just mentioned, God as the one who graciously elects, (2) the elect community (Israel/the church) as his covenant witness, (3) humanity outside this community as the addressee of the gospel of God's gracious election. The threefold pattern adopted here (relating to the "elect community" as God's covenant witness) pertains to the community as attesting (1) God's covenant action, (2) God's covenant revelation, and (3) the addressees of God's action and speaking.

a. What does it mean when Romans 9 speaks of God having mercy and hardening hearts? What does it mean when it says God appoints some, those called from among the Gentiles, to be "objects of mercy" and others, the elect Israel, to be "objects of wrath"? The meaning of this allocation of mercy and hardening of hearts, strange as it is, is disclosed, Barth suggests, only when one notices that Paul (vv. 10f.) portrays it as typical of how God has always dealt with Israel as his people. Because mercy and hardening both take place inside the structure of the covenant, they are not directed against Israel fundamentally. God's action should not be understood merely as his reaction to good or bad human conduct. God's preparation of objects of wrath does not mean the exclusion of people from his covenant. Rather it signifies a divine obliviousness toward all the natural and moral predispositions of this people. God takes their destiny out of their hands and into his own. In his hardening of hearts and in his mercy, therefore, he is not pursuing two conflicting intentions. He is pursuing only the intention of his mercy. The "objects of wrath" are, despite every appearance, embraced by God within the intention "of his merciful will and action."

This peculiar structure of God's covenantal action, formerly enacted within Israel, is something that, on the basis of the Christ event, Paul sees as now being repeated, but between different parties, namely, between the party of divinely called Gentiles and that of Jews outside the church. Nothing foreign to Israel really occurs in this repetition. God acts again according to the same pattern that has always governed his conduct toward Israel. These Gentiles, therefore, should not suppose that God's intention is an anti-Jewish act, as if God had now abandoned Israel. Paul formulated his thesis boldly, however. As such, Gentiles are not Israel, not elect, and therefore, he presumes, not even considered by God as possible objects of wrath. Only the superabundant mercy that God had always shown toward Israel has made it possible for Gentiles now to be called. Paul's apparently anti-Jewish train of thought may thus be distilled, according to Barth, into this twofold statement: First, if God's mercy, as now revealed, is so richly bestowed on the Gentiles, who are subject to his rejection in totally other ways, how much more will it be bestowed upon those to whom it was originally promised. Second, if everything depends precisely on God's mercy toward the fortunate Jews, according to God's covenantal faithfulness, how much more does everything depend on that same mercy for the hapless Gentiles.[65]

---

65. *KD* II/2, pp. 254, 256.

When Barth says Israel (outside of and in the church) bears witness to God's judgment, whereas the Gentile church bears witness to God's mercy, he means the same thing as Paul. With their different testimonies both stand within the same covenant of grace and attest it. Israel attests the divine judgment, but not because of a particular sinfulness. As the witness elected to judgment, it is obedient to its relative position as the first chosen. It testifies to the initial aspect of God's eternal election, his free and gracious election of himself to enter into community with sinners. Israel attests the very judgment on human guilt that it finally does not bear, because God through Christ takes it upon himself. Leo Baeck understood Barth well when he approvingly took up Barth's reference to John the Baptist's finger in Grünewald's painting, pointing toward the Crucified One, and said with Barth, the movement of this hand is the characteristic of Jewish existence.[66] Israel attests God's judgment in the strict sense, because it attests that belonging to God rests exclusively on his free grace, excluding every conceivable worthiness or entitlement. Israel represents what Gentiles and Gentile Christians either do not know or always seem to forget. For by its very existence Israel testifies against natural theology with its assumption of humanity's natural openness toward God.[67] What Israel attests is complete dependence upon God's free election.

If Gentile Christianity is the witness to God's mercy, then that is because it was elected last. In its relative position as subsequent in God's plan, it attests the second aspect of election. Because of God's decision to be in fellowship with sinners, in other words, even those originally excluded from his election can in fact enter into fellowship with God out of pure mercy. For the church not to misunderstand the promise of mercy in a spirit of triumphalism, however, Israel's testimony must still be heard. God's covenanting action excludes every human claim to suitability for membership in this covenant. But it does not exclude God's mercy, so that even the nonelect are gathered in. Just as Israel testifies to "knowing the human reason for God's suffering" which is hidden from the Gentiles, and

66. Leo Baeck, "Die Existenz des Juden: Lehrhausvortrag am 30. Mai 1935," *Leo Baeck Institute Bulletin* 81 (1988): 1.

67. According to Barth, the Jews testify to Gentiles that they are not elect, that one must be Jewish or belong to them, in order to be elect (*KD* III/3, p. 255). This is, he thinks, the thing about the Jews that bothers the Gentiles (cf. I/2, p. 567). Rosenzweig expressed a similar thought: this people "must . . . remain always alien to and an offence to world history." Cf. Rosenzweig, p. 371.

which excludes all human entitlement to covenant membership, so the host of those elected later testifies to the "divine meaning" of God's judgment in the cross of Christ, namely, that God is merciful despite all human ungodliness and wickedness.[68] The church is dependent on Israel's witness. At the same time, it must comfort the Jews with its own witness. The witness of the church is a living reminder to the Jews of what they themselves must not forget as they bear witness to the Gentiles against natural theology, namely, that mercy is valid for everyone. The witness of the church is valid therefore only as it brings comfort to Israel.

b. What does it mean when Romans 10 says Israel is a disobedient nation which strives for righteousness but does not attain it, as opposed to the Gentiles, who attain it but without striving for it?[69] The key lies in seeing, Barth suggests, that Paul's talk of Israel's transgression is "directed to the church." Paul's point is to place the church in solidarity with Israel. The church is to recognize that its own calling rests on God's mercy alone. The church is expected to understand that what Paul states here is not something "against Israel." Rather, it is "for the electing God, and, indirectly, for the elected people and in its election . . . unfaithful Israel as well."[70] But what does Paul regard as the "transgression"? He speaks of it in connection with Isaiah 65. It is certainly not a novelty in Israel, confirmed only in the rejection of Christ. It is a matter of Israel not listening to God's Torah or not striving sufficiently to follow it. As the people of the covenant, they were obligated to follow God's law. The transgression consists of being inattentive, in this legitimate pursuit, to the law within its own law.

According to Paul, Barth explains, Israel neglects that to which it was initially commanded, namely, the work of faith which relies on God's mercy alone. This failing is shown by its disregard of God's mercy in Christ. Israel is thus disobedient to God's gracious election (which is still the source of its life) and not to some alien demand. Therefore this disregard of Christ is not necessary to being a Jew. For a Jew who recognizes God's mercy in Christ confirms his being as Jew, and does not renounce it. Furthermore, since this failing does not pertain to the law, but to its underlying divine mercy, it cannot invalidate the mercy shown to the disobedient. The divine mercy toward Israel cannot be abolished — despite its re-

---

68. *KD* II/2, pp. 227, 229.
69. More precisely, the text under discussion is Rom. 9:30–10:21.
70. *KD* II/2, p. 267.

jection of Christ (and in him reconciliation) as the fulfillment of the covenant. Therefore even its rejection of Christ is an active "confirmation of its election" and a glorification of God's faithfulness.[71] Therefore not even the church can know what transgression means at this point if it does not first know, with Israel, of God's mercy. Finally, therefore not even the church can be certain of this mercy without being in solidarity with Israel.

Barth thus reformulates Paul's idea as follows. Israel attests the Word of God as heard, whereas the church attests it as believed. Israel's transgression does not, Barth underscores, pertain to its hearing the instruction of God. By hearing the divine instruction, the Jews show themselves to be the first elected. As careful hearers of God's Word, they accord with the Word that always precedes the witness of the one community. By signifying the primacy of the Word, the Bible is, in both its parts, "a product of the Jewish spirit."[72] Since hearing always precedes faith, therefore, a church not emulating Israel's appointed service will be a church whose talk becomes "loose speculation." Whether "the Israelites' ('Jewish!') attention to sentence, word and letter" continues in the church is a matter by which the church stands or falls.[73] For "the promise must be heard in order to be believed."[74]

After reading a book by the Berlin rabbi Cohn in 1934, Barth wrote to him that for both the church and the synagogue the basic issue was a new listening to God's Word. Barth asked him, however, why he appeared to call the Jew "more decisively to himself than to his God." He then added: "Is that already the question of a Christian theologian?" For the Christian theologian necessarily asks about faith's essential and "total confidence" in the complete mercy of God.[75] Furthermore, faith's dependence on hearing

71. *KD* II/2, pp. 281, 285.

72. *KD* I/2, p. 566. Elsewhere Barth says that as the "librarians of the church" (Augustine), the Jews are not the antiquarians, but rather "the constantly self-renewing realization and exposition of that human being" who according to those books is the counterpart in God's covenant (III/3, p. 240; ET).

73. *KD* II/2, p. 257. If it did not listen to the Jewish witness, the church would "have nothing more to say to the world."

74. *KD* II/2, p. 263.

75. *KD* II/2, p. 261. On January 28, 1934, Cohn had sent Barth his book *Aufruf zum Judentum,* and stated in the accompanying letter that in synagogue circles Barth's writings were being read with lively interest. The letter together with Barth's response of February 2, 1934, is found in the Barth-Archiv in Basel. What is at stake here becomes clear when we recall Franz Rosenzweig's remark that "Christian faith is 'faith in'" as opposed to that of the

emerges especially in those who are called later, for the Gentiles enter the covenantal community only by God's great mercy. By relying in faith on the mercy extended through Christ, these Gentiles attest that the hearing which precedes and the believing which follows both belong together. And again, the Jews within the church attest to them that the difference between hearing and believing does not inhere in Judaism alone.

c. What does it mean in Romans 11 when by pointing to the existing "remnant" Paul argues that Israel as a whole has not been rejected from God's covenant? This remnant is that segment of the Jews which is now in the church together with those Gentiles who are called. With its faith in Christ and its consequent membership in the church, this remnant does not lose its membership in Judaism. It stands in continuity with the believers of the first Testament. According to Barth, it would indeed be anti-Judaism if Gentile Christians were to see this connection as irrelevant. They would thereby be ashamed of the church's Jewish origin. Since Jews who believe in Christ do not forfeit their membership in Israel, reconciliation in Christ does not mean the renunciation of Israel. Reconciliation in Christ is the verification of Israel's gracious election, not a "new revelation" over against it. This verification means, however, that the remnant stands "for the totality of Israel." It is "the clear proof" that "God's election is not simply transferred to the Gentiles from Israel, departing from Israel as its original object." The remnant confirms the "election of Israel."[76] If, however, Gentile Christians belong together with those Jews who, even as Christians, remain part of Israel, then such Gentiles also belong to Israel beyond the church. And if God has not simply transferred his election from Israel to the Gentiles, then Gentile Christians cannot themselves become Israel and thereby replace it. They can only be grafted into it.

Barth interprets Paul's olive tree metaphor as follows: The (temporary) pruning of the olive tree's natural branches and the ingrafting of wild shoots do not imply that the Gentile church supplants Israel. It enters the place that belongs to Israel. The gospel of God's mercy is not taken away from Israel, to whom the place belongs. Rather, Israel's vacating of its place allows the originally nonelect Gentiles to be implanted where they do not

---

Jew, whose faith concerns "not the content of a testimony, but the product of a begetting. The one who is begotten as a Jew testifies to his faith in that he continues the procreation of the eternal people" (Rosenzweig, pp. 379-80). Barth's question to Cohn apparently concerns this view.

76. *KD* II/2, pp. 298, 301.

by nature belong. There the Gentiles are so dependent upon God's mercy "that they themselves would have been discarded by God, had he truly discarded Israel."[77] Instead of conducting a mission to the Jews, Christianity should stand in alliance with them and attest the gospel among the heathen.[78] Since Israel outside the church does not acknowledge that its gracious election is fulfilled in Christ, and thus also that it is connected inseparably to the church (as the church must confess its connection to Israel), the anomaly certainly "disturbs" the unity of God's community.[79] The resolution of this disturbance lies in God's future, which Paul envisages when he asserts that "all Israel will be saved" (Rom. 11:26). Barth reads this verse together with the following one, that God has imprisoned all in disobedience so that he may be merciful to all (11:32).[80] Although in God's future Israel will "enter into" the church, that does not mean, according to Barth, that Israel's appointed precedence over the newly believing Gentile Christians will be set aside, nor that Israel will be dissolved into the church.[81] Christian anti-Judaism will never be justifiable. What the salvation of all Israel suggests is that the larger portion, like the remnant and those united with it, will confess precisely the mercy of Israel's God in Jesus Christ, seeing in this mercy the basis for the covenantal interconnection between Jews and Gentile Christians.

According to Barth's interpretation of Romans 9–11, what Israel attests is the unbelieving humanity that is passing away, whereas what the church attests is the believing humanity that is coming. Why, however, according to Paul, should there be this reduction in God's elect people to the small remnant, as seen for example in Elijah's isolation, or indeed in the pruning of the olive tree's natural branches? It is precisely by this reduc-

---

77. *KD* II/2, p. 313.

78. *KD* II/2, p. 312.

79. *KD* II/2, p. 289.

80. As the conclusion to the entire argument of Rom. 9–11, just before Paul breaks into his doxology to God's mysterious ways, Rom. 11:32 is for Barth the key to the whole. He understands this statement together with Jesus' word about the first being last and the last being first (*KD* II/2, pp. 330-31). It describes the topsy-turvy law of grace in God's covenantal activity. Because God accepts those who are lost, and because the Gentiles are indeed those who are most lost, the last will be first. Moreover, because accepting the lost Gentiles reveals that the (enduring!) benefit of the Jews' election is based solely upon the fact that God accepts the lost, the first are indeed also the last, without loss of the "Jewish rights of the firstborn."

81. *KD* II/2, pp. 309-13.

tion, Barth suggests, that Israel attests the humanity that is passing away. Recall Martin Buber's words of 1933 regarding a Jewish cemetery, which Barth knew and may well have had in mind: "As I stood there, all the death washed over me, all the ashes, all the silent misery. I lay on the ground, fallen like these stones. But I was not revoked."[82] Barth once said the Jewish cemetery in Prague contains "objectively more true gospel" than all the unbelieving (and much Christian) "goyim-wisdom."[83] Note that Israel does not pass away. It remains elected. Yet it attests the humanity that is perishing. It bears this testimony in the midst of a Gentile world that presumes it can establish itself in the godless idiocy of "unending time."[84] It is this world that wants to push Israel, which disturbs it, out of the way. A Gentile Christianity that does not heed Israel's witness will fall back into sheer paganism. It is as the first elect, and not because of a divine punishment, that Israel attests the God who in his gracious election lets the disobedient "pass away, so that they can receive a real future." Allowing humanity to pass away is therefore a blessing from God, and Israel's testimony to this passing away is "praise to the mercy of God."[85] However, when Israel does not realize that it is already "the people of the risen Jesus Christ," it "brings sorrow on itself."[86] For then it gives its witness, which will certainly continue, "in abstraction." For what its own witness objectively attests is the hopeful "new, gracious beginning" that has dawned in the resurrection of Christ.

From a different vantage point this new beginning is also what the Gentile church attests. It attests the coming humanity whereby the "nobodies" who have no place in God's original election will also be wondrously elected and called. The inclusion of the excluded Gentiles mani-

82. Martin Buber, "Kirche, Staat, Volk, Judentum: Zwiegespräch im Jüdischen Lehrhaus in Stuttgart am 14. Jan. 1933" (with K. L. Schmidt), *Theologische Blätter* 12 (1933): 257-74. Note that in the final part of *KD* I/2, pp. 77-133 (as mentioned in n. 64 above), Barth was undoubtedly thinking of Buber's *Der Kommende: Untersuchungen zur Entstehungsgeschichte des messianischen Glaubens*, vol. 1 (Berlin, 1932).

83. *KD* II/2, p. 260.

84. Cf. *KD* III/2, p. 679. According to Barth, the Old Testament testifies to the limitation of created life (pp. 715ff.). In the New Testament this testimony is then intensified (pp. 728ff.). In the "word of the cross," death itself (as suffered in our place, allowing our "old man" to pass away) takes center stage as the accursed death. Only against this background does Easter hope become visible.

85. *KD* II/2, p. 286.

86. *KD* II/2, p. 289.

fests the power of Christ's resurrection. It discloses a "real future" for the humanity that is passing away. As the church of the resurrection testifies to the coming humanity, it does not move away from Israel. For it will "want to live by nothing else than God's grace directed toward Israel." It thus declares itself for "the unity of humanity which is passing away and which is coming, according to the will of divine mercy."[87] It declares itself for the unity of the enlarged community of God. And so it awaits God's future, in which all Israel will confess this unity. Did not the Jew Franz Werfel also speak of this expectation: "How much longer will this Hell reign here on Earth / with blind hate in the South, West, East and North? / Until the Jews become Christians / and until the Christians have become Jews."[88] This couplet recalls the promise of Revelation 21: "And God will dwell in them, and they will be his people." Somewhat more determinately than Werfel, Barth envisioned the same plurality. In the multitude united with God, consisting in the Jewish people and those who come from the Gentiles, unmixed, and yet inseparable, he foresaw the one community of God.

---

87. *KD* II/2, p. 294.

88. Franz Werfel, "Delphisches Orakel," in *Das lyrische Werk*, ed. A. D. Klarmann (Frankfurt, 1967), p. 527.

Indissoluble Unity

KATHERINE SONDEREGGER

We stand in Professor Busch's debt tonight. In his thoughtful and quietly self-effacing way, he has brought us face-to-face with central questions in the study of Karl Barth, and with central tasks facing Christians in their relation to Jews and to Judaism. With deceptive simplicity Professor Busch has laid out Barth's teaching about the people Israel, organized by historical and exegetical themes. But we should not be deceived: this paper raises the deepest issues in Barth interpretation, especially in matters of epistemology and scriptural authority, and goes to the heart of the matter in the relation of Christianity and Judaism. On reflection, we should not be surprised at such self-effacing seriousness. Professor Busch has shown us this characteristic in his landmark biography, *Karl Barth*,[1] modestly subtitled, *His Life from Letters and Autobiographical Texts*. There too we see Barth's own life and views put forward without the heavy armament of theoretical jargon so familiar to English-speaking audiences — how refreshing that is! — and many rough places in Barth's *Dogmatics* are made plain.

Tonight Professor Busch summarizes views he has developed at greater length in his recent book, *Unter dem Bogen des einen Bundes*,[2] and again carefully and quietly defends Barth against his detractors here and

1. Busch, *Karl Barth: His Life from Letters and Autobiographical Texts*, trans. J. Bowden (Philadelphia: Fortress, 1976).

2. Busch, *Unter dem Bogen des einen Bundes: Karl Barth und die Juden, 1933-1945* (Under the arc of a single covenant: Karl Barth and the Jews, 1933-1945) (Neukirchen-Vluyn: Neukirchener Verlag, 1996).

more prominently in present-day Germany. It is a common human trait, or failing, perhaps, to believe that the evils of the past can be repudiated only by making the heroes as well as the villains of the past share the blame: to make the past a "night in which all cats are gray" as Busch puts it, in a well-turned phrase from Hegel. Some Germans are eager to see in Barth and Bonhoeffer the germ of "totalitarian sympathies," and in Barth, a damning silence about the fate of Europe's Jews. We Americans can recognize the impulse: How many of us long to distance ourselves from the evils of slavery and segregation by exposing Lincoln's hesitation about emancipation and the Kennedys' vacillation about civil rights? It would be hard, I think, to disagree about the corruption and frailty of all our moral acts, and it would be a particular theological blindness not to see the profound relativity of our highest ideals against the surpassing brilliance of the divine justice. But a "little introspection" might also tell us how really pleasing it all is if we can find fault with those who risked their lives for the good: we are no part of that evil generation, we say, and we need not do anything in our day to put off the works of the night! Professor Busch has shown us in his paper how Barth cannot be dismissed so cheaply, and in the midst of all its faults, how his life remains a moral lesson to us of risk, commitment, and Christian courage. Barth remains, I think, in this way too a doctor of the church.

Professor Busch draws our attention to two ways Barth's wartime writings and actions can be correctly understood: as a repudiation of the "two-kingdom doctrine" *(Zwei-Bereiche-Lehre)* of Lutheran moderates; and as a confession of Christian solidarity with Jews[3] on the basis of the authority of Scripture. He articulates three principles Barth draws upon: that our present-day relation with Jews and Judaism must be seen in the light of the Word of God; that it must reflect the confession that Jesus is the Christ of Israel; and that the relation turns on the recognition that we are incorporated in a single community of Jew and Gentile, "unmixed," Busch writes in Chalcedonian language, "yet unseparated." In these three principles the exegesis of Romans 9–11 stands out prominently, forming a good third of Professor Busch's paper and well over half of Barth's discus-

---

3. Like Barth before him, Professor Busch here speaks about "the Jews." Though to be sure we may distinguish a particular social group — the Jews — over against another, the Christians, we might better speak of Jews or Judaisms, as it reflects more fully the complexity and diversity of Judaic history and, at many points, its incommensurability with Christianity.

sion in II/2 of the church and Israel. Paul's letter to the Romans has become the copingstone of recent work by Paul scholars on the apostle's relation to Second Temple Judaism,[4] and formed the locus of Barth's most controversial and "unwieldy" *(sperrigen)* remarks about Judaism. We are brought quickly into the heart of the matter by this royal road, and we might best begin there.

Romans 9:4 and 5 read: "For they are Israelites: they were made God's sons; theirs is the splendor of the Divine presence [*doxa*], theirs the covenants, the law, the temple worship [*latreia*], and the promises. Theirs are the patriarchs, and from them, in natural descent [*kata sarka*], sprang the messiah" (NEB). Now, from these verses Busch's three principles can be seen in germ. But it is striking, and cannot escape the eye of any modern student of Judaism, that these verses do not describe or name present-day Jews or Judaism. It is tempting for Christians to assimilate rabbinic Judaism to these sentiments in Paul; indeed, it is a near catchword in Jewish-Christian relations that Paul taught that all Israel — that is, all Jews — will be saved (Rom. 11:26). Barth himself, as Professor Busch has shown, makes just this association: present-day Jews and Judaism are to be seen in the light cast by these verses. But in my view we cannot make this association so quickly or directly. For the Judaism we know, and Jews themselves practice, is postbiblical or rabbinic Judaism; it is Judaism without the "temple worship." It may seem that this is a small obstacle rather than the stumbling block I have made it out to be. Could we not assume that present-day Jews are simply the kinsfolk of Paul minus the temple? Are not the remaining attributes Paul lists still present: kinship, divine presence, covenants, laws, and promises? Certainly; and I think few scholars of Judaism would deny the historical descent of the rabbinic system from Second Temple Judaism.[5] But it is a historical descent, rather

4. A small sample: E. P. Sanders, *Paul and Palestinian Judaism* (London: SCM Press, 1977); Krister Stendahl, *Paul among Jews and Gentiles* (Philadelphia: Fortress, 1976); Stanley Stowers, *A Re-Reading of Romans* (New Haven: Yale University Press, 1994); J. Louis Martyn, *Theological Issues in the Letters of Paul* (Nashville: Abingdon, 1997); John Gager, *The Origins of Anti-Semitism* (New York: Oxford University Press, 1983); Daniel Boyarin, *A Radical Jew* (Berkeley: University of California Press, 1994).

5. For a classic defense of this claim, see Jakob Petuchowski, *Heirs to the Pharisees* (Lanham, Md.: University Press of America, 1970); and in the nineteenth century, with an eye to the debate over the lineage of the prophets, Abraham Geiger, *Judaism and Its History*, trans. C. Newburgh (Lanham, Md.: University Press of America, 1970).

than identity — just as some of us might say that we are of Swiss or African descent but Americans — because Judaism today does not worship in a temple in Jerusalem, nor practice priestly sacrifice. It would be hard to overestimate the importance of this fact. The temple in Jerusalem was not only the center of the cult, even for diaspora Jews; for centuries after its rebuilding under Ezra, it was *the* worship of Israel.[6] The ritual slaughter and roasting of animals and grains was the means whereby ancient Jews worshiped God and were brought into the divine presence. As was true of all other peoples of the ancient world, temple sacrifice defined for the Jews religious life. Now we can modify this a bit for the Judaism of Paul and Jesus' day. Theirs was a world of synagogue as well as temple; they knew the inwardness of prayer and Torah study, and the communal life of association in clubs, with corporate meals and the reliance of members on one another.[7] Such associations were common in Roman antiquity; both synagogue and church were probably assemblies of this kind. But the temple remained the center of Jewish life and practice.[8] The opposition to Jesus of Nazareth can be best explained, I believe, by his enigmatic proclamations against the temple; his death was a testimony to how vigilantly Jews and Romans defended the temple, even when its legitimacy was undermined by Herod and the Hasmoneans.[9] It is striking, in fact, that in all Paul's deeply conflicted writing about the Law, he never speaks a word against the temple, its practices, cult, or worship. Indeed, his most contested and memorable parable for Christ's justifying work seems to evoke sacrifice: the atonement is God's "means of expiating [*hilastērion*] sin by Christ's sacrificial death, effective through faith" (Rom. 3:25 NEB).[10] Significant, too, is the fact that Paul's hallmark confession —

---

6. For this and a broader account of Second Temple Judaism, see Shaye Cohen, *From the Maccabees to the Mishnah* (Philadelphia: Westminster, 1987).

7. For the social world of Pauline Christianity, see Wayne Meeks, *The First Urban Christians* (New Haven: Yale University Press, 1983), and *The Origins of Christian Morality* (New Haven: Yale University Press, 1993).

8. This is true, I believe, even though the Egyptians built their own temple, closed by Vespasian in 73 C.E. It appears to have been always a "second" temple; Josephus does not mention it.

9. For two accounts of the controversy sayings: Raymond E. Brown, *The Death of the Messiah* (New York: Doubleday, 1994); E. P. Sanders, *The Historical Figure of Jesus of Nazareth* (New York: Penguin Press, 1995).

10. That this is no simple verse to translate or interpret, Stowers, *A Re-Reading of Romans,* makes clear with much helpful detail and historical analysis.

there is no distinction[11] — does not mention, or attempt to relativize, the temple. The apostle appears to assume that the temple will continue, that Jews will worship there in pilgrimage, and pay their taxes for its support. All of this, I think, underscores a point that the Gospel writers themselves make: that the destruction of the temple by the Romans brought the biblical period to a close. A.D. 70[12] marks the end of the Judaism of Jesus and Paul; the end of priesthood, Levites, and temple protocol; the end of the time of revelation; the end of Judaism as a religion that practiced sacrifice, the lingua franca of antique religion.

Now rabbinic Judaism, the Judaism of our world and time, began in the aftermath of this destruction, and developed in Palestine and Asia Minor over the next few centuries of the postbiblical era. This Judaism is characterized by a new system of text and practice: the oral Torah of Mishnah and Gemara; the commentaries by talmudic scholars; the Tosafists; the synagogue worship of prayer, praise, and Torah chanting; the observance of the covenant through Sabbath rest; and taking on the precepts of the law: circumcision, kashrut, family law, private prayer, and moral obligation. This is a different religious system than Second Temple Judaism, though it derives from it; a different religious system than Christianity, though it bears family resemblance. This is the religion Barth called the "Synagogue."[13] He reserved his harshest words of rebuke for this system — the lifeless and joyless synagogue, with no future but destruction, the witness of a people disobedient to their election, stubbornly clinging to their own religion of achievement — and it was the thought, practice, and talmudic argument of this system that Barth found so little time for. Anyone who has read through II/2 of the *Dogmatics* will remember these rebukes. They are the "theological anti-Semitism" *(theologischen Antisemitismus)* Professor Busch referred to, Barth's "anti-Judaism," as English-speakers might refer to them. It is searing to read those words now; sobering to read them as the Christian response to Jews and Judaism during World War II,

11. Between Jew and Gentile, male and female, slave and free, in sinfulness. Boyarin considers this the hallmark of Paul's point of view as a "cultural critic"; in *A Radical Jew.*

12. I speak as a Christian here.

13. Barth would not use the term "religion," of course; that is the fulcrum of his attitude toward Jews and Judaism. His use of the term "Synagogue" as a synecdoche for postbiblical Judaism does not reflect the newer historical assessment that the institution and practice of synagogues in the Roman world were not rabbinic in character or organization, and came under rabbinic jurisdiction only gradually in the common era.

more sobering still to remember that these are words of a Christian *ally* of Jews, a heroic opponent of Nazism and German collaboration. But Professor Busch has brought us to the most serious point, I believe, in our assessment of Barth's teaching about Jews and Judaism: Barth develops this view about rabbinic Judaism in obedience to the authority of Scripture. He hears this teaching in Paul, especially in Romans 9–11, and he finds it echoed and enacted in the passion narratives of the Gospels. Now Barth never shied away from painful and unwanted conclusions, and I think we might honor his example here, by grasping the nettle. Just how does the authority of the Word of God bind and shape us in our relation to rabbinic Judaism? Must a Christian who acknowledges the one Word of God as binding in life and death regard the synagogue — to speak with Barth here — as an impossible possibility, a disobedience to the calling and mercy of God?

Professor Busch argues that Barth viewed his whole work in volume II/2 as a rejection of the "two kingdom" doctrine: that a Christian can separate the confession of faith from the practice of politics, *realpolitik.* We might state that in another way: that Barth rejects the idea that we can understand the world outside the Bible apart from the Bible, its teachings and commands. He would reject the claim that rabbinic Judaism, just because it is postbiblical, and different from the ancient Judaism of Jesus and Paul, can be understood, assessed, and valued *in a Christian way* apart from the authority and direction of Scripture. Our political and moral actions toward Jews and Judaism cannot be formed in a neutral way, as though in this case we could decide to act on the principles of religious tolerance, say, or historical and cultural relativity. Far from withdrawing Christian confession into a private realm of faith and insider narrative, Barth claimed the whole world for biblical authority: there is no world occurrence outside the governance, ruling, and command of God.[14]

Now I think we might make a parallel here with another principle central to Barth's doctrine of Scripture: exegesis may distinguish but not separate the form from the content of revelation. This is the methodological form of Barth's famous doctrine of "secondary objectivity."[15] God is revealed or "unveiled" in the creaturely realm through the "veil," an instrument or "secondary object" of worldly event, human action, and human speech. In our case we would say God is revealed through prophets and

---

14. Barth, *Church Dogmatics* III/3, §49.3.
15. Barth, *Church Dogmatics* I/1, §8.2.

apostles from the people Israel; these ancient Jews are a form of divine proclamation and self-disclosure. Exactly and fully, the form of the divine Word is Christ himself, the inseparable and unsurpassed creaturely form of the Word pleased to dwell with sinners. He is the Jewish flesh of the divine nature. We cannot explicate Scripture apart from this concreteness and particularity. The Bible, Barth argued, was not myth: there was no timeless essence or experience or ideal lying beyond and behind the words of Scripture that we can shear off, leaving the old garments behind. No, they come together, the divine Object and his worldly appearing, not equal partners to be sure — the divine Object must never be equated with its veil — but partners they remain all the same. Now there is great power in these epistemological and methodological claims. And no one makes the form of Scripture seize the heart and enchant the theological mind more than Barth. But Professor Busch has pointed us, too, to the cost such imaginative power exacts. For we are confronted with the possibility here that the self-definition of rabbinic Judaism, the Judaism without temple worship and priest, cannot be given a full hearing by the Christian church because that Judaism is unknown to the Bible. And there is no hearing of the ecumenical partner, no full dignity and autonomy, without self-definition, and self-recognition in its own idiom, institution, and practice. Can we find a way to honor Barth and honor rabbinic Judaism as well?

I believe we might begin this task by taking seriously the event that stands at the edge of the biblical witness: the end of temple worship. To be sure, Christians have not been slow to comment on this event; Barth, like many others, saw it as punishment for Israel's rejection of its Messiah. But we need not see it this way. Indeed, there is nothing in the Gospels, and little in the rest of the New Testament — perhaps Hebrews is an exception — to lead us to hold that the temple was destroyed because its worship was flawed, its worshipers rebuked and judged.[16] Rather, we might examine the rise of rabbinic Judaism, this form of worldly occurrence, as a particular and concrete witness of the centrality of the temple, and its inextricable

16. Heb. 9:1-14 may be a dismissal of the temple and its worship, though the legitimacy of the temple under the Hasmoneans and the Herodians was questioned even — or especially — by those who honored the temple cult. We may well understand Jesus' remarks against the temple in this way. The destruction of the temple in the synoptic Gospels appears in the "little apocalypses," where the desecration of the holy places is a sign of the end times; in John the temple is understood as a sign, pointing to Christ's own body. These need not imply a rejection of the temple itself.

link to its content, the messiah of Israel. Striking and characteristic of rabbinic Judaism is its steadfast decision not to rebuild the temple. Even under the emperor Julian, when Jews were offered the opportunity and means to rebuild, the moment passed and they did not.[17] There has been no Ezra in postbiblical Judaism, even when there was a Cyrus. There have been messianic claimants in rabbinic Judaism, the latest perhaps in the seventeenth century, with followers persuaded of his claims.[18] And there has been a rebuilding of the state or land of Israel, though strikingly political and nonmessianic in character. But there has been no movement to rebuild the temple or begin the priestly sacrifices, even though the priestly laws have been preserved, even practiced from time to time. Indeed, the rabbinic sages are famous for their conviction that the study of Talmud succeeded and complemented — even superseded — the temple cult.[19] Now I believe Christians might look at this enigma of postbiblical Judaism, its tough-minded rejection of the temple cult, as a witness *we* understand through Scripture. Does not the synagogue *obey*, rather than disobey, the call of its Lord through this steadfast rejection? Does it not witness in their own form and voice, to the close of the time of revelation, and to the joining together of temple and Messiah? Jesus Christ is the temple not made by hands; he is our true and high priest: that is the Christian confession. But does not rabbinic Judaism, on its own terms and in its own voice, echo this confession: the time of blood sacrifice is over until the messiah of Israel comes again. Christians and Jews disagree about the Christ of Israel; and every true encounter must have the dignity of disagreement. But Scripture may point us to a deeper agreement: that the time of revelation is closed, and we wait for the Messiah to come with a shout and we will meet him with joy on his appearing.

17. Like other historical events, and especially events from antiquity, this episode is accompanied by ambiguity. The philosophically inclined Julian (331/32–363) hoped, apparently, to discomfit Christians by the offer to rebuild the temple, not endear the Jews. A fire seems to have broken out on the temple mount, and was taken as a sign to desist. But it is by no means clear that Jews, within and beyond Palestine, would have welcomed the renewal of the temple cult. The rabbinic system was now firmly in place, and though the patriarch may have considered such a move, Judaism as a whole had become a religion of prayer and study, not priestly sacrifice. It had entered the postclassical age, and the time for such building, it seems, had passed.

18. Shabbetai Tzevi (1626-76), a messianic claimant with a remarkable and florid career.

19. See the careful discussion in Cohen, chap. 7.

Freedom for Humanity:
Karl Barth and the Politics
of the New World Order

CLIFFORD GREEN

On Barth's first and only visit to the United States in 1962, he was asked about the future of American theology. Fixing his eye on Lady Liberty in New York harbor, he astutely remarked that the statue needed a good deal of demythologizing. Then he went on to say that she could nevertheless be the symbol of a true American theology of freedom. Such a theology, and the church which embraced it, would be marked by "freedom from fear of communism, Russia, inevitable nuclear war and . . . [all other] principalities and powers. Freedom *for* which you stand would be freedom *for* — I like to say a single word — humanity . . . that freedom to which the Son frees us, and which, as his gift, is the one real human freedom."[1]

Freedom for humanity, which is simultaneously freedom for life, is the theme in Barth's politics that I want to explore.

To think about "the *future* of ecclesial theology" means not just quoting Barth but thinking in his spirit about the challenges facing us. Discussing *ecclesial* theology in a concrete way means for most of us focusing on the church in the American context. And thinking about the vast subject of *politics* — with the Bible in one hand and the newspaper in the other, as Barth advised — requires selectivity. The threefold emphasis of

1. Barth, *How I Changed My Mind* (Richmond: John Knox, 1966), p. 79. Note that in 1949 Barth had said that both West and East, in their different ways, "seem to be concerned with 'humanity'"; see Clifford Green, ed., *Karl Barth: Theologian of Freedom* (Minneapolis: Fortress, 1991), p. 316, hereafter *TF.*

89

the World Council of Churches on "justice, peace, and the integrity of creation" in considerable part coincides with Barth's own priorities. So, after some basic perspectives, I plan to discuss: (1) Barth's socialism — economic justice as an imperative of ecclesial theology; (2) Barth's "pacifism" — the peace imperative of ecclesial theology; (3) nature in creation — dogmatic roots for an ecological ethic. These will be followed by a conclusion on church practice as political witness.

Basic Perspectives

1. Anybody thinking in Barth's spirit must immediately take the phrase "new world order" not only with a grain of salt but *cum maximo grano salis*. To be sure, the geopolitical situation has changed in the last decade from what it has been since midcentury. Precisely because Barth fixed his eyes on God's kingdom and God's righteousness, he dealt with human affairs as a great relativizer, and he was certainly a skeptic about all inflated and self-serving claims. He would not encourage churches in the West to join in an orgy of self-congratulation at the demise of the communist Soviet Union and the triumph of capitalism. Rather he would encourage us, as he did in his essay "The Church between East and West,"[2] to cast a critical eye on ourselves, particularly on the injustices of our capitalism and the defects of our democracy.[3] Nor would he encourage us to remain stuck in the dualistic paradigm of the cold war, only substituting Islam now for communism. He would also ask us, I suspect, whether our reading the century in terms of an East-West struggle was not all too parochial; perhaps, after all, the most important political development on the world scene in this century is not the rise and fall of the Soviet Union and the end of the cold war, but rather the throwing off of European colonialism by the nations of Asia and Africa after World War II. And he would doubtless be challenging churches in the wealthy West about our responsibility for global economic justice in the face of the vast disparities in the world. The premise of these challenges is that the church is called to be the church, the

2. In Green, *TF*, pp. 301-18. It is worth noting, incidentally, that nearly everybody in the early 1940s was talking about a "new world order." It quickly turned into the cold war.

3. Barth's critique is similar to Michael Walzer's analysis, in his *Spheres of Justice: A Defense of Pluralism and Equality* (New York: Basic Books, 1983), of the domination of various aspects of life by money.

free people of God for all humanity, in and beyond every nation (another way of saying "one, holy, catholic, and apostolic"); the premise is not Western or American self-interest in religious garb.

2. *Historical thinking* is essential to good political analysis, and the reason for this is fundamental to Barth's theology. His most condensed term for God is "the Lord who loves in freedom." Barth understood God's "lordship" christologically, in the subversive way Jesus defined it in Mark 10;[4] this is the way of the servant, not the way of domination and profane power which was all too evident in the Roman Empire. Barth spelled out God's being and lordship in terms of God's "perfections," the perfections of divine loving and perfections of divine freedom. But there is a term that binds love and freedom together, a term that is highly pertinent to Barth's politics, and one that needs to be given more prominence: the word is "life." Speaking of the being of God, Barth writes: "The definition that we must use as a starting-point is that God's being is *life*."[5] The Creator is the living God, Christ the resurrected Christ, the Holy Spirit the "spirit of life."[6]

One of the consequences of this doctrine of God is that Barth is an astutely historical and contextual thinker. In the field of ethics and politics he quickly dismisses ahistorical thinking as "abstract."[7] This is why the category of "event" is so central to Barth's theology.[8] Revelation is event, not deposit or entity. The church community is event, not an institution. And in ethics God commands freedom, not natural law or principles.

Historical thinking is crucial for the future of American ecclesial theology and its reflection on politics because of the powerful ahistorical tendency in our culture. If Henry Ford is its most colorful representative with

---

4. "You know that those who are supposed to rule over the gentiles lord it over them and their great men exercise authority over them. But it shall not be so among you, for whoever would be great among you must be your servant, and whoever would be first among you must be slave of all. For the Son of man also came not to be served but to serve, and to give his life as a ransom for many." Mark 10:42-45; cf. Phil. 2.

5. Barth, *Church Dogmatics* (hereafter *CD*) II/1, p. 263.

6. Rom. 8:2; Rev. 11:11; cf. Rom. 8:10f.; 2 Cor. 3:6; Gal. 6:8.

7. See Barth's critique of Emil Brunner on the relation of Nazism and communism (Green, *TF*, pp. 297ff.). On a positive note, see his statement with respect to gender: "Different ages, peoples, and cultures have had very different ideas of what is concretely appropriate, salutary, and necessary in man and woman as such" (*CD*, III/4, p. 154).

8. In George Hunsinger's *How to Read Karl Barth* (New York: Oxford University Press, 1991), pp. 4, 30ff., this is the motif of "actualism" and the one he calls "the most distinctive."

his declaration, "History is bunk," George Bush is its most recent exponent with his pronouncement after the Gulf War, "We have kicked the Vietnam syndrome." What did this mean? Unlike Robert McNamara, who at least thought there was something to learn by a self-critical review of the Vietnam War,[9] President Bush told us to put Vietnam behind us. Defeat has been wiped out by a swift and supposedly decisive victory. The cold war is over, America is the world's sole superpower and is standing tall. Apparently we have nothing to learn from misreading an anticolonial revolution in terms of the monistic cold war doctrine; nothing to learn about the limits of military power; nothing to learn from the fact that the Vietnam War compromised the civil rights movement, brought down a president, and caused the greatest division in the country since the Civil War. This was America's "shaking of the foundations," to use Tillich's phrase. And yet the sort of crisis that World War I represented for Europe — and for Barth's early theology — is not to be entertained, according to the presidential pulpit. All the more reason why the Christian church and practitioners of ecclesial theology have to be more perceptive students of history, and better teachers to the nation.

3. Ecclesial theology, third, has to be a more constructive critic and interpreter of the prevailing doctrine of *freedom* in our culture. Why did Barth think we needed to demythologize the Statue of Liberty? This was a gentle critique of the reigning social philosophy in our version of liberal democracy. According to this essentially individualistic doctrine, freedom is our capacity as individuals to choose and to act (within the outer limits of the law) as we see fit. "Freedom of choice" is for many people an ethical trump card — regardless of what one chooses. It's a sort of moral laissez-faire. Indeed, the economic allusion is not accidental: the exercise of choice at the temple of the supermarket is a paradigmatic enactment of this doctrine of freedom. The essence of this doctrine is that freedom is choice, and that freedom itself has no content.

In distinction from this, Barth follows the classical Christian understanding of freedom, which stretches back through Augustine to the New Testament, according to which true freedom is freedom to do the good, to

9. McNamara, *In Retrospect: The Tragedy and Lessons of Vietnam* (New York: Random House, 1995). Cf. p. xvi: "We of the Kennedy and Johnson administrations who participated in the decisions on Vietnam acted according to what we thought were the principles and traditions of this nation. We made our decisions in light of those values. Yet we were wrong, terribly wrong. We owe it to future generations to explain why."

do the will of God, to love God and our neighbor. Here freedom has *content*, which is why Barth filled it out with illustrations: it would be freedom *from* inferiority vis-à-vis Europe, freedom *from* superiority vis-à-vis Africa and Asia, and freedom *from* sundry principalities and powers. Positively he called it "freedom *for* . . . humanity," that is, an imitation of God's freedom in the incarnation — the freedom which, as the gift of Christ, "is the one real human freedom." This is neither an empty freedom nor an individualistic one. It is freedom which is realized in community, the freedom of cohumanity and prohumanity. Can a pluralistic democracy advance beyond our prevailing individualistic, liberal doctrine of freedom? I believe we did for a brief time during the civil rights movement. The cry "Freedom Now!" had real human content. It meant equal treatment, decent housing, good schools, and employment opportunities for African Americans; it did not mean the empty capacity to choose between those goods and their opposites. An ecclesial theology, then, needs to know the fundamental difference between the Christian doctrine of freedom and the empty, individualistic one — which is why Barth always spoke of freedom and responsibility in tandem.[10]

4. Barth's theology is ecclesial public theology. This is the presupposition of everything in this chapter. Ecclesial public theology is an alternative, on the one hand, to that privatized Christianity so common in our culture, what Barth in another context called "pietistic sterility."[11] In a nutshell his view is this: "This gospel . . . is political from the very outset."[12] It is worth pondering what difference it would make if more American Christians were to regard the state not merely as a profane infringement on individual liberty, nor simply as a utilitarian creature of the democratic will, but as an ordinance of God. On the other hand, a truly ecclesial theology will beware of uncritical acculturation to prevailing assumptions, social doctrines, and "realities." It will always be asking about its own distinctive identity, insights, and contributions to political life.

---

10. See, for example, Barth, "The Christian Community and the Civil Community," §19, on political freedom; Green, *TF,* p. 285.

11. Cf. Barth, "Church and State," in Will Herberg's edition of Barth, *Community, State, and Church* (Garden City, N.Y.: Doubleday, 1960), p. 105; Barth juxtaposed to this the "sterility of the Enlightenment [secularism]."

12. Green, *TF,* p. 293.

CLIFFORD GREEN

Economic Justice, Peace, and Ecological Ethics

*Barth's Socialism — Economic Justice
as an Imperative of Ecclesial Theology*

From his early adult years Karl Barth was a socialist. In his 1946 essay "The Christian Community and the Civil Community," he drew the conclusion from Christ's coming to seek and save the lost that politically the church "must concentrate first on the lower and lowest levels of human society. The poor, the socially and economically weak and threatened, will always be the object of its primary and particular concern, and it will always insist on the state's special responsibility for these weaker members of society."[13] There is nothing novel about that — from the Bible's advocacy for the poor, the widow, the orphan, and the stranger to the pastoral letter of the Catholic bishops, *Economic Justice for All*,[14] this is a familiar Christian stance. What is noteworthy, at least to American Christians, is how Barth continues from this premise. "The church must stand for social justice in the social sphere. And in choosing between the various socialist possibilities (social-liberalism? cooperativism? syndicalism? interest-free economy [*Freigeldwirtschaft*]? moderate or radical Marxism?) it will always choose the movement from which it can expect the greatest measure of economic justice."[15] For Barth it was axiomatic that

13. Quoted in Green, *TF,* p. 284.

14. National Conference of Catholic Bishops, *Economic Justice for All: Pastoral Letter on Catholic Social Teaching and the U.S. Economy* (Washington, D.C.: United States Catholic Conference, 1986).

15. In Green, *TF,* p. 284 revised; cf. *CD* III/4, p. 545, where Barth writes that the political task of the Christian community is to "espouse various forms of social progress or even of socialism." Barth mentions several quite different approaches to "socialism" in the passage quoted. *Social liberalism* in Barth's time is about equivalent to "social democratic" in Europe today, namely, a moderate socialist position consistent with liberal democracy. A *cooperative* is a voluntary nonprofit association of consumers or producers for the benefit of its members. *Syndicalism* is a revolutionary strategy for reorganizing society by overthrowing the state which it regards as intrinsically oppressive and substituting the trade union as the key unit of productive labor and government; the motive is socialist in that production is for use, not profit (*Columbia Encyclopedia,* 1963). *Freigeldwirtschaft* is mistranslated "free trade" or "free market economy." It refers to the economic theories of Silvio Gesell (1862-1930) about an economy in which money would be available without interest (hence "free money"), and would also depreciate like other capital assets. According to Andreas Pangritz (Aachen), to whom I am indebted for the following information, Gesell's theories in 1946

94

social and economic justice entailed socialism. At the same time, he was remarkably unideological about the form of it, as the foregoing list of options indicates; he always placed serving concrete human need above theory and political dogmas.

The very mention of socialism in America usually generates severe allergic reactions. So it needs to be said that Barth was a democratic socialist and no Bolshevik.[16] One can find many disavowals of the system of Soviet communism in his writings, and it is not necessary to detail them here.[17] A letter to his son Christoph in 1950 summed up his view: "Anyone who does not want communism — and none of us do — should take socialism seriously."[18] What did socialism mean for Barth? I think it comes down to two things: First, his inability to make peace with the injustices of a sinful world, what Bruce McCormack calls Barth's "revolutionary unrest: constantly being urged forward by the longing for something better than anything offered by this world."[19] The magnetism of the eschatological kingdom of God was for Barth a powerful stimulus to political and economic change in the world. And this connects to the second thing: in the face of those who said "realism" demanded accommodation to capitalism and nationalism, Barth said "we should expect more from God."[20]

Why, a decade after the demise of Soviet communism, is Barth's socialism a crucial challenge to the future of ecclesial theology? First, because it makes us ask ourselves: What do we expect from God? Do we expect "revolutionary unrest" or a complacent and comfortable security in the

were discussed in Swiss anarchist circles and perhaps among the friends of Leonhard Ragaz. Elsewhere in Barth, "radical socialism" meant Soviet communism; cf. *TF*, p. 307.

16. For a summary sketch on Barth's socialism, see Green, *TF*, pp. 41ff.

17. When Emil Brunner asked Barth why he was not combating Communism as he did National Socialism, he replied that though he did not consider that Communism presented the temptation and threat that National Socialism did, he nevertheless did not consider that the Soviet system "conform[ed] to our standards of justice and freedom" and that anyone who wanted from him "a political disclaimer of its system and its methods may have it at once" (Green, *TF*, p. 299). In "The Church between East and West" Barth wrote that "the profoundly unsatisfactory nature" of eastern Communism is obvious to everybody — though, in contrast to National Socialism, he credited Communism with at least having a positive intention of dealing with "the *social* problem"; cf. pp. 315, 313.

18. Cited in Eberhard Busch, *Karl Barth* (Philadelphia: Fortress, 1976), p. 382.

19. McCormack, *Karl Barth's Critically Realistic Dialectical Theology* (Oxford: Clarendon, 1995), p. 109.

20. Barth, in *Die Christliche Welt* 28 (August 15, 1914): 776, cited in McCormack, p. 110.

status quo? After answering that — or perhaps before answering it — we should ponder facts like these in a United Nations report last fall:

> Even in the world's wealthiest countries, the ranks of the poor are growing and many people are being denied the basic rewards of afflu-ence. For example, 16.5 percent of Americans live in poverty, even though the United States leads the world in per-capita consumption of goods and services. Sweden was ranked the best among developed na-tions in spreading the wealth, with fewer than 7 percent of its people in poverty. In the industrialized world, at least 37 million people are un-employed, 100 million are homeless, and nearly 200 million have a life expectancy of less than 60 years.[21]

The picture in our own country is also one of increasing disparities. Income disparity is widening at the extremes: in 1979 the top 5 percent of U.S. earners earned ten times the bottom 5 percent; fourteen years later, in 1993, the top 5 percent earned twenty-five times the bottom 5 percent.[22] According to a recent public television program entitled "Luxury Fever"[23] (based on the book of that name by Robert Frank of Cornell), the wealthi-est 1 percent own 50 percent of the nation's wealth — though one-third of those earning over $100,000 say they can't make ends meet.[24] Meanwhile, the median American income has not increased in the last twenty years, and the earnings of people in the bottom fifth have declined more than 10 percent.[25]

The increasingly interdependent global economy raises more critical issues. Not least among them is the fundamental question: Who controls the global movement of capital? Who benefits and who suffers from this

---

21. *New York Times*, September 13, 1998, sec. 3, p. 2. See United Nations Development Program, *Human Development Report, 1998: Consumption Patterns and Their Implications for Human Development* (New York: Oxford University Press, 1998).

22. Statistics from Robert H. Frank, Cornell economist, quoted in interview on PBS's *The NewsHour with Jim Lehrer,* "Luxury Fever" program, May 20, 1999, and confirmed in Frank's e-mail of June 7, 1999. See Robert H. Frank, *Luxury Fever: Why Money Fails to Satisfy in an Era of Excess* (New York: Free Press, 1999).

23. *The NewsHour with Jim Lehrer,* May 20, 1999.

24. Juliet Schor, Harvard economist, quoted on *NewsHour,* "Luxury Fever" interview.

25. Robert H. Frank, "Our Climb to Sublime: Hold On, We Don't Need to Go There," *Washington Post,* January 24, 1999, p. B1.

movement? This is not solely a question for investors — it also involves responsible and irresponsible borrowing.[26]

Third World debt is another critical issue in the global economy. Both the World Council of Churches at its Harare assembly in December 1998 and the U.S. Roman Catholic bishops in the spring of 1999 issued calls for debt relief to poor nations.[27] In comparison to the burden of Third World debt, just 1 percent of our national budget is devoted to foreign aid, far less than other developed countries.[28]

On the crises of the global economy, here are some comments from an experienced practitioner, worth quoting at length.

> Market fundamentalism relies on an allegedly scientific economic theory. Basically, I think it was Ronald Reagan and Margaret Thatcher who were the main movers in adopting a vulgarized version of laissez-faire economics, turning it into a kind of fundamentalist position. . . . I also worry about inequity. The markets are good for expressing individual self-interest. But society is not simply an aggregation of individual interests. There are collective interests that don't find expression in market values. Markets cannot be the be-all and end-all. These collective decisions, and even individual decisions, must involve the question of right and wrong. I think markets are amoral. . . . But moral values are necessary to prevent their excesses and inequities. . . . In the case of labor markets, work itself is turned into a commodity. As such, the labor markets often work very efficiently. But you can also sack someone even if he has an ailing mother and may have nowhere to turn. People have to be treated as people. . . . I am worried about . . . the replacement of professional values by market values. Turning law or medicine into businesses. I think it changes the character of those activities. In the case of politics, the huge role of money in elections undermines the political process. [The new global economy resembles the internal crises of capitalism in the past.] After each crisis, we made

26. See the four-part *New York Times* series, "Global Contagion: A Narrative," February 15-18, 1999.

27. See Gustav Niebuhr on "A Jubilee Call to Debt Forgiveness" (U.S. Catholic Conference Administrative Board), *New York Times*, April 25, 1999.

28. This is a widely quoted statistic, most recently in the *New York Times*, July 6, 1999, p. A4, in a story on the departure of J. Brian Atwood, director of the Agency for International Development for the past six years.

institutional changes. . . . We have national institutions that keep excesses from going too far. During this period when market fundamentalism has become the dominant dogma, however, markets have become truly global. And we don't have comparable international institutions to prevent the excesses.

This is not some left-leaning, tweed-jacketed, pipe-smoking academic theologian in his ivory tower. This is George Soros, the billionaire New York financier, in an interview about his book *The Crisis of Global Capitalism*.[29]

Christians like Barth who lean to the left will surely acknowledge that the market has won out over state planning as a more efficient way of allocating resources. But those who lean to the right need to recognize that markets have long antedated modern capitalism, and that there are fundamental ethical and policy issues that the market can never answer. Those of us who lean to the left need to recognize that capitalism has proved to be a very successful generator of wealth — which is surely needed to improve living standards among the poor both nationally and internationally. Those who lean to the right need to admit that even moderately controlled capitalism cannot equitably distribute that wealth.

You cannot go to the *Church Dogmatics* and find a Barthian socialist recipe to magically solve these problems. But you will find a passionate commitment to social and economic justice. If socialism as Soviet state capitalism and command economy is dead, socialism as the question of economic justice is more urgent than ever.

Finally I submit that it is precisely in economic theory and practices that we find embedded the operative social philosophy of most people today. This is where the agenda of theological anthropology is actually located. It needs to be engaged in a self-critical way in our theological seminaries and our preaching. What philosophy of religion used to be in the curriculum needs to become economic education.

29. See George Soros and Jeff Madrick, "The International Crisis: An Interview," *New York Review of Books*, January 14, 1999, p. 40.

Barth's "Pacifism" — the Peace Imperative
of Ecclesial Theology

Barth's ethic of peace is grounded christologically, for the command of Jesus that we should love our enemies (Matt. 5:44) is rooted in God's being and action in the incarnation, cross, and resurrection. According to Romans 5:6-11, it is God's enemies who are reconciled to God by the cross; the disciples of Jesus, accordingly, are commanded to love their enemies. For Barth this leads to what he calls his "practical pacifism" — not pacifism as an abstract principle, not an absolute pacifism that ruled out the use of force in certain circumstances, but a definite imperative to peace.[30] From this perspective we can briefly review Barth's course from World War I through the cold war.

Among the various influences that disillusioned Barth with nineteenth-century Protestant theology, what played a decisive role for him personally, he said, was "the failure of the ethics of modern theology at the outbreak of the First World War which led to our discontent with its exegesis, its conception of history, and its dogmatics."[31]

When it came to defeating National Socialism in World War II, however, Barth as vigorously roused Europe to the cause as Reinhold Niebuhr did America. But, typically, as soon as Hitler was defeated, Barth became an advocate for the reconstruction of Germany.

One of Barth's major efforts during the cold war was opposition to nuclear weapons. Working to eliminate these weapons must surely be at the top

---

30. "According to the sense of the New Testament we cannot be pacifists in principle, only in practice. But we have to consider very closely whether, if we are called to discipleship, we can avoid being practical pacifists, or fail to be so" (*CD* IV/2, p. 550). Cited in Hunsinger, "The Politics of the Nonviolent God: Reflections on René Girard and Karl Barth," *Scottish Journal of Theology* 51 (1998): 61-85, esp. 77ff.

31. In his 1956 essay "The Humanity of God"; cf. Green, *TF,* p. 49. The fuller version is as follows: "One day in early August 1914 stands out in my personal memory as a black day. Ninety-three German intellectuals impressed public opinion by their proclamation in support of the war policy of Wilhelm II and his counselors. Among these intellectuals I discovered to my horror almost all of my theological teachers whom I had greatly venerated. In despair over what this indicated about the signs of the times I suddenly realized that I could not any longer follow either their ethics and dogmatics or their understanding of the Bible and of history. For me, at least, nineteenth-century theology no longer held any future." From the essay "Protestant Theology in the Nineteenth Century," in Barth, *The Humanity of God* (Atlanta: John Knox, 1978), p. 14.

of the international agenda for the universal church in the coming century. Perhaps we have been lulled into complacency in the last decade, but there are still an estimated 36,000 nuclear weapons in the world. According to Peace Action, a leading peace organization, the Department of Energy (DOE) plans to begin producing up to eighty nuclear warheads annually for the U.S. Trident nuclear submarine fleet; each of these warheads is twenty times more destructive than the atomic bomb dropped on Nagasaki.[32]

In the 1980s we saw important declarations on peace and atomic weapons by the World Council of Churches Sixth Assembly (Vancouver 1983), the U.S. Roman Catholic bishops, the United Methodist Church, and others.[33] These documents were striking in the degree they diverged from the official national policy of governments of both parties. They declared that the use of nuclear weapons was completely outside the bounds of any Christian ethic, and they urged church members not to be involved in the production or use of these weapons. Barth and his colleagues had reached this conclusion almost thirty years earlier.

In March 1958 people who had been members of the Confessing Church and now led a peace movement in the German churches, like Martin Niemöller, presented a petition to the National Synod of the Evangelical Church. The several hundred signatories "challenged the Synod to declare that atomic war was a *status confessionis* issue for the church," that is, a situation requiring a confession of faith by the church because the heart of the gospel and therefore the very existence of the church was at stake. Further, the petition called on the synod to declare that "the church's position was a categorical No to nuclear war, and that Christians may not participate in any way in preparations for atomic war." A deeply divided synod passed a resolution against weapons of mass destruction and called for the

---

32. Peace Action, "Los Alamos Fact Sheet," February 1999, by Bruce Hall. DOE is planning to spend nearly $50 billion on research, development, and production of nuclear weapons in the coming decade; see the department's "Stockpile Stewardship and Management Plan," which refers to developing "new nuclear options for emerging threats" and "changing military requirements." Sources for the "Los Alamos Fact Sheet" include the DOE budget requests and its "Green Book" on the "Stockpile Stewardship and Management Plan" and analyses of these by the Los Alamos Study Group, the Natural Resources Defense Council (see its August 1997 report, "End Run"), and the Concerned Citizens for Nuclear Safety.

33. The Assembly's "Statement on Peace and Justice" calls the production and use of nuclear weapons "a crime against humanity" and calls on Christians to "refuse to participate in any conflict involving weapons of mass destruction."

end of atomic weapons research, but did not adopt the petition's stance. A rumor circulated that Barth disagreed with the petition. In reply he published a letter in *Junge Kirche* saying: "You may say to all and everyone that I am in agreement with these theses . . . as if I had written them myself." In fact, Barth himself was the author of the petition![34]

A few months later Barth wrote to the European Congress for Outlawing Atomic Weapons. Everyone, including governments, Barth wrote, knows the "evil and danger of atomic weapons," but they still develop and accept them. Intellectuals, including "a large group of church leaders," Barth said sarcastically, "devote themselves to profound philosophical and theological discussions about such problems as the tragic dimension of human existence in the atomic age, but they stubbornly avoid making any specific decision against atomic weapons." Atomic weapons are rationalized by the supposedly greater threat posed by the respective adversaries in the cold war. Therefore every effort must be made to end the cold war, an effort in which Christian faith can bring some creative insights. In the meantime, opposition to "the blasphemous . . . development of atomic weapons" must continue on all levels. Finally Barth asked the congress to consider encouraging active resistance, perhaps by inviting people "to refuse to serve in military units employing such weapons."[35]

If we can never regain our innocence by putting the nuclear genie back in the bottle, it is all the more urgent that we build up international institutions such as the United Nations and the International Court of Justice where raw violence can be sublimated as much as possible into law, politics, and economic sanctions. The posture of the protagonists in the cold war has greatly hindered this development, and outmoded ideas of the nation-state continue to do so. The church, itself an international institution, needs to be both more willing and better organized to mobilize its resources for transcending national and ethnic interests. An international institution like the United Nations will not be able to avoid the use of force from time to time. Particularly in genocidal situations like Rwanda and Kosovo, the need for international police action will continue to arise. But crosscutting political interests in the United Nations will not make decisions to employ force easy.

34. Green, *TF,* pp. 319ff., citing also Busch, p. 431.
35. The text, translated by Robert McAfee Brown, is found in Georges Casalis, *Portrait of Karl Barth* (Garden City, N.Y.: Doubleday, 1963), pp. 73f.

In the history of the church the pacifist and just war traditions have jostled each other for centuries. Just war doctrine — perhaps more aptly called the "just defense doctrine" — intended its canons to constrain violence and sanctioned it only as a last resort under strictly limited conditions. But the self-interests of rulers and states have usually overridden the church's canons of constraint. So sanctioning the use of violence has been the dominant tradition. We are living at the end of the bloodiest of all centuries. From the machine gun at the beginning of the century to the nuclear bomb in the middle, we have proved that every increase in weapons technology will be used for increased death and destruction. And surely we must ask about the connection (as one of several factors) between military violence and the tragic, insane violence in our schools. In light of all this, is it too much to hope that we can shift the balance, that the ecumenical church will become an active peace church, a builder of bridges, an agent of reconciliation, an advocate of economic development? This seems to me the direction of Barth's peace witness.

Nature in Creation — Dogmatic Roots of Ecological Ethics

I take it for granted that the issue of ecology is a self-evident political and global issue. The brevity of this section is itself a symptom of the problem it discusses. I want to mention a critique of Barth's doctrine of creation, as it bears on ecological ethics. Here I am following Paul Santmire and his Harvard dissertation on the status of nature in Barth's doctrine of creation.[36] A concise summary of his analysis is found in his book *The Travail of Nature*,[37] under the rubric "The Triumph of Personalism." The problem here concerns the fundamental status of the natural world — as distinct from humanity — as part of creation in Barth's theology.

Santmire characterizes Barth's position as "radical the-anthropocentrism." In the doctrine of revelation the Word is "*God's* address to *humanity* in Jesus Christ,"[38] and consequently Christian doctrine, Barth says,

36. See Santmire, "Creation and Nature: A Study of the Doctrine of Nature with Special Attention to Karl Barth's Doctrine of Creation" (Th.D. diss., Harvard University, 1966).
37. H. Paul Santmire, *The Travail of Nature: The Ambiguous Ecological Promise of Christian Theology* (Philadelphia: Fortress, 1985), esp. pp. 145-56.
38. Santmire, *The Travail of Nature*, p. 149.

"has to be exclusively and conclusively the doctrine of Jesus Christ as the living Word of God spoken to us human beings."[39]

In Barth's doctrine of election this focus on God and humanity discloses its eternal ground. Election is the eternal basis of everything that happens in history,[40] it is the internal basis — the raison d'être — of the creation. Jesus Christ, the eternal Son, is the electing God. Jesus Christ, as the incarnate Son, is the elect human being. But election also involves, as Santmire puts it, "the ontological prefiguration of a *community of humans* united together in the person of the 'God-Man.'"[41] But the nonhuman creation has no eternal ground. It is rather the "external ground of the covenant," the "theater"[42] where the eternal covenant is played out in history. Santmire summarizes:

> We now see formally speaking that nature for the first time has come into view in Barth's schema, as a kind of stage to allow the eternally founded drama between God and humanity to run its course. So, whereas humanity has a dual status — it is elected in eternity and it is also created "as such," in order to fulfil its eternal determination — the whole world of nature, outside of humanity, has a single status only. It has no eternal determination. Its reality is purely instrumental. It is merely the temporal setting for the really real, for the exfoliation and the consummation of the eternal covenant of grace with humanity. . . . Nature has no divinely bestowed meaning of its own.[43]

This does not mean that the cosmos is evil, inhospitable to humanity, or dualistically opposed to God. It is, Barth says with Genesis, "very good." But, Santmire concludes, "it has no evident permanent meaning in the greater scheme of things, as the human community obviously does."[44] The

---

39. Barth, "How My Mind Has Changed," *Christian Century* 56 (September 1939): 37f., cited in Santmire, *The Travail of Nature*, p. 253.

40. It is "the principle and essence of all happening everywhere" (*CD* II/2, p. 183, cited in Santmire, *The Travail of Nature*, p. 150).

41. Santmire, *The Travail of Nature*, p. 150, citing Barth, *CD* II/2, pp. 116f.

42. Cf. *CD* III/3, p. 48; cf. p. 46, where Barth says its status is "pure service," which means, according to Santmire, *The Travail of Nature*, p. 152, "purely instrumental."

43. Santmire, *The Travail of Nature*, pp. 152f., where supporting citations are given for Barth's argument that humanity is the point of the created world, the meaning and goal of the whole creation.

44. Santmire, *The Travail of Nature*, p. 154.

issue raised all too briefly here concerns the deep structure of a dogmatics and its deficiency as regards ecological ethics. Worth further exploration in this context are two places where ecclesial theology cannot avoid dealing with matter: the human body and the sacraments; this also relates to Barth's understanding of liturgy.

Church Practice as Political Witness

Barth's 1946 essay "The Christian Community and the Civil Community"[45] describes church and state as two concentric circles, of which Christ and the kingdom of God are the center, with the church as the inner circle and the state as the outer. Thus church and state have an analogous relation to covenant and creation, of which Barth said that the covenant of grace is the internal basis of the creation while the creation is the external basis of the covenant. Barth does not advocate a theocratic state. "The tasks of the Christian community in the political realm are secular and profane. . . . Political systems are human inventions, to be tested experimentally to see if, through law and peaceful order, they provide 'an external, relative, and provisional humanization' of existence."[46]

As is well known, Barth regards the state as an "analogue" to the eschatological kingdom of God. Political activity by members of the Christian community should therefore be "parabolic." Christians' work to make law, policy, and practice in the public realm points to and reflects in some degree what the church knows of Christ and the reign of God. Hence the incarnation of the eternal God means putting real living human beings ahead of all causes and ideologies; divine justification points to the constitutional state; Christ's coming to save the lost means a preferential option for the most vulnerable members of society; baptism into one Spirit means the equal freedom and responsibility of all citizens — restricting "the political freedom and responsibility not only of certain classes and races but, supremely, that of women," Barth said, "is an arbitrary convention" which must be abandoned forthwith.[47] These are some of the dozen examples Barth gives of this parabolic politics whereby civic

45. In Green, *TF*, pp. 265-96.
46. Green, *TF*, p. 265.
47. Green, *TF*, p. 285.

life can point to God's kingdom for which the church hopes, prays, and works.

Well and good. But now let us ask about turning this procedure back on the life of the church itself, that is, looking to *the actual practices of the church as enacting the doctrines it proclaims.* I am asking about the church which is not only a community of the Word and the Spirit, but also an economic and political community. I am asking how the Christian community, in its own life and practice, can better become *itself* a sociopolitical parable of the gospel, an enacted parable of God's reign and realm.

I am prompted in this direction by the season of Pentecost we now celebrate. According to Luke in the Acts of the Apostles, the coming of the Holy Spirit created a new political and economic community in the world.[48] *A new political community:* the Christian community was first constituted by devout Jews "from *every nation* under heaven."[49] Their nations are all listed, from Persia in the east to Libya and Rome in the west. The first form of the church was not, *pace* my colleagues in "congregational studies," the local congregation — the dominant form of church life in our land — but a new international community, the first "united nations." *A new economic community:* I find it very suggestive that Luke links liturgy, and specifically the eucharist, to economics. "And they devoted themselves to the apostles' teaching and fellowship, to the breaking of bread and the prayers. . . . And all who believed were together and had all things in common; and they sold their possessions and goods and distributed them to all, as any had need."[50] They distributed bread, the body of Christ, and they distributed goods and money to those in need — they did this, it says a little later, "with glad and generous hearts." (Those who celebrate the Eucharist only infrequently, or in the modern, individualistic way, should ponder the economic implications of their liturgical practice.)

Now let us not get sidetracked by arguments about the early church and "primitive communism," let us recognize that Luke is not talking about "primitive capitalism" either, and let us admit that structuring a just economic order in a global economy is a complex and demanding task. Here I want us to focus on the economic life of the church as political wit-

---

48. I wish those who talk so much about "spirituality" would recognize the intrinsic connection between faith in Jesus Christ and political world transformation as Luke presents it.

49. Acts 2:5ff.

50. Acts 2:42ff.

ness. And let us remember that there is a long tradition in the church of making direct connections between economic life and the gospel — I am thinking of monastic communities on the one hand, and communities like Mennonites and Hutterites on the other.

We can begin by recalling that churches are already engaged in a great deal of economic activity. Recall church-based insurance companies such as the Aid Association for Lutherans and Lutheran Brotherhood; recall millions of dollars given annually for humanitarian aid and disaster relief; think of revolving loan funds supporting sweat-equity, low-income housing, and people donating their labor to build houses through Habitat for Humanity; think of trusts and foundations administered by congregations and denominations; and we should certainly highlight the corporate responsibility movement spearheaded by the Interfaith Center for Corporate Responsibility which assembled sufficient church funds to influence major banks and corporations in their policies on apartheid in South Africa, for example. Subsidizing with church offerings parochial schools, hospitals, and homes for the elderly is also a substantial economic activity.

Yet all this is unsystematic and relatively modest in scale compared to the actual economic resources under the control of church members. What might a more ambitious organization of churches as an economic institution be able to accomplish, and in a way that embodies church priorities and addresses social injustices in some significant measure?

1. A "Workers of Conscience" fund for church members who resign their jobs making nuclear weapons to assist them while they find new employment.
2. A church-based health insurance scheme for the very poor — church members and nonmembers — at least some of them.
3. A vigorous affirmative action hiring program by businesses owned by church members.
4. A training and loan program to help minority young adults start businesses in poor city neighborhoods.
5. Establishing a substantial ecumenical foundation to support activities such as the above.
6. A retired executives organization to volunteer expertise in support of the above.
7. Research and education projects on the church as an economic institution — its resources and activities.

What about parables of a new political community, a polis that more nearly reflects Pentecost and a new humanity and less the class and racial and other conflicts of our cities and world?

1. A top priority has to be racial reconciliation, as a parable of the reconciliation of the world with God. We could begin with a major migration of white, suburban church members to black, urban congregations.
2. Institutionalize the sanctuary movement, along the lines of the German church-based organization Asylum in the Church, which provided legal defense to foreign workers the government was illegally trying to deport.[51]
3. Promote systematic church support of the United Nations and the International Court of Justice.
4. Expand dramatically church programs of international exchange and travel seminars, especially to places of ethnic, religious, and political conflict such as the Middle East, Sudan, Korea, Russia, Vietnam, Rwanda, Ireland, and the Balkans.
5. In Christian-Jewish relations, inaugurate a ten-year, church-wide program of theological research, dialogue, and congregational education.
6. Establish Muslim affairs offices in the main denominations to educate church members about the complex realities of Islam and to counteract media stereotypes.

These are just a few initiatives that churches can take themselves, independent of and *in addition to* the direct service of Christians in the public world of economics and politics. Let Barth himself have the last word in a concluding passage from "The Christian Community and the Civil Community."

The real church must be the model and prototype of the state. The church must *set an example* so that by its very existence it may be a

---

51. The church-based organization is Asylum in the Church (Asyl in der Kirche), in Berlin-Kreuzberg and connected to the Kirche zum heiligen Kreuz. The address is: Asyl in der Kirche, Nostilzstrasse 6/7, 10961 Berlin (phone 49-30-6914183). The pastor who is in charge of the project is Pfarrer Jürgen Quandt (49-30-8550440/41). I believe the organization is funded by the Ev. Kirche. (Information from Dr. Ralf Wüstenberg, Berlin.)

source of renewal for the state and the power by which the state is preserved. The church's preaching of the gospel would be in vain if its own existence . . . were not a practical demonstration of the thinking and acting from the gospel which takes place in this inner circle. How can the world believe the gospel of the King and of his Kingdom if by its own actions and attitudes the church shows that it has no intention of basing its own internal policy on the gospel? . . . Of the political implications of theology which we have enumerated there are few which do not merit attention first of all in the life and development of the church itself. So far they have not received anything like enough attention within the church's own borders.[52]

52. Green, *TF*, p. 294.

Freedom for Humanity

DAVID HOLLENBACH, S.J.

Clifford Green's essay raises several important challenges by theology to the emerging world order, and by the emerging world order to theology. In this response I want to focus on three points: (1) Barth's theology of freedom in community challenges the two major pseudosovereignties that threaten to become demonic in our time — the market and narrowly defined in-groups such as national, ethnic, or religious communities; (2) this theological challenge has major importance for our understanding of justice; and (3) it will significantly affect the way we think about the use of force, specifically about the question of humanitarian intervention for the defense of human rights.

First, Barth's challenge to the pseudosovereignties of nation and race is of course at the heart of his role in the Confessing Church and his authorship of the Barmen Declaration. The challenge continues to be most relevant today, though it has a somewhat different focus. That only God, and not any ethnic or national community, is God remains a crucial theological contribution to the new world emerging today. This challenge is linked with Barth's christological and covenantal insistence that the freedom of the human person is essentially relational and realized only in community. This has important economic and political consequences. Let me briefly point to these consequences in light of the second challenge — the way we understand justice.

The importance of the way we conceive of justice is forcefully indicated by the international financial crisis on the current agenda of governments of the developed world and major international financial institutions. This crisis concerns the value of currencies, interest rates, and potential returns on investments. The response commonly heard in the U.S. Treasury Department and the International Monetary Fund (IMF) is that the solution to the crisis lies in further expansion of free markets, not their contraction. But James Wolfensohn, president of the World Bank, has recently sought to put what he calls "The Other Crisis" on the agenda of these bodies. This other crisis is the one that affects the well-being and the very lives of millions of people worldwide, especially the poorest. Here are Wolfensohn's words in an address to the governors of the World Bank:

> Today, while we talk of financial crisis — 17 million Indonesians have fallen back into poverty, and across the region a million children will now not return to school.
>
> Today, while we talk of financial crisis — an estimated 40 percent of the Russian population now lives in poverty.
>
> Today, while we talk of financial crisis — across the world, 1.3 billion people live on less than $1 a day; 3 billion live on under $2 a day; 1.3 billion have no access to clean water; 3 billion have no access to sanitation; 2 billion have no access to power.
>
> We talk of financial crisis while in Jakarta, in Moscow, in Sub-Saharan Africa, in the slums of India, and the barrios of Latin America, the human pain of poverty is all around us. . . .
>
> Mr. Chairman, we must address this human pain. We must go beyond financial stabilization. We must address the issues of long-term equitable growth, on which prosperity and human progress depend. We must focus on the institutional and structural changes needed for recovery and sustainable development.[1]

Wolfensohn concludes his description of this "other crisis" with the appeal that "we must focus on the social issues." I would put it this way: we must focus on the way the globalizing economy leads to greater justice or to greater injustice, to greater well-being or to increasing poverty for the majority of the human race. Solutions to the financial crisis are important, to

---

1. James D. Wolfensohn, "The Other Crisis" (address to the Board of Governors of the World Bank, Washington, D.C., October 6, 1998; Internet resource: http://www.worldbank.org/html/extdr/am98/jdw-sp/am98-en.htm; accessed November 6, 1998).

be sure. But they are not enough. Indeed, Wolfensohn himself observed that in some countries that followed IMF and World Bank recommendations and accepted free market adjustments to their social systems, the lot of their people has declined. Development of a new architecture for the global economic system must take these concerns into account. The market cannot be treated as the new sovereign.

Let me suggest several ethical guidelines that are drawn from the United States Catholic bishops' pastoral letter *Economic Justice for All,* issued in 1986 in the heyday of enthusiasm for free markets. Clifford Green refers to this document in his paper and sees it as compatible with Barth's theology. I agree. But I also think it articulates ethical norms more concretely than Barth often does. It can be especially helpful to us for this reason.

The bishops' ethical stance toward markets, I would argue, is the result of a theology that is simultaneously incarnational and eschatological.[2] It is a theology that takes the human reality seriously enough to keep alive the memory of what actual living people have undergone and achieved in the past. It remembers the pain caused by laissez-faire capitalism in the days before the emergence of the welfare state in the North Atlantic region. This incarnational theology also pays attention to the present effects of institutions and the values that undergird them on people in different present-day societies. Thus the bishops did not focus only on the negative effects of state socialism in the Soviet bloc and its epigones. They also paid attention to what was happening to the poor in American cities and in the favelas of Latin America and the rural regions of Africa. The eschatological orientation of the theology led them to affirm that whatever positive achievements could be attributed to the market, these achievements were not enough, for they left large groups of people behind when the benefits were being doled out.

This theology is at the basis of an ethic of some specificity. Let me highlight what can be called the three pillars that support the overall architecture of this ethic. The first pillar is the central claim that every economic decision, institution, and policy must be evaluated in light of its impact on the dignity of human persons who are created in the image of God.[3] This

2. See National Conference of Catholic Bishops (NCCB), *Economic Justice for All: Pastoral Letter on Catholic Social Teaching and the U.S. Economy* (Washington, D.C.: National Conference of Catholic Bishops, 1986), esp. nos. 53-55.
3. NCCB, no. 28.

means paying serious attention to the human effects of markets, and promoting what can be called a people-centered vision of economic activity. This may perhaps seem a truism. But Wolfensohn and the World Bank seem to have taken a bit longer than the bishops to reach it. In Wolfensohn's recent words, "development is about getting the macroeconomics right — yes; but it is also about building the roads, empowering the people, writing the laws, recognizing the women, eliminating the corruption, educating the girls, building the banking systems, protecting the environment, inoculating the children."[4]

The second pillar is that the dignity of the person is realized only in community.[5] This, of course, is central to Green's Barthian argument. It means that human interdependence is valued positively, as an opportunity for enhanced human dignity and well-being. The bishops thus approach the reality of globalization of the economy from a standpoint that is essentially positive and hopeful. The movement from self-sufficiency to genuine interdependence provides an opportunity for growth in well-being for all involved.

But here the third pillar is crucial: the obligation to support the dignity of all in community means that those who are left out have the single most urgent claim on our consciences, and on the policies of governments and international financial institutions also.[6] Over a decade ago the bishops argued that far too many people were simply being left out of the benefits generated by markets. Their eschatological vision was that of an inclusive community from which no one is excluded — namely, the reign of God. Their theology led them not to expect this fullness of community to be entirely realized in history. But it also led them to insist that getting the macroeconomics right is not enough when the number of millions who have literally nothing is growing, not declining. The World Bank seems to be gradually waking up to this reality, at least in the rhetoric of its president. Whether this can be said of the U.S. Treasury secretary or the head of the IMF is another matter. Something has gone wrong when many countries that have adhered to World Bank and IMF free market conditions over the past decade are worse off today than they were ten years ago. Not only is this not good enough, the direction is wrong. It is time, in other

4. Wolfensohn, "The Other Crisis."
5. NCCB, no. 77.
6. NCCB, nos. 86 and 252.

words, to build the option for the poor into the international financial architecture that shapes the lives and well-being of all of us today. That
would be the beginning of the incarnation of at least one aspect of the eschatological vision in which Christians hope. It also seems increasingly to
be a condition of political stability of the new globalized world we live in
today.

This leads to my third point: the political and human rights aspects
of this theological ethic, which have been especially important in debates
about the NATO intervention in Kosovo. Freedom in community is at the
basis of the U.S. Catholic bishops' definition of human rights. They call
human rights "the minimum conditions for life in community."[7] They also
affirm that the community relevant for the protection of human rights is
the human race as a whole. This means that human rights are global concerns, not simply the internal affairs of sovereign nation-states. Indeed, the
very notion of national sovereignty must be discounted when this understanding of human rights is taken seriously. This opens up the possibility
of ethically legitimate intervention across national boundaries by the international community when gross violations such as genocide or ethnic
cleansing are under way.

There are conditions on the use of force, of course, as the just war
theory has long affirmed. In particular, the role of international organizations as the "legitimate authority" for such intervention is more important
than in the past. If the limitation of sovereignty legitimates intervention,
the judgment of a particular nation such as the United States must also be
subjected to multinational scrutiny. In my judgment, NATO as a regional
multinational organization in proximity to the Kosovo crisis in fact provided such legitimate authority for intervention in a just cause in Kosovo.
Some of the means used, however, were more dubious, for some of the air
war tactics seemed disproportionate and indiscriminate attacks on innocent noncombatants. Such attacks are themselves violations of human
rights. But my main point is that when we take both the limits on national
sovereignty and the importance of human rights in the global community
as seriously as we should today, a new possibility of legitimate intervention
arises. Indeed, I think the international community failed to exercise its re-
sponsibilities in this regard in a reprehensible way in the face of the
Rwandan genocide of 1994. France and the United States bear particular

7. NCCB, no. 79, section title.

responsibility for this failure because of the central roles they played in blocking U.N. action to prevent the horror of the 800,000 deaths that occurred in Rwanda in less than three months' time.

In sum, I think the central themes of the limits on national and market sovereignty and the conception of freedom in community as the basis of a definition of human rights remain lasting legacies of Karl Barth to the new world we are living in today. My hope is that an ecclesial theology that takes Barth's insights seriously will be a fully ecumenical and fully public theology as well. I have tried here to suggest a few ways we might move toward such an ecumenical, public approach to theological ethics and the social witness of the church.

"I See Something You Don't See":
Karl Barth's Doctrine of Providence

CAROLINE SCHRÖDER

Under the heading "The Christian and the Universal Lordship of God the Father,"[1] Barth offers this characterization of what it means to be a Christian: "He sees what the others do not see. . . . The Christian sees in [the world process] a universal lordship. . . . The Christian sees in it the universal lordship of God, of the God who is the Father, who is the Father to him, his Father. He sees the constitutive and organizing center of the process. What makes him a Christian is that he sees Jesus Christ" (p. 241).[2] Imagine two children who must pass time in the waiting room of a doctor's office.

---

1. All parenthetical page numbers in this chapter and its notes, unless otherwise noted, are from Barth's *Church Dogmatics* III/3.

2. "And so the belief in God's providence undoubtedly consists in the fact that man is freed to see this rule of God in world-occurrence, this secret history of his glory. This does not mean that faith becomes sight. . . . When a man believes in God's providence, he does not know only in abstracto and generally that God is over all things and all things are in his hand, but he continually sees something of the work of this hand, and may continually see God's will and purpose in very definite events, relationships, connexions and changes in the history of created being. He notes in this history disposings and directions, hints and signs, set limits and opened possibilities, threats and judgments, gracious preservations and assistances. He knows how to distinguish between necessary waiting and pressing on, speech and silence, action and passion, warfare and peace. He perceives always the call of the hour, and acts accordingly. He is free for this intercourse with the divine providence. But it is not a philosophy of history which gives him this freedom" (p. 23).

This essay was translated by Arnold Neufeld-Fast, Ph.D., and edited by George Hunsinger.

They look around and explore every corner, piece of furniture, and object in the room. To fill the time they create a game with simple rules: "I see something you don't see" or "I spy." One child secretly chooses an object somewhere in the room which the other child must guess. The other child must at least have the possibility of seeing the object, and with adequate description, be able to recognize and name it. The game ends when the object is correctly guessed, that is, when both can see and name the same thing. Two points may be made. First, the statement "I see something you don't see" is actually incorrect. To be more precise, it should read: "I see something you also can see, but in a place where you aren't looking, because you don't yet know what I see." Appropriate descriptions are needed if the object is not to be disclosed simply by pointing to or naming it. Second, the not-quite-accurate statement that starts the game implies a certain superiority of the player who chose the object, but also a concern to communicate in order to remove the superiority, since out of a solitary seeing, so to speak, a common seeing should sooner or later occur. Barth's doctrine of providence seems to parallel both aspects of this story — a certain superiority by the one who sees, and yet also a sincere effort to communicate and thus to remove the superiority. In other words, the danger exists that the statement might be translated: "I see something you don't see, because you do not see as I see, nor can you see as I see, even if you were to look in the same direction." Or even worse: "I see something you don't see, because the object shows itself only to me, and not to you, and nothing can be done about that."

Providence within the Doctrine of Creation

The doctrine of providence, according to Barth, does not belong in the doctrine of God (as does predestination), but in the doctrine of creation. For Barth God's electing activity is necessarily nearer to God than is God's providential action. Election is an aspect of the doctrine of God. Barth speaks of election as logically prior to creation, reconciliation, and redemption. Jesus Christ and creation can be spoken of in the same breath, but not divine election in the same breath as the work of creation.

Providence is not seen as a further chapter in the work of creation, as a *creatio continua*, since a clear division exists between creation and providence. The Creator and the creature are at once distinguished and connected. The sovereignty of the Creator is guaranteed, but in such a way that the continual mutual turning of the Creator and the creature to each other must be simultaneously expressed and unfolded. The creature exists in and through this turning, which Barth describes as coexistence.[3]

> God the Creator co-exists with his creature, and so his creature exists under the presupposition, and its implied conditions, of the co-existence of its Creator. . . . Hence whatever may take place in the history of the creature, and however this may appear from the standpoint of its own law and freedom, it never can nor will escape the lordship of its Creator. . . . And so the creature co-exists with [God] as the reality distinct from [God], and in its own appropriate law and freedom, as [God] precedes it at every turn in his freedom of action and with his work. (pp. 12f.)

Though Barth rejects the idea of anchoring providence in the divine being, he does not reject anchoring it in God's first work *ad extra:* "The power of the *Deus providebit* is that of the *Deus creavit*" (p. 9). The power of the Creator has not vanished with the work of creation. God did not dissipate himself in his first work. His power remains present with his creature. "Providence" means that God is not displaced to an enclave beyond space and time. Talk of God's providence means viewing oneself as close to the Creator in the present. Whoever gives up talk of God's providence renounces this viewpoint — though God's proximity is untouched by such renunciation. God's providence points to the faithfulness of the Creator,[4] and this divine faithfulness is the root of the one relationship which unfolds itself in all times and places.

The relationship between Creator and creature is not a matter of

---

3. Later, in connection with the topic of *concursus,* Barth expresses the twofold specification of the relationship between Creator and creature in a manner which, though obvious for conventional theology, is disputed in contemporary discussions. "But the order of precedence of the eternal love of God and the creature as the object of this love is absolutely irreversible, for God does not need the creature, but the creature has absolute need of God" (p. 108).

4. "Between Creator and creature in the sense of biblical theology there is a connexion which makes it impossible for the Creator to leave his work to itself, and makes immediately necessary the reality and knowledge of a second action of the Creator following the first, i.e., his action in the sense of the concept of providence" (p. 9).

tracing abstract eternal truths, though the times of creation are grounded in God's eternity. This relationship can be considered only as a history, as an ongoing event which arouses expectations and breaks them open, an event in which no one can hide by virtue of abstract knowledge. By contrast, a *creatio continua* corresponds better to the idea of an eternally unchanging and therefore indiscriminate presence of God. In that context the real and suspenseful presence of God is harder to sustain.

If we can speak of God only because his electing action in Jesus Christ has made him known to us, then we have a history — a covenant history[5] — which must be told above all other stories. This history discloses something of the dynamic which takes place in God prior to all creaturely action. In any case, more can be said about God's free decision of election than about the traces of providence in the world. Election, as accessible to faith, is the only legitimate starting point for speaking of divine providence. Theologically we find ourselves on a one-way street.

Linking Doctrine to Belief

Belief in providence, Barth argues, is distinct from the doctrine itself: "Belief in God's providence is the . . . joy of the confidence and the willingness of the obedience grounded in this reality and its perception" (p. 14). Belief in God's providence means confidence and obedience, thus a coherence of inner and outer conduct. In this coherence, belief unfolds its life-forming possibilities.

Barth understands Christian belief in providence as "faith in the strict sense of the word," and thus sees it oriented to the Word of God (p. 15). He thus prepares (48.2) for the final part of section 49, "The Chris-

---

5. "What follows this unique act is first and decisively the history of the covenant which is the meaning, basis and goal of this act. It is the execution of the eternal decree of God's eternal election of grace. This is the occurrence which can be called a new creation in Gal. 6:15 and 2 Cor. 5:17. But this new creation belongs to the order of the reconciliation with God of a world in need of reconciliation. It is not a repetition of the first creation. It transcends it by a distinct and radical alternation and even transformation of the creature in which its existence as such is presupposed but not re-established. A second thing which follows that unique act, however, is the rule of divine providence which accompanies, surrounds and sustains the history of the covenant, the fulfilment of divine predestination, as what we may and must call a second history strictly related to the first and determined by it" (p. 6).

tian under the Universal Lordship of God the Father" (49.4). Faith in its different dimensions pertains only to the community of faith, where God's Word through the Holy Spirit can be heard. Faith has its own dignity. Resting on the effective connection of Word and Spirit, it does not stand at human disposal. This dependency pertains to faith in Christ generally, and so no less to faith in providence. Being neither arbitrary nor merely subjective, faith, insofar as it is given, is irrefutable. That faith in providence is logically unavoidable and not at human disposal corresponds finally to the theological insight that God's free decision of election takes priority over his providential action. For the believer this insight is a matter of self-understanding — of not having chosen faith in God's lordship oneself, nor of being able to choose it or even to preserve oneself in it.[6]

Faith in providence, as the gift of grace, makes God's lordship certain: "The lordship of God over the history of created being is not therefore a problem, but an objective fact which is far more certain than anything else we think we know about this history or even ourselves" (p. 16). Barth compares this certainty with that of axiomatic knowledge, though here he expresses himself cautiously. Yet even in relation to this knowledge, the knowledge of God's lordship forms "a class apart" (p. 16). Nevertheless, the parallel with axiomatic knowledge can indicate where we must begin when we look toward God and the world, and in the process struggle for knowledge. Every possible advance in knowledge is questionable compared with the given certainty of God's lordship and is accountable to it.

It is of the greatest importance for Barth to distinguish belief in providence from every type of worldview.[7] Yet in this connection he confesses that faith in providence also has to do with conceptions, which humans, "not without the divine appointment, will and permission," use as "masks" in order to see the other "masks of God."[8] The relationship of belief in providence to abstract conceptions, which can be transformed easily into "isms," is not fully explained. Barth admits their validity within limits.

6. "Man has not elected himself, but is elected, to believe in the lordship of God" (p. 17).

7. In this regard he recalls Albrecht Ritschl's interpretation as an example of how one may not take up the theme of providence theologically: "According to A. Ritschl (*Unterricht in d. chr. Rel.*, 1875, §60) it is the glory of 'faith in the fatherly lordship of God' that it is 'the Christian worldview in a nutshell'" (p. 18 revised).

8. Barth adds: "The belief in providence embraces these conceptions, but it also limits them" (p. 21).

The classification of conceptions as "masks of God" achieves two things. First, the same pertains to them as for the other masks of God, namely, that they do not fall outside the framework made possible and limited by God's permissive will. Second, the masks of God do not achieve an unmasking of the world, but in contrast they actually serve to increase the distance of humans from the world and themselves, further complicating the relationship. With the intention of unmasking, humans only distance themselves further from the reality of their concrete being before God and in the creation by means of their conceptions. Humans produce new masks which virtually offer them places in which to hide themselves (p. 21). Echoes of Genesis 3 are unmistakable here. In any case, with such conceptions humans reach neither God nor the fellow creature.

Yet belief in providence need not be limited to conceptions if it looks at the world from the view of God. Its characteristic perception is clearly unique, a perception which in turn is dependent on the special presence of God in his Word. For if humans are claimed by God's Word — "apprehended and freed" — then in view of that which occurs around and with them, as dark as that may be, they are "not without light."[9] Here Christian existence is addressed as an existence which is granted insight in very modest measure, in portions, as it were, "again and again." Insight into providence forbids all attempts at conservation. Like the manna in the wilderness, it must always be expected and received anew. This is the prophetic aspect of Christian existence and its perception of history.[10]

Three Classical Terms

"God the Father as Lord of His Creature" — this is the title of section 49, in which Barth interprets the classification of the doctrine of providence

---

9. "Basically and structurally this prophetic relationship to history is also that of the belief in providence. It consists in the fact that the man who is apprehended and freed by the Word of God is not without light and therefore always sees light in the obscurity of world occurrence" (p. 24).

10. "What man can receive through the Word of God in this respect is knowledge for life. It is daily bread, manna from heaven, which must be gathered and eaten but not kept. We cannot boast of having it, or become complacent. If it is not to be given in vain, we can only live with it, stretching out our hands for a further gift that we may always have it afresh" (p. 24).

according to the first article of the confession of faith through the three descriptions of the conventional (i.e., Protestant orthodoxy's) doctrine of providence: God preserves *(conservatio)*, accompanies *(concursus)*, and rules *(gubernatio)* his creation.[11] This exposition of the doctrine of providence with the assistance of traditional terminology forms the "lion's share" of the Barthian doctrine of providence. It is followed by the chapter mentioned above, "The Christian under the Universal Lordship of God the Father," which serves as the conclusion to section 49. In this brief account I must limit myself to just a few aspects that make up Barth's reception of the theological tradition. It is a sympathetic connection with the path of doctrinal development prior to its being squeezed into a Christian worldview, but it also involves certain noticeable accentuations. The wealth as well as the heterogeneity of Protestant orthodoxy's doctrines of providence are not always properly noticed. Such accentuations can be found in all three sections — of divine preservation, accompaniment, and rule — and it is noticeable that as a rule they carry a pastoral tone. This is especially true for the discussion of divine preservation. Creation and preservation as differentiated divine actions have, in a certain sense, assisted *that-which-negates (das Nichtige)* — i.e., that which God did not will and does not will — to find its own actuality. This power of negation has a shadowy godlike existence. It asserts itself by unfolding a strange, threatening effectiveness not over God, but over his creation.[12] Barth's account achieves two things. First, evil is denied any type of reality before God. Second, human inclinations toward evil, indeed, to be tempted by evil, especially when they concern God, are taken seriously. The pastoral tone of the doctrine of *conservatio* corresponds to these themes, given that limitedness is a fundamental determination of createdness. The creature is protected from falling back into an apparent

11. "God fulfils His fatherly lordship over His creature by preserving, accompanying and ruling the whole course of its earthly existence. He does this as His mercy is revealed and active in the creaturely sphere in Jesus Christ, and the lordship of His Son is thus manifested to it" (p. 58).

12. "That which is not [*das Nichtige*] is that which God as Creator did not elect or will, that which as Creator he passed over, that which according to the account in Genesis 1:2 he set behind him as chaos, not giving it existence or being. That which is not is that which is actual only in the negativity allotted to it by the divine decision, only in its exclusion from creation, only, if we may put it thus, at the left hand of God. But in this way it is truly actual and relevant and even active after its own particular fashion" (pp. 73f.).

(schein) or substanceless existence.[13] Assurance is given by God's preserving action that the creature cannot fall outside the frame of divinely affirmed life — even as the creature reaches its own limit in death — and thus assurance is given in view of the fear of being ensnared, sooner or later, in that which God has excluded from the beginning.

The accentuation and pastoral tone become even clearer in the contexts of divine accompaniment and rule, even though these sections are focused on the relationship of God's will to everything which occurs.[14] Barth now confronts the difficulty of having to express God's intimate proximity to creaturely events as well as his distance from them. He does this precisely by addressing the open texture of human life, and seeing this life as textured or accompanied by divine action.[15] That which human beings suffer and do is enlisted for service by God, and before God all human life is fragmentary and incomplete. Its broken character is thus really the creaturely counterpart of God's omnipotent operation.[16] With the topic of *gubernatio* Barth posits God's active sovereignty precisely at the point where we perceive ourselves as sovereign, in particular where we seem to act in accord with our own will, striving after goals and acting toward their realization.[17] In any

13. "And that which was no appearance he will not allow to become appearance even when it is over. If it did become appearance, this would mean that the non-existent had triumphed over the creature of God, that by giving such power to the non-existent God had finally revoked his own work, and that he had finally retracted that Yes and given himself to isolation" (p. 89).

14. "But creaturely events take place as God himself acts. As he himself enters the creaturely sphere . . . his will is accomplished directly and his decisions are made and fulfilled in all creaturely occurrence both great and small" (p. 133).

15. "God was, and was at work, even when the creature had not commenced its work. God is, and is at work, in the accomplishment of this work. God will be, and will still be at work in relation to this work, when the creature and its work have already attained their goal" (p. 151).

16. "God's arm remains outstretched even when that of the creature has been allowed to fall. . . . The act could only begin with God, and it can only end with God. And in the one case as in the other 'with God' means in the service of his omnipotent operation" (p. 152).

17. "The moment it is produced, the effect which I produce is no longer mine. I did produce it, and the fact of it is irrevocable. . . . But just because the effect is brought into being under the divine lordship, it does not belong to the creature to appoint or fix the form and compass or the meaning and range of this effect, no matter how ineluctably the effect follows from the most personal being or activity of the creature. Nor does it belong to those other creatures who experience that effect to appoint or fix its character, no matter how deeply they are affected by it or how thoroughly they make it their own" (pp. 152f.).

case, if the doctrine of *gubernatio* is correct, God cannot be surprised by what human beings do. God never experiences human action passively, but always precedes the occurrence in foresight and preordination.[18] Human beings cannot depart from the circle of the divine will. Sooner or later every effect, both the willed and unwilled, is taken from human hands and in a sense returned to God. God remains the real author, the actual agent. In that case it would not be talk of God's agency that is inauthentic, but talk of human agency. Creaturely history, together with what has been suffered and done, with intentions disappointed and realized, appears in a certain sense to be the modeling clay of divine agency.

Suffering often seems to confound us more than action. In contrast, Barth's doctrine of predestination indicates what makes action theologically confounding as well — not because action is interrupted by suffering, passivity, or helplessness, but because it is taken out of the hands of the most active and successful. Human action is, no less than all creaturely occurrence, vertically and horizontally relativized.[19] So everything which happens — including that brought about by human beings — is provisional and dependent on the context. Nonetheless, Barth guards against allowing the meaning of human action to disappear in a closed system. God, stresses Barth, is not the whole.[20] It is due to God's limitless joy in detail and concern for his creature that the particular cannot be absorbed by the whole or be instrumentalized from the perspective of a higher level within a process. To the extent that human action is directed toward a telos in God, the dignity and integrity of the particular remains

18. "Both in general and in particular God himself fixes for the creature its goals, that is, the goals that it will actually attain. In one way or another it will ultimately realize the divine decree" (p. 167).

19. "In the most literal sense creaturely occurrence is only preparatory [*vorläufig*], i.e., it is engaged in a process. . . . It is his [God's] action which determines the world-process in its true and definitive form. This is in a sense the vertical relativisation of creaturely occurrence. . . . The individual thing is as it were a word or sentence within a context. It is indispensable to this context. But only within this context does it say what is really intended. Only within this context can it be read and understood rightly. And this is in a sense the horizontal relativisation of creaturely occurrence" (p. 170).

20. "But the relation between the divine and creaturely activity cannot be reversed as the relation between the individual activity and the totality of creaturely activity can be reversed. And this is what distinguishes the divine activity from the totality of creaturely activity, no matter how highly we may rate the totality in relation to the individual, or how greatly superior it may actually be" (p. 122).

intact.[21] Here too the pastoral tone is unmistakable. The doctrine of providence's horizon of expectation is not determined by a closed system or totality, but by God's acceptance of the particular in its particularity — or of what *coram mundo* does not appear capable of being integrated without damage or loss.

Two further motifs in Barth's doctrine of providence may be mentioned. Both concern the horizon of expectation connected to belief in providence, and both involve the doctrine of *gubernatio*. The first prevents the horizon of expectation from being limited by either continuity or contingency. The second may be summarized in Barth's own words: "The King of Israel is the King of the world" (p. 176).

The doctrine of providence has traditionally related God either to continuity or else to contingency, whereby the experience of contingency was generally given precedence. Basically either relation is possible, since each in its own way astonishes people — analogous to the astonishment that there should be something rather than nothing, the first life-breath of philosophy. If God is viewed more as sustainer, then continuity, constancy, and regularity will be seen as signs of divine faithfulness.[22] The orders that defy chaos and dangers of annihilation will also be significant in this regard. By contrast, if God is viewed more as the coming One who has promised to make all things new and who is present to his creation as the promised One, then significance will be accorded to the unexpected and the contingent, to that which cannot be derived from what has been or from the existing orders of the status quo. From experiences of both continuity

---

21. "In this whole there is nothing which at its own time and place and according to its own function is simply instrument, material, cannon-fodder, in the fulfilment of this or that development, or the establishment of this or that *bonum commune*; which in practice, then, is merely a means to further the ends of certain favoured creatures, a ruling class within this whole. But as each individual with its own being and activity is co-ordinated with all other individuals and God and according to the will and plan of God (and certainly not without this subordination and co-ordination), by this very fact it has its own independent significance and validity, its own independent value and dignity, being granted that which is good, which is indeed the very best, for it, attaining its own individual ends, and in this way the common end of all creatures" (p. 173).

22. These tendencies are found Barth's work as well. Though Barth refuses to equate the two, he apparently sees a closer proximity of the laws of nature and their observance to faith in creation and providence than to chance, which connotes arbitrariness, irrationality, and infidelity. Natural laws are an expression of "order and form," and so testify to God's "constancy" and "faithfulness" (p. 128).

and contingency, Barth makes a twofold distinction related to God, reminding us that each has its own appeal and persuasiveness, but that each can also seduce us to an attenuated set of expectations. In any case, for Barth the concept of history includes the two moments of continuity and discontinuity, which also mark the limits of our vision. The vitality of our historical perception extends only as far as the manifest opposition between the two. It belongs to the world rule of God, however, that "we can believe in this rule but cannot see it," because it overlaps the two moments while transcending each.[23]

In relating God's universal lordship to God's being the king of Israel, the horizon of providential expectation is not constricted but more closely specified. In this way Israel is included in the doctrine of providence, and God's free decision of election is taken up in its entirety.

It seems surprising that for Barth a middle ground seems to exist between the history of the covenant and general creaturely occurrence. This middle ground has, if not a revelatory quality, then at least a directional character. Barth finds four traces of this middle ground. "Away from this center [i.e., Jesus Christ] in the midst of world-occurrence generally, they do not prove to us, but they do testify, confirm and demonstrate, from where and by whom that occurrence is ruled" (p. 176). These traces function only for those who already confront world occurrence with eyes and ears open, and thus they are apparent neither of themselves nor equally for

---

23. "Because he rules alone, and because he himself is the goal. . . . He is uplifted both above the necessity which rules and is revealed in this history, and also above its real and obvious contingency, above the continuities and discontinuities, above the various uniformities and the various freedoms of world-occurrence: and not merely above the necessity which is known to us, but also above the necessity which is concealed from us or only suspected by us; not merely above the contingency which is known to us, but also above that which is concealed from us or only suspected by us. . . . It belongs to the world-rule of God that this is the case, and this is one of the most cogent reasons why we can believe in this rule but cannot see it. What we can see is only necessity and contingence, continuity and discontinuity, law and freedom, which exist side by side with each other and in opposition to each other. . . . One day it will be granted to us to see what now we cannot see — that beyond the antithesis God is the true King and World-ruler, the Lord of all things and everything, the Lord of the general and also of the particular. But we ourselves are not beyond the antithesis. Only God is that, and he always was and always will be. . . . The general and the particular . . . are as it were the two basic sounds by which God wills to manifest his wisdom, to declare his Word and therefore himself, in the works of creation. Not only does he rule over the antithesis. He also rules in it and by it. For it is in and by the antithesis, . . . that there arises creaturely history in time as opposed to a timeless existing" (pp. 159-60).

all. But their discovery is not limited to particular times and places. "They can be heard and seen at all times and at all places" (p. 200). To the perception of faith, these traces step out of the sphere in which God is concealed. They offer a sort of guidance system that points to the actuality of divine revelation and lets it be anticipated anew. The four traces of God's revelation are (i) the history of Holy Scripture, (ii) the history of the church, (iii) the history of the Jews, and (iv) the limitation of human life.

Barth accords special significance to the third trace of God's world rule. It allows him to speak not only about a plurality of histories,[24] but also about the rudiments of theological anthropology. Specifically, he suggests that the Jewish person is the one who holds out to humanity the disturbing truth about humanity. Precisely because for Israel the self-evident dimensions of human life are fundamentally disrupted, Israel is a "a people which is no people," with a history which is "no history."[25] What makes this trace of God's providence distinctive is its being composed precisely of such paradoxes, as well as the strange necessity of its continuance. Israel's existence is so intertwined with God's being as God that Israel's continuance through time assumes — openly or tacitly[26] — the character of a

24. "Finally, even the concept of the history of the Jews as we ourselves have made use of it is a most ambiguous one. Since the year 70 there have been many different and disconnected histories of the Jews, that of the Polish Jews, the Spanish Jews, the Portuguese Jews, or the German Jews. There has, of course, been the history of the Jewish Synagogue and its various ramifications, the history of its scriptural exegesis, its worship, and its piety. There have been the histories of countless Jewish groups and individuals. There have been the histories of Jewish movements and undertakings, as, for example, modern Zionism. But there has never been a connected history of the Jews as a single community, a history which itself has helped to form this community" (p. 214).

25. "They are . . . a people which is no people, and as such is the people, the people of God; a people which has no history, and as such, with all the problems which it raises in world history, has the only truly human history, the history of man with God" (p. 218).

26. "But the real thing itself is the one natural proof of God adduced by God in the existence of the Jewish nation amongst other nations. It is hardly seen by Anti-Semites and liberals, but here a part of world-history gives the most direct witness to the biblical witness of revelation, and therefore to the God who is attested in the Bible. To this very day Israel confronts us as a people of God rejected by God. To this very day Israel shows us that it is only in judgment that God exercises grace and that it is his free decision that he exercises grace in judgment" (*Church Dogmatics* I/2, pp. 510-11). "At this point we are almost tempted to speak, not of an indication of the world-governance of God, the God of the Bible, but of an actual demonstration of it. . . . It is easier to turn away unenlightened from the history of the Bible and that of the church than from this history" (III/3, p. 210).

proof for God's existence. At the same time, Israel makes perceptible "the theme of creaturely occurrence in all ages,"[27] namely, God's steadfast turning to his creature along with the character of human existence as an attack on God's free grace.[28]

The history of the Jews as the clearest trace of God's providence also indicates what it means to speak of election from the perspective of those God has passed over.[29] According to Barth, God's election must finally be spoken of as "the election of another." Christian faith is concerned from beginning to end with the fact that another steps in for us. The root problem in the complex interconnection between the concepts of election and providence here emerges. It is precisely Barth's presentation of the doctrine of providence which shows again and again how God's electing action reaches beyond the elect. The elect are so to speak the medium through which God effects certain ends.

A "twofold rule" for understanding God's governance shows how Barth sees the interconnections of election, providence, covenant history, and the history of God's creature. To understand divine governance, Barth proposes, we need to observe a twofold rule. First, we need to look from the

27. "They are the only people that necessarily continues to exist, with the same certainty as that God is God, and that what he has willed and said and done according to the message of the Bible is not a whim or a jest, but eternally in earnest, and the theme of creaturely occurrence in all ages" (pp. 218-19).

28. "Hence it is revealed in this people what man is, man in his relationship with God, man before the judgment seat of God, sinful man: the man who resists and opposes the grace of God; the man who counts it too mean a thing to live only by the grace of God; the man who wants another king instead of this King; the man who does not want to be elected by God, but wants to elect God, and secretly wants to be his own God; the man who wants to preserve and help and save himself by his own efforts, taking to himself all the glory. And is this only the Jewish man? Not by a long way. This is every man, without exception" (p. 221).

29. "From the existence of this people we have to learn that the elect of God is [another]. . . . For in the existence of the Jew we stumble upon the fact that the divine election is a particular election, that we ourselves have been completely overlooked in the particularity of this divine election. What the history of the Jews tells us is that the divine election is the election of another. Our election can be only in and with this other. . . . And who is this other? The Jew? . . . But really it is the one Jew Jesus Christ who is looking out upon us from the desolation and persistence of the existence of the Jews. He is this Other who is for us. He is the one Elect as the new Head of the whole human race. It is true, of course, that he actually looks at us face to face only when we first encounter him in the Gospel, in faith, in his community. . . . The sign and testimony of the history of the Jews is waiting for open eyes and unstopped ears" (pp. 225f.).

particular events attested in the Bible to world events in general. Those particular events do not take place simply for their own sake. They form the inner basis of all creaturely occurrence. They are not a constriction, but an original and pattern of events in general. They are not an end in themselves, but a ministry in and to creation as a whole. Second, we need to look back from general events in the world of nature and history to the particular events attested in the Bible. The second rule means looking to the history of the covenant of grace with Israel, from the promise that initiated it and with an eye to its final fulfillment. There is finally no such thing, Barth argues, as secular history in the serious sense of the word (pp. 183f.).

The elect cannot remain among themselves, because election does not mean isolation, the separation of a few survivors in a watertight ark high and dry above those doomed to destruction. In electing God connects with humankind and with all creatures. Our problem, however, is that an intensified sense of one's election always opposes a movement toward the universal. The complexity of the relationship — between providence and election, between creaturely occurrence and the history of the covenant, between the universal and the particular — slips from view. Indeed, it might be said more pointedly that the beneficiaries of election are not the elect, but the others whom the elect overlook and despise.[30] In this way talk of God's lordship lures faith out of isolation and disregard for the world, and shares the gift of prophetic historical perception, as already mentioned, which keeps more in view than just itself. The particular may have noetic priority, but it occurs for the sake of the universal, which still awaits its profile, its face, or — one could say with Romans 8 — it awaits being brought to speech; but is it speech that is still in becoming?

Thus the theme of the doctrine of providence is ultimately not about what occurs, but about rather the manner in which God's communication with humans and human communication with what is creaturely grow out of what occurs. For this, more is required than simple factuality — namely, Word and Spirit — which are not identical with what occurs.[31] What oc-

---

30. Compare "the secret of the 'thirty-six righteous ones' whom, according to Jewish lore, the world shall never lack. . . . Their hidden holiness can outweigh countless guilt, redress the balance of a generation, and secure the peace of the invisible realm" (Hans Jonas, "The Concept of God after Auschwitz," in *Mortality and Morality: A Search for the Good after Auschwitz*, ed. Lawrence Vogel [Evanston, Ill.: Northwestern University Press, 1996], p. 142).

31. The "doing of the will of God" does not let itself be identified with the multiplicity and confusion "of the lines of creaturely occurrence" (III/3, p. 44). However, "every time that

curs is neither self-explicable nor self-generating; in this theological sense there are no "brute" facts. Independent of human speech and understanding, everything which occurs in speech and understanding is also put in brackets, as it were. It is subordinated to the bidding of God's Word and brought to completion by hearing as enabled by the Spirit, and everything depends on this.[32] However, God's Word is, according to Barth, crucially and essentially Word in the singular (cf. Barmen Declaration, art. 1), and what our hearing may receive is finally nothing other than this one Word. Therefore Barth can also say, "The fact that the Lord of the world is our Father stands or falls with the fact that even in the world his activity is the activity of his Word and Spirit" (p. 143).

The Complexity of Christian Agency

Outside the area of influence common to both Word and Spirit, thus "outside" in the world, there is just — but still! — the Holy Spirit alone. Here one can see something like the pneumatological grounding of faith in providence, that is, as soon as this faith steps beyond its ecclesial home onto the stage of creaturely occurrence, a movement which it is constantly obliged to make. In view of inconsistencies, groundlessness, and uncertainty, faith in providence lives from an ongoing dependence on God's Spirit.[33] The only

---

God shows forth his power to the men of his choosing, and through them to others, every time, then, that he acts, he does so in the following way: his Word goes forth to these men, to be received by them in the power of his Spirit; his Spirit is given to these men, to receive his Word of power" (p. 142).

32. "Unless I am mistaken, it is the merit of the school of Cocceius to have introduced the concept of *iussio* into the discussion of the *concursus.* . . . Everything that happens can be traced back to a Word of God. Therefore 'the Lord God will do nothing, but he revealeth his secret unto his servants the prophets' (Am. 3:7). And conversely: 'The word that I shall speak shall come to pass. . . . I will say the word, and will perform it, saith the Lord God' (Ezek. 12:25, cf. 37:14)" (p. 143).

33. "It is only of the Holy Spirit that he can learn to understand situations, to recognise opportunities, to choose possibilities and to distinguish them from impossibilities. The situations and opportunities and possibilities and impossibilities of the world-process with which he is called upon to wrestle do not as such contain within themselves or proclaim any divine and infallible Word. In the midst of them he can direct his path only with a provisional certainty. It is only the Holy Spirit who can command him, giving the orders and prohibitions which he must and can obey. It is only the Holy Spirit who can really guide him" (p. 258).

chance to escape the confusion of interrupting, powerful voices is provided by the external Word: How can it remain perceptible as an address from outside of ourselves? It must fundamentally disturb our own self-certainties and the self-certainties of world occurrence, which is ultimately the case for communications of the Holy Spirit as well. These communications come neither from us nor from the self-certainties given to us but, as it were, "from above."[34]

Now the Christian community lives from that which distinguishes it from the world, namely, that it knows something the world does not yet know. This distinction is located nowhere else but in the unity and togetherness of Spirit and Word. This unity is the basis for the binding nature of ecclesial directives. Only here can the *deus revelatus* be found. For this reason the church's proclamation is the pillar, as it were, for faith in providence. The church's proclamation has an exceptional responsibility for its members' faith in providence, insofar as this faith is called to that discernment of spirits, which is necessary "outside." Schooling people for this expected capability either happens in the church community or not at all.[35]

Thus as "an integral part of the Christian confession," the doctrine of divine providence is indeed directed to the individual, but it is not left to one's own discretion. It is directed to the individual insofar as he or she "is the living member of the Christian community" (p. 239). Whoever sees himself or herself in faith within the frame of the church's doctrine of providence, perceives something he or she can no longer dispense with. Faith in providence is not a private matter, but a common asset of the church, one in which everyone will participate, that is, as a creature who has learned to say yes to his or her creatureliness. This is the unique feature of Christian faith: "the Christian makes the affirmation that is demanded of man."[36] And in

---

34. "The Holy Spirit is holy in the fact that he does not come from us but to us, and that he does not come to us from our own environment but from above" (p. 264).

35. "At this former point he has to learn to know what will be the bearing of his subjection to the will of God at the latter. At this former point he has to become so familiar with the life and authority of the Holy Spirit in the Word of God as to be able at least in some measure to differentiate him from all other spirits at the latter. At this former point he has to accustom himself to obedience to him, and exercise himself in this obedience. Any gap in his development, his schooling in active righteousness, in this inward sphere will necessarily avenge itself at once in a refusal to exercise it in the outward" (p. 257).

36. "Of all the Christian is the one which not merely is a creature, but actually says Yes to being a creature. Innumerable creatures do not seem to be even asked to make this affir-

this yes-saying the structure and complexity of Christian existence are summarized.

There are expectations of Christian existence: it realizes the unity of truth and actuality, of divine providence and universal lordship in the dynamic unity of faith, obedience, and prayer. These characteristics of Christian existence cannot be reduced to each other, but mutually interpret one another.[37] In them the believer is pulled further and further into God's trust as servant, child, and friend,[38] and in this growing relationship of trust the form of Christian conduct *(Verhalten)* becomes recognizable. The fruit of this intimacy is the participation of Christian existence in the universal lordship of God.

> In virtue of what he (and only he) can see, the Christian is the one who has a true knowledge in this matter of the providence and universal lordship of God. This providence and lordship affect him as they do all other creatures, but he participates in them differently from all other creatures. He participates in them from within. Of all creatures he is the one who while he simply experiences the providence and lordship of God also consents to it, having a kind of "understanding" — if we may put it in this way — with the overruling God and Creator. (p. 242)

It is necessary here to identify the characteristics of prayer. Prayer "is the most intimate and effective form of Christian action" (p. 264) which expresses the great astonishment that one is a child of this Father.[39] In the

---

mation. Man is asked. But man as such is neither able nor willing to make it. From the very first man as such has continual illusions about himself. . . . But the Christian makes the affirmation that is demanded of man" (p. 240).

37. "If the divine providence and lordship are reflected in the Christian as in pure glass, . . . then this obviously means that the occurrence which proceeds from God and embraces heaven and earth is repeated in the narrow sphere of his own creaturely existence, of his own thoughts and will and deed, of his own life. The providence and universal lordship of God are not merely true to him, but in this repetition they are actual. . . . They are actual to him in faith, in obedience, and in prayer. These are the three forms of this dynamic and totally Christian attitude" (pp. 244-45).

38. "In obedience the Christian is the servant, in faith he is the child, but in prayer, as the servant and the child, he is the friend of God, called to the side of God and at the side of God, living and ruling and reigning with him" (p. 286).

39. "In prayer, he makes use of the freedom to answer the Father who has addressed him, or, to put it in another way, to go to meet the Father from whose goodness he proceeds,

most personal way, prayer safeguards the distinction between God and humanity, that is, between the Creator and the creature, for in it the person "desires and expects something [of God], because he hopes to receive something which he needs, something which he does not hope to receive from anyone else, but does definitely hope to receive from God" (p. 264). Therefore prayer, especially as supplication, is an expression of faith in providence. It occurs in the certainty that God lets himself be addressed, that God lets himself be moved and determined by this address.[40] Thus it occurs with the expectation of being heard. In this expectation it becomes a sign of advent: "The Christian asks, and by this asking the doors are opened wide, and the gates are lifted up, that the King of glory may come in" (p. 264). As those who pray bring their personal concerns and needs before God with this expectation, they also reach beyond their own concerns and needs as well, and join in the spirit-inspired stammering in which already the apostle Paul saw the Christian community taking up the speechless groaning of the creation (p. 279).

A Contemporary Reception: Potential Hindrances

It could be concluded from reading III/3 that nothing new exists under the sun. Does Barth's doctrine of providence really go beyond the fundamental distinctions that he borrows from Protestant orthodoxy? Doesn't he seem to use them without any special originality or explosive effect? Can his doctrine of providence be received without subscribing to a backward-looking view of dogmatics? Doesn't Barth connect a conventional doctrine with metaphors and expressions that have long since become politically unacceptable in academic circles? As Barth takes up the language of God the Father without any inhibitions, so too he makes use of the biblical met-

---

or, to put it in yet another way, to give direct and natural expression to his great surprise that God is his Father and that he is the child of God" (p. 265).

40. "It is a genuine and actual share in the universal lordship of God. The will of God is not to preserve and accompany and rule the world and the course of the world as world-occurrence in such a way that he is not affected and moved by it, that he does not allow himself to converse with it, that he does not listen to what it says, that as he conditions all things he does not allow himself to be determined by them. God is not free and immutable in the sense that he is the prisoner of his own resolve and will and action, that he must always be alone as the Lord of all things and of all occurrence" (p. 285).

aphor of "king" in order to express the significance of God's universal lordship. Is it really worth the effort to retrieve "providence" as an expression of divine sovereignty?

A theology, for example, which sees the standard doctrine as shattered because of failed theodicies, will likely search for radically new orientations. Efforts at Jewish-Christian dialogue can be stimulated by ideas like those of Hans Jonas, according to whom the doctrine of "God ruling the universe," which belongs to "Maimonides's Thirteen Articles of Faith," must be given up, especially after Auschwitz.[41] Barth would find this kind of atmosphere for dialogue distasteful, insofar as he moves in a tradition which connects lordship and power with the concept of God. God's lordship, however, must be distinguished from capriciousness, inscrutability, and randomness. An insistence on "meaning and purpose, plan and intention" might seem sufficient to address the problem. God's lordship does not manifest itself as a domineering force before which the creature must shrink, but rather as a qualified lordship.[42] Is Barth's definition of divine lordship adequate, or should the concept be rejected altogether?

A further obstruction could be that how Barth presents the history of Israel — as a trace of God's providence and a clue for theological anthropology — is felt to be anti-Jewish. How should one judge his decision to see "Jewish history" as culminating in Christ? Is this simply a repetition of the old doctrine of disinheritance? In any case, the idea of parallel paths and of equally valid witnesses is hardly possible here. Can we look upon "the Jews" through Christ alone?

These are concerns that could be raised against Barth's doctrine of providence. However, I would like to emphasize an objection regarding Barth's removal of providence from any possible connection with a worldview. Barth could be seen as breaking off discussion, as questionably restricting theology's area of responsibility, especially at a point which increasingly demands dialogue. As Christian Link has observed, providence for Barth is not the object of a worldview. Consequently it is removed from the problems of scientific thought and from the negativity of the modern

---

41. Jonas, p. 141.

42. "The power of God over all things is not a blind power. He does not rule merely for the sake of ruling. He rules as a Father. His ruling is the ruling of his definite and conscious will. Behind it there is meaning and purpose, plan and intention. . . . He directs it to the thing which . . . it has to do and to be in the course of history in time; to the telos which has to be attained in this history" (III/3, p. 155).

experience. "Barth transposed providence to a level where it can no longer be discredited by the modern demand for the verification of hypotheses. It no longer stands in service of explaining the world."[43] Not even the perception of faith will be able to evade pressure from other perceptions over time. The distinction of providence from a worldview should therefore be thought anew.

Just what does the Christian see that others don't see? And how is understanding or agreement over this seeing possible? Is a shared understanding even imagined? How does the believer see herself in relation to the other? "We see something you don't see," Barth seems to claim, "because the object appears only to us and not to you, and we can't change anything about that."

For Barth the subject of the seeing is not Christian faith as such, but the Christian. Isn't this an expression of spiritual arrogance combined with a lack of self-understanding? Have Christians grown so fond of faith in providence that they could elevate themselves into authorities on matters related to divine providence and universal lordship? One who believes in his or her own invulnerability will tend to belittle the vulnerable and be incapable of sharing their pain — unless it is used to indicate the latter's weakness and one's own superiority, that is, as material to build up one's own feelings of self-worth. And what does it mean to participate in providence "from within"? That one's own will is congruent with the will of God? Doesn't this agreement transgress the necessary boundary between God and humankind, and particularly between God and the Christian? As if countless chapters of church history would not speak against the claim that Christians have an advantage over others.

Conclusion

"I see something you don't see" — on its own this would be a fatal summary of the doctrine of providence. The perception of faith never looks directly in the face of God's providence; if anything, it looks at divine provi-

43. Christian Link, "Gestalt and theologischer Ort der Vorsehungslehre Karl Barths," *Zeitschrift für Dialektische Theologie* 10 (1994): 113-15, on 113. Providence "is not an object of a possible worldview. Consequently it is largely removed from the pressing problems of scientific thought (and one may see this as a disadvantage) and of the negativity of the modern experience of reality" (Link, p. 113).

dence from behind, so to speak. If the church knows "what the world does not know" — namely, that "the King of the Jews has himself come on his people's behalf" and that "only because in his coming on his people's behalf he has come on behalf of the whole world" (p. 181) — what should this knowing mean if not a tremendous expansion of the horizon of expectation, which is not identical with the claim to a privileged form of awareness? Perhaps it is a task of the doctrine of providence to impress upon the church, its capacity to remember and its horizon of expectation, how far the free grace extends with which God turns to creation. Faith in providence is a freedom for which human beings must first be liberated. It wastes away when human beings attempt to realize it on their own, or demand it as a kind of basic right. It is a fragmentary seeing, whose most basic word can only be "Nevertheless."[44] Its light is insufficient for the further reaches of expectation and hope.

With prayers of supplication faith in providence gains a profile that distinguishes it from stoic apathy, from self-sufficiency, and from the unassailability of a rational ideal that can exist without passion, come what may. Prayer "is the most intimate and effective form of Christian action" (p. 181). Through prayers of intercession people become aware of their own reality over against God and of their togetherness with all other creatures, full of needs. Then they can hear in others a sign, a word, a language which announces God's further activity, God's still outstanding coming. In this way they may learn to speak that language of hope for themselves. It is God's Spirit, in unity with the Father and the Son, who breaks into our words and our speechlessness, and who places us in our supplications at the side of a creature tormented by anticipation — and so assists our perception of faith toward an undreamed of horizon of expectation.

---

44. "This Nevertheless is the problem of the belief in providence and the doctrine of providence. It can only be a Nevertheless. What man sees is simply the multiplicity and confusion of the lines of creaturely occurrence, which in itself and as such — for creation is not God — cannot be identified with the doing of the will of God. . . . There can be no question of a transparency proper to this occurrence as such, or of an inherent ability of man to see through it. . . . The belief in providence maintains and confesses this with its Nevertheless. It has itself the character of a 'foreseeing.' In faith in God's particular revelation man sees God before he sees the general history of creation" (III/3, p. 44).

"I See Something You Don't See"

RANDALL C. ZACHMAN

Caroline Schröder has conducted an insightful and provocative examination of Barth's doctrine of providence, and of the ways we may or may not wish to receive his doctrine today, especially in light of what she calls its special attractions and dangers. The title of her paper places the emphasis on the way the doctrine of providence expresses a particular perception of faith, which sees, albeit in a fragmentary and ever-new way, the activity of God in the world which is otherwise imperceptible to others. The attraction of this doctrine appears to be that it claims that faith perceives something of the governance of God in the otherwise perplexing and vexing flux of world occurrence, and that such faith even participates in the governance of God by its obedience and prayer. The danger seems to be that believers will derive smug satisfaction from their superior insight into something otherwise hidden from others, and will therefore look down on their blind brothers and sisters with contempt, or even disregard them altogether.

The danger Schröder points toward may tell us more of her own assumptions about the Christian community and the temptations it faces than it illuminates the concerns of Barth in this part of his dogmatics. Schröder seems convinced that Christians as individuals and a group are tempted by what she terms spiritual arrogance, based on their claim to know and see something others do not, or perhaps cannot, know and see. This arrogance may be fueled by providence, but it seems especially fortified by election. Schröder thinks the elect "overlook and despise" those who are not yet elected, and that the elect community suffers from isolation and world blindness from which it needs to be forcefully summoned. However, providence may reinforce this spiritual arrogance, since faith's perception of providence may lead the faithful to say to those who do not believe, "I see something you don't see, because the object shows itself only to me, and not to you, and nothing can be done about that." The elect who discern the providence of God may view themselves as invulnerable, and Schröder tells us that "one who believes in his or her own invulnerability will tend to belittle the vulnerable and be incapable of sharing their pain — unless it is used to indicate the latter's weakness and one's own superiority, that is, as material to build up one's own feelings of self-worth." Hence Schröder seems to read Barth's doctrine of providence with an eye to the ways it might be "an expression of spiritual arrogance combined with a lack of self-understanding," which would make communication and agreement with unbelievers impossible.

According to Schröder, if the doctrine of providence is to be of any pastoral and theological use today, it must be presented in such a way as to thwart and undermine the spiritual arrogance which threatens the Christian community. Hence, although she enumerates at least five distinct purposes for the doctrine of providence, the primary purpose of the doctrine is to reveal that the horizon of election extends well beyond the elect. "It is precisely Barth's presentation of the doctrine of providence which shows again and again how God's electing action reaches beyond the elect." This doctrine awakens the elect from their smug self-satisfaction by showing them they are not the beneficiaries of their election, but precisely "the others whom the elect overlook and despise" are the beneficiaries. The doctrine of providence is not meant to turn the Christian community inward in smug self-satisfaction; rather, "talk of God's lordship lures faith out of isolation and disregard for the world, and shares the gift of prophetic historical perception . . . which keeps more in view than just itself." Hence, over against the narrow particularism of election, the doctrine of providence has as its task "to impress upon the church, its capacity to remember and its horizon of expectation, how far the free grace extends with which God turns to creation." This doctrine will give rise not to a faith which says, "I see something you can never see," but rather to a prayer of supplication, in which the vulnerability and pain of the world beyond the church are lifted up to God with Spirit-guided sighs too deep for words. "It is God's Spirit . . . who breaks into our words and our speechlessness, and who places us in our supplications at the side of a creature tormented by anticipation — and so assists our perception of faith toward an undreamed of horizon of expectation."

I would like to respond to the following three points raised by Schröder in her paper. First, I will consider her interpretation of the relation of election and providence in Barth's theology. Second, I will examine Barth's relation to the Reformed tradition in the development of his doctrine of providence. Third, I will consider her thesis concerning the function and purpose of faith's perception of God's providential work. I will conclude with the question Barth raises for me as I think of the contemporary reception of his doctrine of providence.

Election and Providence

If Schröder's interpretation is correct — and if I have correctly understood it — then Barth's doctrine of providence would have as its purpose the revelation of the horizon and goal of God's electing work in Jesus Christ. If this is true, then it is hard to see how Barth could really distinguish between the doctrine of election and the doctrine of providence. Moreover, such an interpretation actually reverses Barth's own position. Barth claims that election reveals the goal and purpose of providence, not vice versa. The self-revelation of God in Jesus Christ reveals that God has taken on himself the future that sinful humans have chosen for themselves, in order to give himself to humans as their future. This is the content of divine election, and it reveals the full extent of God's saving will, which is universal in its reach. There is no way that Barth's doctrine of providence could make any more universal his doctrine of election — nor is there any way that faith in election as Barth describes it could ever be inwardly directed as Schröder seems to suggest. The elect are called to witness to the rest of the world the world's election which is already and eternally true de jure, but not yet revealed to be true de facto.

Barth's Relation to the Previous Reformed Tradition

The doctrine of providence is situated precisely in this time between the revelation of God's election of the world in Jesus Christ and the universal revelation of Jesus Christ in and to the world. Barth insists that the very same God who is revealed in Jesus Christ to be the future of the world is now the lord and governor of the world. He makes this claim in an intensive and serious disagreement with the "older theology" of providence, which he traces from Zwingli and Calvin to the orthodox scholastics. "But we have to take note of the astonishing fact that the older Protestant theology was guilty of an almost total failure to ask concerning the Christian meaning and character of the doctrine of providence, let alone assert it. Even in Calvin we seek in vain for a single pointer in this direction" (*Church Dogmatics* III/3, p. 30). Barth accuses Zwingli and Calvin of abstracting from the self-revelation of God in Jesus Christ when they spoke of God the creator and governor of the universe, leading them to develop the concept of a "supreme being" characterized primarily by omnipotence, over against the God of mercy and love revealed in Jesus Christ. Indeed, Barth claims that Calvin's doctrine of providence, based on an abstract concept of divine omnipotence, led directly to Schleiermacher's God as the Whence of the feeling of absolute dependence. Hence I do not think it is at all accurate to say, as Schröder does, that when one reads Barth, one could conclude that "nothing new exists under the sun." Far from embracing a concept of God connected with power and lordship, as Schröder suggests, Barth offers a thorough and radical critique of the traditional view of divine lordship and power, and categorically rejects the way Calvin and the orthodox understood both concepts. For Barth the lordship and power of God, even in providence, are revealed to be the lordship and power of eternal love, not of human concepts of omnipotence: "the majesty of the operation of God consists in the fact that it is the operation of his eternal love" (III/3, p. 107).

However, if it is the God who is eternal love, the Father of Jesus Christ, who is the Lord and King of all world occurrence, and this God is only revealed in the Christian community by the Word and Holy Spirit, then the activity of God in the world is not revealed, but hidden. The activity of the one God is thus clearly distinguished by Barth into two distinct spheres, the sphere of God's revealed activity, the covenant fulfilled in Jesus Christ, and the sphere of God's hidden activity, the lordship of the Father of Christ over all creaturely history. "And this means that the context, the economy, the disposition is not only revealed in the history of the covenant and redemption whose center is Jesus Christ. In a hidden form it is also present and active in world-occurrence generally. The two spheres are distinguished only by the fact that in the one case it is hidden and in the other it is revealed" (p. 196). Since the providential activity of God is hidden, there is no way that it can be read off the appearance of world occurrence. "For as the history of God's glory takes place in, with, and under that of creation, it is a hidden history, which is neither felt, seen, known, nor dialectically perceived by man, but can only be believed on the basis of this Word of God" (p. 19). Indeed, according to Barth, "God laughs at all our attempts to see His rule with the eye of human reason" (p. 160). Since God is at work in a hidden way in world occurrence, not even believers directly see God at work in the world. "What man sees is simply creation in all the regularity and contingency of its own movement and development" (p. 44).

The Purpose of Faith's Perception of Providence

This brings us to the other central question posed by Schröder in her examination of Barth's doctrine of providence, which she also claims is the one question Barth always considers: What is it humans get to see when they believe, and within which limits? Schröder seems to take it as self-evident that believers do in fact see the providence of God in the world, but there are many statements in Barth that would lead us to think that all such seeing is impossible. "Its revelation is not world-occurrence itself, but the Word of God, Jesus Christ. On the basis of this Word, in the freedom created by it, it may be believed, but prior to the consummation of the time of the world it can never be seen" (III/3, p. 20). Thus we are to have faith in God's lordship "even at points where there is no such revelation, where to all appearances we have to do only with creaturely occurrence" (pp. 43-44). However, it soon becomes clear that faith is not entirely blind. Even though they can never see the universal plan or total rule of God, the faithful can nevertheless continually see "something of the work of his hand, and may continually see God's will and purpose in very definite events, relationships, connections, and changes in the history of created being" (p. 23). The faithful may do this only as they move from the revealed God in Jesus Christ to the hidden God in world occurrence, "for if we did not know him already in this revelation, how could we ever perceive him in world-occurrence as a whole?" (p. 197). Such partial recognition of the activity of God even in the realm where God is hidden is possible because the two realms are not simply parallel to one another — again in direct contradiction to his reading of "the older theology" — but rather correspond to one another. "But we cannot overlook or deny the fact that creaturely history is still similar in every respect to the history of salvation, as a reflection resembles the original" (p. 50). Because Christians know the original, i.e., Jesus Christ, they can also come to recognize the activity of God in the world which corresponds to that original, although, as Schröder notes, this recognition is always partial, in need of correction, and needs to be sought anew every day, under the guidance of the Holy Spirit. "Man has always many new things to see even when he ostensibly made a serious beginning long ago, and has acquired no little genuine skill, in having open eyes for the ways of God in creaturely occurrence" (p. 57).

However, the question is, what is the purpose of this partial recognition of the God of Jesus Christ even in the realm where God is hidden? Schröder takes it as self-evident that the purpose is related to our ability and willingness to communicate what we see to others who do not see what we do. "How does the believer see herself in relation to the other?" she asks. However, this seems to me to miss the objective Barth sets for faith in the providence of God. The goal of such faith is not communication — that is the goal the whole community has as the elect community of Jesus Christ — but is rather practical decision (as opposed to speculative reflection). "Hence it is not a theoretical seeing but a practical, not a programmatic but a free, not an infallible but one which stands in need of correction" (III/3, p. 26). This emerges in Barth's first description of belief in providence, in a phrase Schröder omits from her citation of this passage. "Belief in God's providence is the practical recognition *(die praktische Erkenntnis)* that things are as we have said" (III/3, p. 14). Hence Barth's concern with what faith perceives of God's work in the world is not to play a game of "I Spy" with others who do not see what we see, but is rather with the concrete decisions such perceptions summon forth. "He [Barth] notes in this history disposings and directions, hints and signs, set limits and opened possibilities, threats and judgments, gracious preservations and assistances. He knows how to distinguish between great and small, truth and appearance, promise and threat. He knows how to distinguish between necessary waiting and pressing on, speech and silence, action and passion, warfare and peace. He perceives always the call of the hour, and acts accordingly" (p. 23). One thinks in particular of the free and various ways Barth responded to the kaiser's war effort in WWI, the rise of Hitler in WWII, and the invasion of Hungary by the Soviets. So long as one has this provisional and practical goal in mind, Barth does not object to the development of pictures or worldviews of God's activity here and now, like those he developed about the meaning of events in the nineteenth and twentieth centuries. "It will certainly be a modest insight. Probably it will not usually concern itself with larger or total issues. It will be content to be a clear perception of individual points and questions making possible practical decisions for the next stretches of the way" (p. 56). However, it is precisely with regard to the practical decisions to which we see ourselves summoned by our partial perception of God's activity in the world that Barth raises the issue of communication and agreement about which Schröder speaks. "It will not become so easily the basis of a programme or party, or an object of debate. It will be the instrument to promote understanding with as many others as possible. But within these limits it will always be sure of itself and fruitful" (pp. 56-57). As is clear from his writings in *Against the Stream,* however, the understanding and agreement we seek is not necessarily with the unseeing outside world, but rather with our fellow Christians who think they see something different in God's activity in the world, and feel called to make very different decisions on the basis of what they perceive.

Conclusion

The question with which I am left when reading Barth's discussion of providence is this: To what practical decisions is God calling the church today, not only in terms of the events of human history — of which Barth was an especially keen observer — but also in terms of God's governance of, and care for, the world in which we live, and the universe our world inhabits? Unfortunately, Barth can provide us with no help on the latter question; but we can turn, yet once again, to Calvin. For Calvin not only attended to the signs of God's providence in history, as did Barth, but also delighted in pondering, contemplating, and meditating on the wisdom, goodness, and care of God manifested in the heavens above and in the smallest plant below, and urged his followers to imitate God's care for every living thing, in gratitude to and praise for God, the fountain of life itself.

What Wondrous Love Is This?
Meditations on Barth, Christian Love,
and the Future of Christian Ethics

CAROLINE J. SIMON

Preliminaries

"Nothing is so difficult in philosophical writing as to get people to be sympathetic enough to what one is saying to understand what it is."[1] This observation by the late British philosopher R. M. Hare can be as aptly applied to theology as to philosophy. I am a philosopher, trained in the Anglo-American analytic tradition. That training is little help, and perhaps a handicap, in developing the amount of sympathy necessary for understanding the theology of Karl Barth. Barth himself says that at least *some* sorts of philosophers might rightly look at theological ethics as an invasion of their traditional turf and an "annexation comparable to the entry of the children of Israel into Canaan."[2] From some philosophers, then, Barthians might expect hostility rather than the sympathy requisite for understanding. However, in recent years I have become something of an eccentric within the field of philosophical ethics, operating at the margins among philosophy, theology, and literature. Eccentricity, being de-centered, is one characterization that Barth gives of Christian love.[3] I hope my particular brand of eccentricity will make ruminating on Barth's view of love a useful enterprise.

1. R. M. Hare, *Moral Thinking* (Oxford: Clarendon, 1981), p. 65.
2. Karl Barth, *Ethics*, ed. Dietrich Braun, trans. Geoffrey W. Bromiley (New York: Seabury Press, 1981), p. 19.
3. "So seriously is love self-giving that his life is an 'eccentric' life, i.e. one which has its center outside itself" (Barth, *Church Dogmatics* IV/2 [Edinburgh: T. & T. Clark, 1958],

Love is at the center of Barth's theology, as well as at the heart of his ethics. I make this statement knowing that writers on many of the topics Barth addresses could view their subject as at the heart of Barth's theology. There is a kind of breathtaking organic unity to Barth's theological vision that makes almost any topic a fitting, and nondistorting, "central focus" to that vision. However, love *is* the center of Barth's theology, because Barth understood that God is love. God's triune nature is eternal love, for, says Barth, "even in Himself God is God only as One who loves" (IV/2, p. 755). Moreover, Barth's christological stance maintains that there is no knowledge of God apart from knowing the God who so loved the world that God came into the world to redeem the world. And Barth understood love as the center of Christian ethics, of the Christian way, and truth, and life, because "love is the life-act of the Christian" (p. 832). To be a Christian is to be transformed into a lover by the creative love of God (p. 776). Love is what calls us out of our old, isolated, unreal selves, re-creates us as "new and loving" people (p. 777). Love is what knits us together into the *ecclesia*. The church is the church only to the extent that its Christian witness is lived out in the world in a way that prompts the world to say, "Behold, how they love one another" (II/2, pp. 719, 814).

What will the centrality of love in Barth's theology have to do with the future of Christian ethics? Dictionary definitions of "ethics" and "morality" point to thinking about and conforming to systems, principles, and rules. When I teach ethics courses, my students are often looking for answers to specific ethical questions; the media prime their questions. Television and radio talk shows and the covers of newsmagazines lead them to ask: What should an ethical person think about genetic engineering or abortion or euthanasia or preserving old-growth timber or raising state revenues through gambling or U.S. involvement in the Balkans? Some students are easily frustrated if a particular ethicist does not give a clear answer to such questions. Other students will reject an ethic that does give a clear answer to a question if the answer contradicts what the student already believes on the issue. Christian students, I find, want *the* Christian answer to these questions; they want the Christian ecological ethic, the Christian sexual ethic, the Christian economic ethic. And they mean by this that they want Christian principles, Christian answers.

---

p. 788). All parenthetical references in the text are to Barth, *Church Dogmatics*, ed. G. W. Bromiley and T. F. Torrance (Edinburgh: T. & T. Clark).

I think the future of Christian ethics, to the extent it is shaped by the theological vision of Karl Barth, will disappoint these students. Barth can at times sound as if he is sketching a Christian code of conduct. For example, when commenting on the Heidelberg Catechism's questions 104-112, he says, "That (and only that) human action is obedient to God's command which keeps holy the right of man established in Jesus Christ in such a way that it also respects human dignity, preserves and furthers human life in every form, brings honor to the relationship between man and woman, creates a real community of work and compensation, and makes human speech to be an instrument of truth."[4] However, I do not read Barth's theology as yielding, or even pointing to, a calculus for "solving" ethical quandaries. Ethics rooted in Christian dogmatics will, says Barth, "certainly not become legalistic or casuistic ethics."[5] Moreover, he tells us: "No idea, no principle, no traditional or newly established institution or organization, no old or new form of economy, state, or culture, or moral system, no idea of education and upbringing, no form of the church, can be for [Christians] the a priori of what they think and speak and will, nor can any negation or contesting of certain ideas and the social constructs corresponding to them. Their a priori is not a cause, however great, necessary or splendid it may appear to be or is. It is the righteousness of God in Jesus Christ." Moreover, as Barth makes clear in his *Ethics*, Christian ethicists settle for something less than a truly *Christian* ethic if what they put forward is "a compendium of highly probable correct answers."[6] What Barth's theology will yield is not a calculus but a call: a call to self-examination, both for individual Christians and for the church, and a call to meet our as-yet-unknown future as Christ's church in God's world with prayerful,[7] open inquiry concerning how to be God's lovers in those particular, concrete places and shifting times.

4. Karl Barth, *The Heidelberg Catechism for Today*, trans. Shirley C. Guthrie, Jr. (Richmond: John Knox, 1964), pp. 114-15.

5. Karl Barth, *The Christian Life: Church Dogmatics*, Volume IV, Part 4, *Lecture Fragments*, trans. Geoffrey W. Bromiley (Grand Rapids: Eerdmans, 1981), p. 6.

6. Barth, *Ethics*, p. 452.

7. It is significant that when Barth turns to the task of ethics as it arises from the doctrine of reconciliation, in what was to be part 4 of volume IV, he focuses his attention on the Lord's Prayer as the prayer of the church. It is in meditatively and seriously praying this prayer that the church understands what its task, work, way of life, in other words, its ethic, is to be.

This does not mean that Barth's Christian ethic says *only* "Love, and do as you please." For part of what Barth calls us to examine is the nature of our love. What we call love is often self-assertion. We love in order to appear loving and hence lovable. We love in order to fulfill our needs and to control our loved ones. In one memorable simile Barth compares us when we love this way to "the wolf when it has swallowed up and consumed . . . both Red Riding Hood and her grandmother" (IV/2, p. 734). We want our "beloveds" to become part of our life, our plans, to satisfy our needs. We too often want what is good for those we love only insofar as it fits with getting what we want or need from them. Thus, as is well known, Barth shares suspicions of eros (his term for natural human love) with Nygren (pp. 734ff.)[8] and Kierkegaard (pp. 781-82). However, though Barth often mentions the command of God in the context of Christian ethics, in contrast to Kierkegaard he is suspicious of love as a duty, of loving others only because we are commanded to. Barth characterizes such love as "an *eros* with its back to the wall" (p. 782).[9] Barth also warns us to guard against a "love that is mere philanthropy, a sympathetic and benevolent concern and assistance which we can exercise with zeal and devotion without taking even a single step away from the safe stronghold of being without our fellow-man, but in a deeper withdrawal into ourselves." In yet another vivid image, Barth says a dehumanized love as philanthropy grasps the other by a "cold instrument" or a "paw with sheathed talons" instead of our human touch. Such philanthropy isolates, and humiliates; it does not reconcile and restore (p. 440). It is like the charity that Simone Weil speaks of in *Waiting for God:* "It is not surprising that a man who has bread should give a piece to someone who is starving. What is surprising is that he should be capable of doing so with so different a gesture from that with which we buy an object. Almsgiving when it is not supernatural is like a sort of purchase. It buys the sufferer."[10] Much of the American welfare and social service system exemplifies this sort of philanthropy. Barth would ask Christians involved in aid, relief, or social service work to ask how

---

8. As a careful reading of this section of the *Dogmatics* makes clear, Barth, while endorsing the general distinction between *eros* and *agape*, has plenty of criticisms of Nygren's particular exposition of these concepts.

9. "Love and joy have it in common — and therein reveal their profoundly necessary interconnection — that neither of them is ordered or can be produced or practiced to order" (IV/2, p. 789).

10. Simone Weil, *Waiting for God,* trans. Emma Craufurd (New York: Harper and Row, 1951), p. 147.

much of what we do fits this description. For when we love erotically, or dutifully, or philanthropically, we do not practice Christian love.

Well, then, when do we practice Christian love? Barth tells us that we practice genuine Christian love when our love has its basis in a free response to "a mighty act of the Holy Ghost for whom we can only pray, whose presence and action can only cause grateful astonishment even to those who are active in love, let alone others" (IV/2, p. 785). God's love for us, which is the sole basis of our ability to act in Christian love, is an electing love that seeks us out while we are defiant enemies (pp. 766ff.). God's love for us is a purifying love, cleansing us from the sin that alienates us from God (pp. 771ff.). God's love is a creative love that transforms us from "those who cannot and will not love (for [we] are sinners)" into people "who do actually love" (pp. 776-77). Actually loving is like coming out of the dark cave in which we hoard and safeguard our unregenerate self. Barth says this love

> is a matter of giving ourselves to the loved one, and therefore, as we continue to be ourselves, of renouncing the false idea that we belong to ourselves and being ourselves together with the loved one, in relationship to him. This relationship is the open into which the cave-dweller emerges when he is made one who loves by the love of God, by the work of the Holy Spirit. When he does not keep and maintain but gives himself, he does not exclude himself in relation to the loved one, but at all costs and whatever else betide he includes himself in the being of the loved one. (pp. 787-88)

When we emerge from the cave, we encounter the reality of God and the reality of God's presence in our neighbor. Barth says, "We love . . . when God and the neighbor are real entities for us which are to be distinguished from ourselves, as their desires are from ours, so that we cannot find them in ourselves nor can we translate their desires into ours nor reconcile them with ours; entities which persistently and definitively resist all our attempts to identify them with our own entity and to which we are bound in such a way that we *must* submit to them."[11] Thus, one sign that we are practicing Christian love is that it comes in opposition to our natural inclinations; what it calls us to do is costly indeed, may cost us *everything*. Paradoxically, another sign that we are practicing Christian love rather than

11. Barth, *Ethics,* p. 457.

dutiful or philanthropic love is that joy will be Christian love's natural accompaniment (IV/2, p. 789).

Barth's realism leads him to temper this glorious picture by maintaining that the Christian life is a perennially mixed bag; for even the best of Christians, actions of Christian love are often frail, puny, and weak,[12] and are almost always also shaped by other forms of love (p. 735). "We are told," says Barth, "that we are to be sinners saved by grace, not that we are to be as gods."[13] In the end for Barth, the only unalloyed example available of a human being who lived a life of Christian love is "the man Jesus" (IV/2, p. 822).

Barth is surely correct that the man Jesus is the great and paradigmatic lover. Nevertheless, we will be well served if we can have our sense of what Christian love looks like tutored by examples of ordinary Christians — people in many ways like us, yet people who have lived in ways to call us to self-examination. To the extent that Barth influences the future of Christian ethics, Christian ethics will be more concerned with loving praxis than with elegant theorizing. Barth would be appalled if we were to use talking and wrangling about details of his ethics as a diversion from living the life of Christian love. "The Word of God," says Barth, "is not just spoken but is spoken for you, to you." A person who thinks he is attending to *Christian* ethics and thinks that "while it may be true, it does not apply to him, the reference being to some other or others and not himself," is self-deluded.[14] Christians must not only discuss the problem of Christian love; we must also live it (IV/2, p. 751). And Christian love, says Barth, is "the concrete and not the abstract loving of someone who is concrete and not abstract" (pp. 802-3). Concrete examples from the past can help us face

---

12. "Christian love, as we have had to indicate already, is not a kind of prolongation of the divine love itself, its overflowing into human life which man with his activity has to serve as a kind of channel, being merely present and not at bottom an acting subject. It is not the work of the Holy Spirit to take from man his own proper activity, or to make it simply a function of His own overpowering control. Where He is present, there is no servitude but freedom. This false conception is contradicted by the great frailty of that which emerges as love in the life of even the best Christians. If it were merely identical with the flowing of the stream of divine love into human life, if our little love were a manifestation or particle of the love of God, it could not and would not be so weak and puny. But the work of the Holy Spirit consists in the liberation of man for his own act and therefore for the spontaneous human love whose littleness and frailty are his own responsibility and not that of the Holy Spirit" (IV/2, p. 785).

13. Barth, *Ethics*, p. 453.

14. Barth, *Ethics*, p. 16 (for this quotation and the one in the preceding sentence).

into and prepare for our own unknown future. So in the remaining three parts of this presentation I will do three things: (1) I will set out a narrative that I think embodies much of what Barth says about Christian love; (2) I will reflect on questions that this narrative raises about one aspect of Barth's theology of Christian love; and (3) I will talk about directions for the future of Christian ethics.

A Love Story

As is well known, 1934 was the year Barth played a principal role in organizing the Barmen Synod and in framing the Barmen Declaration. It is less well known that during that same year, Pastor André Trocmé arrived in the French village of Le Chambon. Four decades later Philip Hallie, an American Jewish philosopher, would find himself moved to tears by a simple newspaper account of an incident in Le Chambon. Hallie would set himself the task of finding out how goodness happened in that small, isolated village. His book, *Lest Innocent Blood Be Shed,* is one telling of the story of Le Chambon.

What Hallie's book testifies to is that goodness happened in Le Chambon because Christian love happened. I take the very existence of *Lest Innocent Blood Be Shed* to be a surety of that fact. Hallie, an academic who had specialized in the skeptical philosophy of Montaigne, had no predisposition toward, and no vested interest in, recognizing and commemorating Christ's *ecclesia* in action, yet in 1993 when he was writing the preface to the second edition of this book, he said,

> I have come to believe that if a miracle is a marvelous event involving spiritual power at its vital center, the efficacy and the survival of the village were miraculous. Whether God used Trocmé and his fellow villagers as instruments, and whether God protected the village from destruction, I leave up to the theologians. But a belief in God certainly motivated Trocmé and the villagers, and the love the villagers displayed was indeed effective. For me and for others it was beautiful and beyond all quotidian understanding, like the rainbow after the Flood.[15]

15. Philip Hallie, *Lest Innocent Blood Be Shed: The Story of Le Chambon and How Goodness Happened There* (New York: Harper and Row, 1985, 1993).

Hallie started his investigation of Le Chambon after reading of an incident during the German occupation of this French village when Vichy French police demanded the surrender of all the Jews sheltered in the village. The authorities knew full well that the villagers had for some time systematically concealed Jewish refugees. Failure to cooperate, it was said, would mean arrest. Yet the village, led by its French Reformed pastor, refused to cooperate. It is a testimony to the effectiveness of the villagers' methods of concealment that an involuntary search of the village by the police turned up only one Jew. As the Jewish man sat alone waiting to be taken away on the bus, which was surrounded by police guards, one after another of the villagers came and handed him chocolate and other scarce food items to take with him.

Hallie set out to understand what made these people act this way, and he concluded that it was beyond ordinary understanding. He also found that they were motivated by their pastor's conviction that to stay close to Jesus meant to love as Jesus loved. Trocmé's view here is very similar to that of Barth, who says the impetus to Christian love is in our not wanting to be without God, and therefore not wanting to be without our neighbor.[16] André Trocmé, expositing Old Testament texts concerning the "cities of refuge" that the people of God were to provide for those hounded during incipient blood feuds, had taught his congregation that love was inconsistent with "standing idly by the blood of one's neighbor." Trocmé's congregation lived out that lesson.

Barth tells us, "[T]he Christian community can and must be the scene of many human activities which are new and supremely astonishing to many of its own members as well as to the world around because they rest on an endowment with extraordinary capacities" (IV/2, p. 828). The activities of Le Chambon astonished Hallie, as well as Pierre Sauvage. Sauvage made the film *Weapons of the Spirit* as a testimony to the village that had sheltered him as a Jewish child fleeing the Holocaust. The citizens of Le Chambon did not set out to astonish; they set out to follow Jesus and to help those in need of their help. If a refugee came to a door in Le Chambon, the person would not be turned away. A network of farmhouses was set up in which refugees would be sheltered, with instructions to flee into the woods if patrols showed up looking for Jews. "In the course of the first two years of the Occupation, Le Chambon became the safest place for

---

16. Barth, *Ethics,* p. 455.

Jews in Europe."[17] As its reputation for welcome spread and the situation in Europe became increasingly dangerous, more and more people sent their children to Le Chambon to be cared for. Over the course of four years the villagers saved hundreds of lives. But they did it in a way that did not attract notice until years later. Theirs was a quiet, enduring goodness.

Not everyone recognized at the time that those who sheltered Jews acted appropriately. Their own mayor chided the rescuers for endangering the existence of the whole village for the sake of strangers. Moreover, a high official in the Reformed Church of France sought to discipline Trocmé because his teachings were endangering the existence of the Protestant church in France.[18] Trocmé and his followers refused to be deterred by their detractors.

The quiet goodness of André Trocmé and his wife, Magda, reached beyond nonviolent resistance to the Nazis and Vichy to active love of their enemies. When the police came in 1943 to arrest André Trocmé for his role in sheltering Jews, his family invited the two policemen to sit down and have supper with them. Magda Trocmé was asked later, "How could you bring yourself to sit down to eat with these men who were there to take your husband away, perhaps to his death?" She responded: "It was dinner time; we were all hungry. The food was ready." What Madame Trocmé took for granted moved one of the policemen to tears. As he took Trocmé away he said, "I'll tell this story later. Yes, I'll keep it alive."[19] Hallie's book has helped to fulfill this policeman's commitment.

Who Is My Neighbor?

The people of Le Chambon lived out an answer to the question, Who is my neighbor? Their neighbor was anyone in need of help. Their neighbors were Jews who came seeking shelter. Their neighbors were also Vichy police, if such officials happened to have come to make an arrest at dinnertime. They loved the stranger within their gates;[20] they loved their enemies

17. Hallie, p. 129.
18. Hallie, pp. 212 and 143.
19. Hallie, pp. 20-23.
20. They also went out and sought strangers to come within their gates, by contacting the American Friends Service Committee and asking them to send Jewish children in need of refuge to their village. See Hallie, pp. 131ff.

and those who spitefully used them. And it is here that this narrative does more than illustrate all that Barth says about Christian love. The story of Le Chambon also interrogates distinctions Barth draws within his account of Christian love.

In the *Dogmatics* Barth makes a distinction between love, which we are to have for our fellow partners in the covenant, and what he calls humanity or friendliness, which we are to have for all. Barth says that in the New Testament, "The closed circle to whose members the command to love refers is no longer that of the people of Israel and strangers casually associated with it. But — however irksome this may be to those who regard Christian love as a human virtue — it is still a closed circle: the circle of disciples, brothers, the saints, members of the body of Christ; the circle of the community of Jesus Christ gathered by the Holy Spirit from Jews and Gentiles, and ruled and quickened by Him. . . . As the recurrent expression has it, Christians love one another" (IV/2, p. 804). Barth seems to have three sorts of reasons for making this claim. First, his reading of the Old and New Testaments leads him to think that the scriptural emphasis is characteristically on the "household of faith" as a sphere of special obligation to love. Second, Barth's abhorrence for the abstract and his emphasis on particularity lead him to flee a love had for "fellow-man as such" toward a concrete relationship with *"this particular fellow-man."* Third, in explicating the interconnection between Christian love of God and Christian love of neighbor, Barth calls on the concept of *mutual witness.*

The relationship between Christian love and mutual witness requires explanation. Barth says neighbors are such to one another because and insofar as they "continually proclaim to one another by their human activity the love of God which constitutes Israel, the community and the existence of each individual in Israel and the community, and this love as the basis of their freedom to love God in return" (p. 812). Love of neighbor is the horizontal axis of a love of God that is rooted in and is a living proclamation of the vertical axis of a love of God. And "love of God" here signifies a reciprocal love of God for us and love of ours for God. If Christian love is rooted in this *mutual* witness, my relationship to the non-Christian is at most *"latent love"* (p. 805) and love for "my neighbor or brother of tomorrow" (p. 809). Barth urges Christians to reach out to the person outside the circle of the household of faith in humility and in hope. Christians are to reach outside the circle in humility, because, for all we know, the person we assume is not of the faith is, unbeknownst to us, in reality already a member of the household of faith. Christians are to reach outside the circle in hope, because the person who in reality is not now our brother or sister will, we hope, become one. But this reaching out will not be love, but humanity or friendliness.

Now, Barth in no way wants this to lessen the obligation we have toward our not-yet-neighbors.

> I love neither God nor my brother if I do not show openly to every man without distinction the friendliness emphatically recommended and even commanded in so many New Testament passages. The New Testament does not call this "love." And what the New Testament calls "love" is in fact other and more than this friendliness. But the latter is a kind of anticipation of it. . . . It is the position of readiness of the Christian as he looks and moves to the neighbor or brother of tomorrow in each of his fellows, even including the "enemy" of the people and the community. . . . They must be ready and on the way to love for all. (p. 809)

So Barth is telling us that we seriously love our neighbor only if we also, and equally seriously, extend humanity toward our not-yet-neighbor. Given this, there may in the end be no practical difference between the Christian who sees himself, when extending aid to those outside the household of faith, as loving a neighbor and the Christian who under such circumstances sees himself as being friendly toward a human being.

This may be so, but I am not so sure. André Trocmé read the biblical refrain to "love one another" through the lens of the parable of the Good Samaritan.[21] This parable is, after all, the "answer" Jesus gives to the question, "Who is my neighbor?" The lens of this parable led Trocmé to believe that "there are no important divisions between human beings such as 'Jew' and 'non-Jew.' The main distinction among people is between those who believe that those in need are as precious as they themselves are, and those who do not believe this."[22] Over the door of the Reformed Temple of Le

---

21. Hallie, pp. 110, 170.

22. Hallie, p. 194. Trocmé took this so seriously that he refused to try to convert Jewish refugees being aided in Le Chambon to Christianity. To do so, he thought, would be aiding them for ulterior motives. See pp. 54-55. Barth would certainly honor Trocmé's wish to avoid instrumentalism here: "We cannot love in order to achieve something. . . . Love is betrayed if we try to make it the object of this type of calculation" (*CD* IV/2, p. 783).

Chambon was carved the inscription "Love One Another." From the beginning of his pastorate there, Trocmé tutored his parishioners in looking for ways to apply this by reaching out to others. For Trocmé the essence of Christian witness had its foremost application in how *outsiders* were treated; the love of the parishioners for one another was rooted in their joint adventure of aiding those outside their circle that needed their help. For Barth the order of emphasis is the reverse: the foremost obligation is toward the *insider;* outsiders are aided by the witness of mutual love insiders share for one another and are given help as potential or nascent insiders.

It does not seem to be accidental, then, that some of the actions Barth is famous for taking led to a document like the Barmen Declaration. Barmen sought to decry the encroachment of the Nazi state into the Protestant churches in Germany. It sought to guard the purity of the church, but it had nothing to say about the Nazi state's treatment of those outside the Protestant church. Later Barth would look back on the Barmen Declaration and say,

> Even it was not a total resistance against totalitarian National Socialism. It restricted itself to repelling the encroachment of National Socialism. It confined itself to the Church's Confession, to the Church service, and to Church order as such. It was only a partial resistance. And for this it has been properly and improperly reproached. . . . In proportion to its task, the Church has sufficient reason to be ashamed that it did not do more, yet in comparison with those other groups and institutions it has no reason to be ashamed; it accomplished far more than all the rest.[23]

The framers of Barmen exhibited a courage and theological seriousness that can and should challenge us as we face our future. Barth's involvement with Barmen did, after all, cost him his chair in Bonn and his doctorate at the University of Münster. However, the courage and seriousness behind Barmen was of the sort to be expected of Christians who thought first of all of those within the household of faith. The courage and seriousness of those in Le Chambon who risked their lives to save Jews was of a somewhat

---

23. Quoted in Jack Rogers, *Presbyterian Creeds: A Guide to the Book of Confessions* (Philadelphia: Westminster, 1985), p. 191.

different sort. It was the courage and seriousness to be expected of Christians who, tutored by Jesus' story of the Samaritan, thought first of those lying by the side of the road, hardly remembering to notice anything but a particular person in need.

It is appropriate to anticipate two rejoinders. The first is that my description of Barth's account of Christian love does not do justice to the amount of balancing he does, in his characteristic theologizing. Barth's characteristic patterns are *"x* but also *y"* and *"a* nevertheless *b."* This pattern is evident in his discussion of Christian love. Barth is clear that while the people of God form a circle within which mutual love is practiced, the mutuality of brotherly love is practiced *for the sake of* the world (IV/2, p. 805). He is also clear that "while the circle of vital Christian love for the neighbor is not the sphere of all men indiscriminately, it is not a hermetically sealed circle within this sphere but one which continually broadens out into it" (p. 809). This is all quite true, but it does not undercut my point. My point has been to raise a question: Will it make some practical difference where the accent in this balancing falls? From the point of view of Christian practice, *"x* but also *y"* may very well not be equivalent to *"y* but also *x."* Barth himself uses such an asymmetry to make a distinction between Christian theology and Christian philosophy. "Theology," says Barth, "speaks about God but not without reference to the brother, and philosophy speaks about the fellowman for God's sake."[24] I think the differing actions of those involved in Barmen and those involved in rescuing Jews in Le Chambon give us an example of a practical difference that a person's (or group's) particular emphasis can make on action.

The second rejoinder is that I have not given due regard to Barth's point that what love requires, what love or friendliness looks like when lived out, is a function of concrete people and places and times. The response of the Synod of Barmen to the Nazi threat may look different than the response of Le Chambon to the Nazi threat because Germany in 1934 was a different place and time than a village on a plateau in southeastern France in the 1940s. The Barmen Declaration may have been but an early stage in what would have been a widening circle of involvement on Barth's part, leading, for all we know, to personal resistance to the German treatment of the Jews, if he had not been deported back to Switzerland in 1935. Sharing Barth's views about whether the Christian's response to the non-Christian can be

24. Barth, *Ethics*, p. 45.

one of Christian love may have little or nothing to do with the differences in actions I have adumbrated. Trying to discern which of these hypotheses is a more likely explanation of the phenomena would take careful historical work and, perhaps, a kind of supernatural insight into the hearts of the particular Christians involved. Since my goal has been to raise a question for the church to use in present and future self-examination, rather than to answer a question, I am relieved not to have to settle this issue here.[25]

Our Future

What I have attempted to do in the first three parts of this paper is to lay out what can now be seen as two models of Christian love. The first model, which we can call the Barthian model, answers the question, "Who is my neighbor?" by saying, "Those within the household of faith, but also (seriously but latently) any in need." The second model, which we can call the Trocmé model, answers the same question with: "Any in need, but (perhaps) especially those within the household of faith." As we look to the future of Christian ethics, especially given what we know from the church's past and present, I think we should not say "either/or" to these models, but rather "both/and."

The Barthian model will be of use in self-examination when the particular challenges facing the church seem to make it excruciatingly difficult not to give the lie to our claim to be Christian by failing to love our fellow Christians. After setting out his model, Barth wryly observes, "If — unlike the Bible — we want to say more than this, we must be careful that we do not say less" (IV/2, p. 809). Certainly the church has often in the past said less by its actions. All too often in the present our actions say less. I do not know what your academic institutions, congregations, denominations, and Christian organizations are like. If they are anything like my own, Barth's model can remind those of us who call ourselves Christians of how far short we fall of our calling in Christ to love one another as God has loved us. The Barthian model chides us to face the reality of the differences

25. I am also aware that I have, throughout the paper, ignored developmental issues regarding Barth's thought. It may, for example, be that by the time Barth was writing *The Humanity of God* (Richmond: John Knox, 1960), his own emphasis would have been more like Trocmé's. I have neglected this matter mainly because I am very poorly equipped to tackle such questions. I hope that this neglect has not led to too much distortion.

among Christians over theology, over social issues, over polity, over taste in liturgy, and to love in spite of those differences. It asks us to beg God for the grace to love one another even when we would prefer that our brothers and sisters were different, better, easier to get along with — in sum, more like our fantasy versions of ourselves. The world has not often been astonished at how Christians love one another. The world has more often had a right to look on in jaded wonder at our pettiness.

The Trocmé model will be of use when our temptation is to be an enclave, to let our boundaries become, if not hermetically sealed, at least more resistant than welcoming. This model will become especially necessary in times when Christianity has cultural hegemony and "Christian" is culturally identified with a particular race or class or ethnicity. As we know from the church's past and our present, such situations all too easily lull Christians into indifference to the plight of those on the margins. Such situations may even lead to outright hostility, and that hostility may even masquerade as zeal for the Lord. In such situations we should habituate ourselves to Trocmé's kind of blindness, the kind of blindness that responds to a demand to hand over any Jews with the retort, "We know of no Jew; we know only human beings."

Whatever the future holds, Barth is right in saying that Christian love is a call for action that leads the Christian into the complexities of his or her time and situation (IV/2, p. 801). We can know from our past that as we are led into the complexities of our future we will often be confused and fumbling and wrongheaded in our attempts at loving. The church's future will be like the church's past, bearing out Augustine's observations in the *City of God.*

> Our righteousness, too, though true in so far as it has respect to the true good, is yet in this life of such a kind that it consists rather in the remission of sins than in the perfecting of virtues. Witness the prayer of the whole city of God in its pilgrim state, for it cries to God by the mouth of all its members, "Forgive us our debts as we forgive our debtors." . . . [W]ho but a proud [person] can presume that he so lives that he has no need to say to God, "Forgive us our debt?" And such a [person] is not great, but swollen and puffed up with vanity.[26]

26. Augustine, *The City of God,* trans. Marcus Dodds (New York: Random House, 1950), p. 708.

Repentance, forgiveness, and reconciliation are so central to Barth's theology because they are such primary tools in the repair kit that is essential to the Christian life. Jesus' prayer that he taught us to pray displays how few are the things we need: a sense of God's glory, presence, and care; enough food to keep body and soul together; forgiveness; and protection from being cursed with an intractable pattern of repeated blunderings. With the faith and hope that God will heed our prayer, we can face our future knowing that love will abide, with its frailty and fumbling purified and redeemed by God's grace. We can live as those who know that our lovelessness is "not set aside but is refuted by" God's seeking us, finding us, loving us, reconciling us, and transforming us into lovers, for Christ's sake.[27] As we look to the future, it is perhaps fitting to end by reminding ourselves of Barth's words on a New Year's theme from a sermon he preached in Basel Prison:

> God always gives us strength for one leg of the journey at a time. At each stage we are promised that he will continue to provide additional and greater strength as needed on our way into the future. The powers we receive each time somehow enable us to do the very things we had been incapable of doing so far. God does not distribute the full ration all at once. He apportions it from one day to the next. You will not be a rock of strength overnight. Neither will you remain a weakling, worth nothing but writhing, throwing up your hands in despair and falling on your face (that will happen often enough!). God gives you strength and power to become a man, modestly yet determinedly, who goes his way, humbly yet courageously, and is strong and grateful: strong because it is God's almighty grace for which he is grateful.[28]

---

27. Barth, *Ethics*, p. 458.

28. Karl Barth, *Deliverance to the Captives* (New York: Harper and Brothers, 1961), pp. 113-14. I am grateful for helpful comments on drafts of this paper from Michael Hayes, Stephen C. Simon, and J. Jeffery Tyler.

What Wondrous Love Is This?

JOHN WEBSTER

Professor Simon has given us a lucid and quietly provocative reading of Barth, one whose cogency derives in part from being set alongside the humbling story of Christian people who did what the gospel commanded and looked after those around them. It is especially gratifying to me that such a respectful account of Barth should be offered by a self-confessed analytical philosopher of religion in the Anglo-American tradition. Where I come from, the analytical philosophers are of a rather more obdurate frame of mind when it comes to Barth, whom they regard as a joke in several volumes. Without having read him, they hate him; and so Professor Simon's courteous account is all the more welcome, even if she feels that taking Barth seriously has meant drifting into eccentricity.

There is a good deal in the paper which invites further conversation and reflection. We could spend some time thinking through Barth's refusal of an ethical calculus, to which Professor Simon rightly draws attention early on in her paper, and which is both deeply significant and routinely misunderstood. Both the significance and the misunderstanding derive from the fact that Barth's repudiation of moral calculation is an aspect of his controversial moral anthropology — an anthropology in which conscience and consciousness are not allowed to become coterminous, and in which the faculty of judgment is itself chastened by the gospel and reintegrated into an account of moral selfhood as responsible and active assent to the vocation the gospel announces. Or again: Professor Simon draws attention to those passages in which Barth offers a merciless exposure of the perversion of love into philanthropy, and she asks whether modern welfare technologies can stand up to such scrutiny. We might also spend time pondering the relations between Christian love and, on the one hand, the presence and activity of the Holy Spirit and, on the other hand, the activity of prayer. Both these relations are central to Barth's ethics — and both, we might add, are often conspicuously absent from a good deal of contemporary writing on ethics, even, mirabile dictu, from those styles of ethics which make a good deal of the ecclesial character of the Christian moral life. Lastly, there is much to be discussed about the necessary coordination of the theological testimony of Barmen and the practical testimony of the Reformed community in Le Chambon. How, Professor Simon asks, may concern for the purity of the church and its teaching be protected from closing in upon itself? What are the *moral* aspects of the act of confession?

From this range of issues, it is an aspect of that last question that I would like to pursue, the relation of morality to confession. I take it that a central concern for Professor Simon's paper is interrogation of the distinctions Barth draws between the love which is proper within the household of faith and the humanity or friendliness the covenant people are required to demonstrate to all. The paper invites us to reflect on two somewhat divergent accounts of the boundary between insiders and outsiders which is established by the Christian confession. For Trocmé and the community of Le Chambon, the love command is interpreted through a certain reading of the parable of the Good Samaritan, one which finds the foremost application of that story in undiscriminating treatment of all, and especially of outsiders. For Barth, on the other hand, it is the fellow member of the covenant community who is the proper object of the Christian's love; outsiders are what Professor Simon calls "potential or nascent insiders," and thus objects of what Barth himself calls "nascent love" (IV/1, p. 805).[1] What might be said about that representation of the matter? A couple of reflections may help us proceed along the paths of inquiry which Professor Simon has indicated to us.

The first reflection builds on a hint in Professor Simon's paper that Barth's account that the *proximus* is primarily the covenant partner is not to be interpreted as some kind of ecclesial introversion. Barth resists any neat identification of the object of Christian love with membership in the

---

1. All parenthetical page references in this chapter are to Karl Barth, *Church Dogmatics* (Edinburgh: T. & T. Clark).

visible Christian community. It is certainly true that in *Church Dogmatics* IV/2 Barth defines the neighbor thus: "the one who in Christian love is loved apart from and side by side and together with God is the fellow-man who stands next to the one who loves in the historical context of the existence of Israel or the existence of the community of Jesus Christ" (p. 805). But a page or two later Barth enters a vital qualification. Of course, he says, "There can be no question of an extension in principle of Christian love for the neighbour into a universal love with the hidden presence, and emergence, of these 'foreign' children"; or again, "I have not to be closed but open to the possibility that the circle of the brothers whom I must love may prove tomorrow, or even within the next hour, to be wider than I now realize" (p. 808).

All this is much more than a concession, a softening of what Barth admits to be a seemingly "harsh" (p. 802) identification of the neighbor with my covenant partner in the church. Nevertheless, "this positive fact does not involve the negative one that we must in no case love the fellow-man whom we do not know or think we know as our neighbour in this specific concrete sense. Baptism and visible fellowship in confession are for us an inclusive sign, but they are not for this reason *a limine* an exclusive sign. *Tertium datur*" (p. 802). What surfaces here, in fact, is the deep dogmatic structure of Barth's anthropology and ethics, above all the christological aspects of that structure. The reason it is not enough simply to say that the primary person who claims me as a neighbor is my fellow believer is christological: in Jesus Christ, each person, inside but also outside the church, can be my neighbor. This argument has already been made in *Church Dogmatics* I/2. There Barth insists, as he does in IV/2, that the neighbor is ordinarily the fellow Christian, for the neighbor is commissioned to act as such in my regard "[t]o the extent that there is within the world a Church, created by the Word and Spirit of God, to be the earthly body of the heavenly Head, Jesus Christ. . . . It is the Church which introduces the Good Samaritan" (I/2, p. 421). But the church is *representative;* that is, it is not only a congregation bounded by a confession, but also "a summons . . . to the humanity which is around it but does not belong to it" (p. 422). The logic of Barth's christological grounding of the neighbor is thus threefold. First, in Jesus Christ's taking flesh, the new destiny of humankind is secured; second, that new destiny is operative in the church of the apostles and prophets; but third, that church is representative, and so "we must . . . be prepared and ready for the fact that man, our fellow-man generally, can become our neighbour, even where we do not think we see anything of the Church" (p. 425). The fact that for the New Testament the neighbor is properly and primarily the companion in the faith "does not exclude, but includes the fact that in every man we have to expect a brother. . . . What man is there who might not one day meet us as a messenger of the Word of God?" (p. 427). Such neighbors, we might say, were the Jews of Le Chambon.

All this amounts to a suggestion that, viewed from one angle, the Trocmé and Barth models may not be so far apart after all, especially since for Barth the boundary between insiders and outsiders is provisional, very porous, and usually runs in unexpected places. Professor Simon is an attentive reader of Barth, and none of this has escaped her paper, which seeks not to force a choice between these two accounts of the neighbor, but to raise a question about the practical difference made by accenting one model or the other, and to identify the different sorts of self-examinations to which they may give rise.

However, matters cannot rest here: a second line of reflection is necessary. For all that he repels a kind of ecclesio-centrism, Barth remains explicit in giving priority to the covenant partner as the neighbor who claims my love. Why does he do this? Why is it the fellow Israelite or the member of the community of Jesus Christ who claims me in a particular way? A number of things need to be said at this point to extend the analysis Professor Simon has laid before us.

First, for Barth the neighbor is not simply the person in need, but rather the person who does good to me. On Barth's reading, in the parable of the Good Samaritan it is the Samaritan (not the man who fell among thieves) who is the neighbor, and thus "the primary and true form of the neighbour is that he faces us as the bearer and representative of the divine compassion" (I/2, p. 416); "My neighbour," he writes, "is my fellow-man acting towards me as benefactor" (p. 420). The point here is, of course, not simply a disagreement in interpreting the parable; what is at first glance a mere exegetical difference opens out into a much deeper point which concerns the basic shape of Barth's moral anthropology, and which underlies what he says about the neighbor.

We can best see the difference when we remember that Barth is very hesitant about generalized benevolence, that affirmation of the duty of "universal love of humanity" (IV/2, p. 807) which is often thought to provide the interpretative key to the parable of the Good Samaritan. Why is he so hesitant here? Partly it is (as Professor Simon indicates) his particularism, his preference for "a very definite and specific proximity" (p. 803). But something more fundamental is at play here. Barth refuses to think of humanity in isolation from the history of salvation which is enacted in the person and work and word of Jesus, and which bears fruit now in the history of the church. There is for Barth no full and authentic humanity outside that history. To think of humankind in isolation from that history is on Barth's terms not to think truthfully. That is why for Barth all human persons are either confessing members of the household of faith or latent, potential, and future members of it. It is this which presses Barth to assert that the Christian is my neighbor as the representative human being, humankind on its way to becoming what in Christ it has been made. The stress on the Christian as neighbor is not driven by sectarianism (indeed, both by temperament and by theological conviction Barth was in many respects a secular person, for whom the internalities of Christian culture held little attraction). The limitation of the term "neighbor" to my fellow believer is a rejection of the idea that there is any reality we might call "humankind as such," humankind considered in abstraction from the gospel. The Christian is my neighbor because, as one in whom life in Christ is especially manifest, the Christian refers me to Jesus Christ, the bearer of the mercy of God.

This means that while Barth would surely have praised the actions of the good people of Le Chambon, his grounds for doing so would not be that the parable of the Good Samaritan requires that we be neighborly to those in need, whatever their relation to the Christian confession. For Barth, such an account of the matter would tend to presuppose an account of the neighbor undisciplined by the gospel. The Christian, according to Barth, is to act in response to the needs of another because that other may be a silent witness to me of the mercy of God. Undergirding this are some fundamental features of Barth's ontology of the human — most of all, his conviction that human beings have a given teleology, that they are not simply discrete units of personal need, but are what they are as they belong to an order of reality with certain ends. To love the other as a latent Christian is not to do violence to his or her integrity; still less is it to set up barriers to compassion. It is nothing other than a matter of affirming the other's teleology, to treat the other as what he or she already is in Christ. My neighbor is "ordered" to be the witness to me of Christ's mercy; that mercy is confessed in the church, and therefore it is the members of the church who are the especial realization to me of neighborliness. This does not exclude the "foreign" witness, nor does it mean that those others can be considered as if the gospel calling were not true for them also, as if Christ were not their destiny, too.

To conclude: In his discussion of the neighbor in *Church Dogmatics* I/2, Barth quotes (p. 412) a little phrase from Calvin's commentary on 1 Corinthians 10:15f.: *la vraye charité procède de ceste source là.* A theological account of love is governed by the source of love, God in Christ present in the Spirit. That source is boundless, and human love which stumbles along behind the love of God will be boundless too. But it will also be a love which is ordered by its source, that is, put in a right relation to reality. Why am I obliged to protect the persecuted? Why may I not stand idly by when the strong hurt the weak? Barth's answer, I suggest, is in part because not to offer help would be untruthful; it would be to act in a way which is false to the nature of the reality which Jesus Christ established in taking flesh, and whose universal scope is now anticipated in his church. Because he is true, I may not pass by on the other side; but also, because he is true, I must learn to find my neighbor in my fellow members of his church, and then in all who do not yet know that he is their neighbor who presents to them the mercy of God.

Mysterium Trinitatis:
Barth's Conception of Eternity

GEORGE HUNSINGER

"What, then, is time?" asked Saint Augustine. "I know well enough what it is provided that nobody asks me; but if I am asked what it is and try to explain, I am baffled."[1] Among the familiar puzzles involved in trying to explain time is the paradoxical nature of what we call the present. On the one hand, the present seems to be nothing but a fleeting moment. "The present is time," Augustine observed, "only by reason of the fact that it moves on to become the past." If so, "how can we say that even the present *is*, when the reason why it *is* is that it is *not to be?* In other words, we cannot rightly say that time *is*, except by reason of its impending state of *not being*" (p. 264). From this point of view, the present is an elusive instant. It cannot be divided into parts, because it has no duration. A mathematical point would seem an apt analogy for this "flowing now" *(nunc fluens)*, since each present instant is indivisible; yet because the present flows, it would also seem analogous to a river or, perhaps more precisely, to a straight line constituted by a steady succession of contiguous indivisible points.

On the other hand, the present also seems to be a real duration that persists without interruption, indeed the only moment that actually endures. Since the future is not yet and the past is no longer, it seems that past and future do not strictly exist, and that what actually exists is the present alone. Only the present is what we directly experience, and only

1. Augustine, *Confessions* 11.14, trans. R. S. Pine-Coffin (London: Penguin Books, 1961), p. 264. Parenthetical page numbers cited in the following text refer to this work.

the present abides. Since neither the past nor the future can be said to exist, "it might be correct," stated Augustine, "to say that there are three times, a present of past things, a present of present things, and a present of future things" (p. 269). If past and future exist, in other words, it is only as functions of present consciousness. The past is a function of memory, the present a function of attention, and the future a function of expectation. "Some such different times do exist in the mind," Augustine concluded, "but nowhere else that I can see" (p. 269). From this point of view, the present is not a fleeting instant, but a persisting duration. A circle or a sphere might offer a possible analogy for this abiding present *(nunc stans)*, since the present of our consciousness is continuous and encompassing, like the periphery of these mathematical objects.

Broadly speaking, there are two main views of eternity, and they correspond, more or less, to these two different facets of the present. One view resembles the abiding present of unitary consciousness *(nunc stans)*, while the other aligns itself with the flowing present of successive instants *(nunc fluere)*. Until modern times the former view was most familiar in Christian theology. Associated with Augustine, Boethius, and Anselm, it posits eternity as an abiding present but with a difference. What is present to human consciousness as a sequence of moments, one after another, is present to divine consciousness simultaneously. Past, present, and future are not successive for God as they are for us. The divine eternity is an "eternal now" *(nunc aeternitatis)* that embraces our temporal past, present, and future comprehensively *(totus)*, holding them together in God's consciousness or knowledge all at once *(simul)*. God's eternal now is in one sense more like a mathematical point than a straight line, since it cannot be divided into parts; yet it also seems analogous to a circle or a sphere, since it encompasses all temporal moments simultaneously within itself.

The eternal now as traditionally conceived gives rise to many conundrums. If God knows the future before it happens, for example, doesn't that entail fate or determinism? Under these circumstances, how can human freedom and temporal contingency really exist? If all temporal moments are encompassed simultaneously in eternity, furthermore, doesn't that finally make temporal sequence itself into an illusion? How can past, present, and future be real in themselves, or else how can their sequence be real in eternity for God? Questions can also be raised from the standpoint of Scripture. Is the biblical God really eternal in the sense of this "eternal now"? According to the Bible, Oscar Cullmann has argued, God's time is something more like "everlastingness." It is much like our time, only indefinitely extended. The real contrast is not between time and timelessness, but between limited time and endless time.[2]

In the modern period considerations like these have led to the exploration of another model for eternity. Eternity, it is proposed, is distinct from time but not separate from it. Eternity is a transcendent, transhistorical dimension that runs along in tandem with time while yet being immanent within it. Eternity is not a stationary present over against time that incorporates all time simultaneously, but a flowing present that accompanies the succession of time as it occurs. Eternity shapes or directs the temporal process largely by possessing the plenitude of a larger essence and a greater amplitude for the future. This processional view of eternity has its philosophical forebears in Whitehead and Hegel, and its theological descendants in recent interpreters like Ogden and Tracy on the Whiteheadian side, and Pannenberg, Moltmann, and Jenson on the Hegelian. In either case eternity, like time, is a flowing now, a *nunc fluens,* that not only moves along with time but also requires time for its own self-actualization.

From the standpoint of the more traditional view, this later point is damaging. A God who needs the world for the purpose of self-actualization is not the biblical God. A Creator whose being is conditioned and restricted by the creation is not Israel's Lord. An eternity dependent upon and limited by its interaction with time is not compatible with the God of free and sovereign grace. The processional view of eternity evacuates God of his deity, it is thought, and makes eternity dwindle into some sort of finite infinity. For God's eternal being is seen as inextricable from the temporal being of the world. Both are essentially implicated in one and the same process of becoming. Although Whitehead and Hegel differ on whether the process is organic or dialectical and on just why God needs the world, both agree that God's being is in the process of becoming along with the world, that God's being is composite, that God is more fully actualized at the end of this process than at the beginning, and that without this or some such process God would not and could not be fully actual as God.[3] God needs the world, or at least some world, in order to achieve self-actualization.

---

2. Oscar Cullmann, *Christ and Time* (Philadelphia: Westminster, 1951), p. 46. For this and other references I am indebted to William C. Placher's fine essay, "The Eternal God," in *Narratives of a Vulnerable God* (Louisville: Westminster/John Knox, 1994), pp. 27-52.

3. For an excellent technical discussion, see Brian Leftow, "God and the World in

Karl Barth's conception of eternity does not fit neatly into either of these standard views. His conception overlaps elements of each while transcending both. More precisely, although Barth stands mainly in the tradition of Augustine, Boethius, and Anselm, he modifies this tradition in order to appropriate what is valid in Hegel. His primary motivation, however, is not to reconcile these divergent traditions. It is rather to think through the conception of eternity in thoroughly trinitarian terms. Eternity for Barth is not the container in which God lives. It is a predicate of God's triune being. For that reason eternity exemplifies and guarantees God's full and sovereign freedom. Nowhere is Barth's focus on God's freedom as the Lord more significant than in his trinitarian conception of eternity. By granting primacy to the divine freedom at the heart of God's trinitarian life, Barth can side with the traditional view on eternity's radical otherness and perfect transcendence while also incorporating themes of dynamism, teleology, and immanence that characterize the more modern view.

A terminological headache may be noted at the outset. When discussing eternity, Barth's use of the word "time" can be quite ambiguous. The word's meaning sometimes shifts, it seems, from one sentence to the next. A more vexing case would be difficult to recall unless it were Paul's slippery use of the word *nomos* in Romans 7–8. Barth can say in one place, for example, that "Time has nothing to do with God,"[4] while also asserting that "God . . . is supremely temporal" (III/2, p. 437). A careful reading shows, however, that Barth intends at least three points. First, in some strong sense eternity is timeless. Second, eternity is a mode of time that is peculiarly God's own. Finally, the eternal temporality of God is the condition for the possibility not only of our having time at all, but also for time's redemption. The vagaries of the word "time" reflect, perhaps, the agony and the ecstasy of theological language as Barth used it in general. "God is light," Irenaeus once remarked, "and yet God is unlike any light that we know" (*Adversus haereses* 2.13.4). Barth knew this dictum and cited it (II/1, p. 190). It offers a possible paradigm for his use of the word "time." It is as though he were saying: "God is temporal, and yet God's temporality is unlike any time that

---

Hegel and Whitehead," in *Hegel and Whitehead,* ed. G. Lucas, Jr. (Albany: SUNY Press, 1986), pp. 257-67.

4. Karl Barth, *Church Dogmatics* II/1 (Edinburgh: T. & T. Clark), p. 608. References to this multivolume work are included in the text.

we know." The time peculiar to God is at once the presupposition of creaturely time and yet so utterly different as to be ineffable.

Barth's Conception of Eternity: Its Trinitarian Background

God's time is as ineffable for Barth as the doctrine of the Trinity that gives it form. Barth makes perhaps the first sustained attempt in history to reformulate eternity's mystery in fully trinitarian terms. The mystery of eternity becomes in effect a subtopic in the mystery of the Trinity. Eternity holds no perplexities that cannot be stated in trinitarian terms, and the Trinity has no formal aspects irrelevant to the question of eternity, so that the form of the Trinity and the form of eternity coincide. Barth unfolds the mystery of God's eternal time within a fully trinitarian framework.

How to relate God's oneness to God's threeness and vice versa is, needless to say, at the heart of trinitarian doctrine. Three aspects of this question are relevant in Barth's reformulation of eternity. The Trinity as Barth understands it means that God is self-identical, self-differentiated, and self-unified. God is self-identical in being *(ousia)*, self-differentiated in modes of being *(hypostases)*, and self-unified in eternal life *(perichoresis)*. The *perichoresis* presupposes God's self-differentiation as Father, Son, and Holy Spirit, even as those three *hypostases* in turn presuppose God's self-identity as the Lord. To oversimplify for a moment, we may say that the one divine being correlates with God's freedom, that the three divine modes of being correlate with God's love, and that their perpetual unification correlates with God's eternal life. The trinitarian God is thus the living God who loves in freedom, or more technically, the Trinity is the *perichoresis* of the three *hypostases* in the one *ousia*.

The depth of the divine *ousia* is, for Barth, a single, self-identical subject, an acting I, the Lord, who is free and sovereign in trinitarian self-differentiation. The Lord does not exist in abstraction, for the one divine *ousia* exists in and only in the three divine *hypostases*. The three *hypostases* are, in turn, God's free subjectivity as the one Lord. The acting divine subject differentiates himself into three while yet remaining indivisibly one. He also unifies himself as three in the communion of his eternal life. This communion takes the form of mutual indwelling. *Perichoresis* means that the Father is in the Son, and the Son is in the Father, in the communion of the Holy Spirit, to all eternity. It means that each *hypostasis* participates in

169

the other *hypostases* completely. It means that they dwell in one another more closely, if possible, than a mathematical point, while yet retaining their essential identifying distinctions. In the trinitarian communion of God's love, the otherness of the other is not lost but enhanced. The Father remains the Father, the Son remains the Son, and the Spirit remains the Spirit in the midst of their mutual indwelling. Note that Barth does not see the divine *ousia* as a function of the *perichoresis,* as do some recent theologies, but rather the reverse. The *perichoresis,* states Barth, is "a further description of the *homoousia* of Father, Son, and Spirit" (I/1, p. 485). Although there is no *ousia* without the *hypostases,* and no *hypostases* without the *perichoresis,* the divine *ousia* is, in Barth's judgment, logically prior and determinative (I/1, p. 351).[5]

The relation between the one *ousia* and the three *hypostases* cannot, Barth contends, be captured by a single, unified thought. This contention, which separates Barth from all standard philosophical theologies and all theologies that seek ordinary coherence, is of far-reaching significance. Barth frankly acknowledges the "great difficulties" at this point that have typically beset trinitarian doctrine. "We, too," he states, "are unable to say how in this case 3 can really be 1 and 1 can really be 3. We, too, can only state that in this case it all has to be thus, and we can state it only in interpretation of the revelation attested in the Bible and with reference to this

---

5. Although Barth has sometimes been labeled a "modalist," the charge is mistaken. Two reasons seem to lie behind the mistake. First, Barth uses the term "mode of being" to translate *hypostasis.* He seems to prefer "mode of being" to "mode of existence," partly because "existence" is a term he usually reserves for human existence, and partly because he sees the *hypostases* as essential determinations of God's eternal *being (ousia).* "Mode of being" in this sense obviously has nothing to do with "modalism." The second reason relates to the way Barth connects God's Lordship and free subjectivity ("I am the Lord") with the divine *ousia* itself, to which he seems to grant logical and perhaps ontological precedence (though he sees both the *hypostases* and the *ousia* as primordial and ontologically basic). Modalism, however, means that the trinitarian *hypostases* are merely manifestations of God in history, but not essential distinctions within the eternal Godhead itself. For Barth, however, the trinitarian *hypostases,* each of which is fully God, coexist in, with, and for one another eternally and essentially. Barth repeatedly states that the living God would have been an eternal communion of love and freedom between the Father and the Son in the unity of the Holy Spirit, whether the world had been created or not. Nothing could be farther from modalism. "Social trinitarians," on the other hand, who are usually the ones making this charge, might ask themselves whether they can do as much justice as Barth can to the clear biblical witness to God as a single acting subject who is the Lord. In any case, modalism can be charged against Barth only out of ignorance, incompetence, or (willful) misunderstanding.

object" (I/1, p. 367). All our concepts are inadequate in the face of this trinitarian mystery. They are "radically ill-suited to this object" (p. 368). They
can only point beyond themselves to a truth they cannot properly express
(p. 429). The unity of God's oneness-in-threeness and threeness-in-
oneness is, states Barth, a unity for which "we have no formula, but which
we can know only as the incomprehensible truth of the object itself"
(p. 368).

Any attempt at conceptual closure at this point will, Barth argues, be
profoundly unsuitable. Either God's oneness will be stressed at the expense
of God's threeness, or God's threeness at the expense of God's oneness.
Barth's drastic alternative is a strategy of juxtaposition. The Lord God, he
asserts, is at once a single, indivisible subject, and yet also Father, Son, and
Holy Spirit. No harmonization of these predications is either possible or
worthwhile. No systematic unity or principle that resolves the antithesis
between them can be descriptively adequate. Adequacy at this point is a
higher virtue than consistency. By switching back and forth dialectically
between statements about God as one and statements about God as three,
Barth proposes to provide as descriptively adequate an account as might
be possible of a reality that is, by definition, inherently ineffable. "Theology," he writes, "means rational wrestling with the mystery. But all rational
wrestling with this mystery, the more serious it is, can lead only to its fresh
and authentic interpretation and manifestation as a mystery." On all sides
good care must be taken to see "that the *mysterium trinitatis* remains a
mystery" (p. 368). Since the reality of God's oneness and God's threeness
cannot be reconciled in thought, a "trinitarian dialectic" must be devised
in which statements to the one side are continually "counterbalanced" by
statements to the other. When the one is in the foreground, the other can
only be tacitly presupposed, and vice versa. In practice, therefore, the concept of God's triunity "can never be more than the dialectical union and
distinction in the mutual relation between two formulae that are one-
sided and inadequate in themselves" (p. 369).

Barth carries this basic dialectical strategy into many theological
questions. Two will be of special interest when we return to consider his
conception of eternity more directly. One concerns his understanding of
God's eternal life, and the other his understanding of God's perfection.
"Life," Barth writes, "is the fundamental element in the divine being" (II/1,
p. 322). To describe God as "the living God" is "no mere metaphor" (II/1,
p. 263). Nor does it merely describe God's relation to the world. It de-

scribes "God himself as the One he is" (p. 263). God lives first of all in and for himself. He would still be the living God even if he had never created the world and even if he had not acted to redeem it. In either case, "nothing would be lacking in his inward being as God in glory, as the Father, Son and Holy Spirit, as the One who loves in freedom" (IV/1, p. 213). God in no way needs the world in order to be who he is: the living God who loves in freedom. "God seeks and creates fellowship between himself and us, and therefore he loves us," writes Barth. "But he is this loving God without us as Father, Son and Holy Spirit, in the freedom of the Lord, who has his life from himself" (II/1, p. 257).

God's life takes a particular form. It resides in the "process of generation" whereby God "posits himself as the living and loving God" (II/1, pp. 305, 302). That is, God's life is the process by which he posits himself as the Holy Trinity. His life is a life of free distinction and communion in the *perichoresis* of the Father, the Son, and the Holy Spirit. In the freedom of his eternal love "God lives as he who is" (p. 307). God is the One who lives in the *perichoresis* of the three *hypostases,* "in their being with each other and for each other and in each other, in their succession one to another" (p. 297). Therefore, God's being, Barth concludes, does not exclude but includes becoming. If it is possible to speak of "an eternal self-realization" in God (p. 306), it can only be in the sense of a perpetual movement from perfection to perfection. The unity of the triune God is "the unity of a being one which is always also a becoming one" (I/1, p. 369). It is a unity always becoming one because perpetually positing itself as three. With respect to the Trinity Barth writes: "What is real in God must constantly become real precisely because it is real in God (not after the manner of created being). But this becoming (because it is this becoming) rules out every need of this being for completion. Indeed, this becoming simply confirms the perfection of this being" (I/1, p. 427). God's life in and for himself, his inner life in love and freedom, his being in the process of becoming, his one *ousia* in three *hypostases* in the process of *perichoresis,* is a perfect work *(opus perfectum)* that occurs in perpetual operation *(in operatione perpetuus)* (p. 427). In the dynamism of his one eternal life, God, who is his own basis, his own goal, and his own way from the one to the other, continually becomes who he is.

When speaking about God's perfections, Barth adopts the same dialectical method. Again, the unity of God's being is seen as so ineffable that it cannot be properly expressed by the concepts at our disposal. Instead of closure or a unified conception, Barth resorts once more to the strategy of dialectical interconnection and juxtaposition. Instead of a conceptual synthesis, he leaves us with an unresolved antithesis. What the antithesis describes is an ineffable unity-in-distinction. Theological description moves back and forth, repeatedly, from unity to distinction and back again, the one counterbalancing the other. Both the unity and the distinction describe God's being as a whole, not two separate parts that constitute the whole. Note that Barth does not think God's being is dialectical or antithetical in itself, only that our minds are incapable of grasping its unity through a single principle or system. Although the divine reality is unified, constant and stable in itself, it is also endlessly vibrant in its life. The best theological grammar available to describe it is dialectical and full of reversals.

Where other theologies speak of God's properties or attributes, Barth prefers to speak of God's perfections. "We choose the latter," he explains, "because it points at once to the thing itself instead of merely to its formal aspect, and because instead of something general it expresses at once that which is clearly distinctive" (II/1, p. 322). Other realities may have attributes, but only God has perfections. Note that his perfections are perfections of the Holy Trinity. God is the one Lord who distinguishes himself eternally as Father, Son, and Holy Spirit, and God is also the three divine "persons" who perpetually become one in the communion of their eternal life. God is, that is to say, the One who loves in freedom. "In this," says Barth, "he is the perfect being: the being which is itself perfection and so the standard of all perfection; the being, that is, which is self-sufficient and thus adequate to meet every real need; the being which suffers no lack in itself and by its very essence fills every real lack." The one true perfection of God, states Barth, is his loving in freedom as such, but this perfection is really lived out by him "and therefore identical with a multitude of various and distinct types of perfection." The one being of this God is "eternally rich." "To know him means to know him again and again, in ever new ways — to know only him, but to know him as the perfect God, in the abundance, distinctness and variety of his perfections" (p. 322).[6]

6. Barth specifies "the perfections of the divine loving" as grace, mercy, and patience (paired respectively with holiness, righteousness, and wisdom in correlation with God's freedom), and "the perfections of the divine freedom" as unity, constancy, and eternity (paired respectively with omnipresence, omnipotence, and glory in correlation with God's love).

The one God who posits himself as three is also the same God who posits himself as many. The three are his *hypostases* or concrete modes of existence; the many are his perfections. The many perfections of God confirm and glorify his oneness. "He is who he is and what he is," writes Barth, "in both unity and multiplicity. He is the one who is this many, and the many who are this one. The one is he who loves in freedom. The many are his perfections — the perfections of his life" (p. 323). At this point Barth sees "an exact parallel" to the doctrine of the Trinity (p. 326). "As it is of decisive importance not to dissolve the unity of the Godhead [*ousia*] tritheistically into three gods, but to understand the three modes of being [*hypostases*] strictly as the modes of being of the one God with whom we have to do in all his works, so it is of equal importance to interpret God's glory and perfections, not in and for themselves, but as the glory of the Lord who alone is able to establish, disclose and confirm them as real glory." Like the doctrine of God's *hypostases*, "the doctrine of God's perfections consists at every point only in the development and confirmation of the doctrine of his being [*ousia*]" (p. 327).

In drawing this trinitarian parallel, Barth separates himself from the venerable theological tradition that regards simplicity as more basic in God than multiplicity. Traditionally, it has typically been held that because God's simplicity is proper to his being, multiplicity can only be ascribed to his being improperly. "The life of God was identified with the notion of pure being," but this identification only shows that at this point "the idea of God was not determined by the doctrine of the Trinity" (p. 329). "The fundamental error of the whole earlier doctrine of God is reflected in this arrangement: first God's being in general, then his triune nature — with all the ambiguities and sources of error which must result from this sequence" (pp. 348-49). Barth agrees with this tradition about simplicity, but disagrees about its exclusion of multiplicity as supposedly improper to God. God's "simplicity" means that God's being is both singular and indivisible (pp. 442-45). The singularity and indivisibility of God are not denied, however, but upheld in traditional trinitarian doctrine. "The name Father, Son and Spirit," writes Barth, "means that God is the one God in threefold repetition. . . . He is God in this repetition, but for that very reason he is the one God in each repetition. . . . Identity of substance implies the equality of substance of the 'persons'" (I/1, pp. 350-51). The mystery of the Trinity at this point is precisely this: that because God's being in its simplicity admits of no parts or degrees, each of the three divine *hypostases,* in simultaneity with the other two, is fully and perfectly God.[7]

By carrying the trinitarian pattern over into his discussion of how simplicity and multiplicity are related in God's inner being, Barth again exemplifies the dialectical logic of his theology. "In God," he writes, "multiplicity, individuality and diversity do not stand in any contradiction to unity" (II/1, p. 332). Just because God's inner being is that of the Trinity, "God's being transcends the contrast of *simplicitas* and *multiplicitas,* including and reconciling both." Barth concludes: "If God is the God who is rich in himself, and if he is the one true God even in his works *ad extra,* we cannot emphasize either his *simplicitas* or his *multiplicitas* as though the one or the other *in abstracto* were the very being of God, as though the one inevitably excluded the other. We can only accept and interpret God's *simplicitas* and *multiplicitas* in such a way as to imply that they are not mutually exclusive but inclusive, or rather that they are both included in God himself." Moreover, just because God's inner being is that of the Trinity, the multiplicity of God's perfections must also be thought through in terms of the *perichoresis.* From this standpoint the unity of the divine perfections is not static but dynamic. The multiple perfections of God maintain their distinctive identity — not only for us but for God[8] — even as they perpetually become one (p. 333). What Barth says in a slightly different connection would apply also to the divine perfections: God's reality is of such a character that any one perfection exists with all the others, in the others, alongside of and after the others, in "an eternal simultaneity and successiveness" (p. 343). From this point of view once again, the unity of God — the unity of the one *ousia* in three *hypostases,* the unity of his freedom in love, the unity of his *simplicitas* in *multiplicitas* — "is dynamic and to that extent, diverse." Barth summarizes the dialectical logic: "What

---

7. It was essentially this insight into the divine mystery which enabled Athanasius to resolve the Arian crisis. See T. F. Torrance, "The Doctrine of the Holy Trinity according to St. Athanasius," in *Trinitarian Perspectives: Toward Doctrinal Agreement* (Edinburgh: T. & T. Clark, 1994), pp. 7-20.

8. Parallel to the distinctions among the *hypostases,* Barth sees the distinctions among God's perfections as real for God and not merely for us. In scholastic terminology, they are therefore *distinctionae formalis* and not merely *distinctionae rationis ratiocinatae.* In other words, these distinctions are not merely mental conveniences, but inherent in the being of God. See Richard A. Muller, *Dictionary of Latin and Greek Theological Terms* (Grand Rapids: Baker, 1985), p. 94.

we have here is, then, a complete reciprocity in the characterization of the one [divine] Subject. Always in this reciprocity each of the opposing ideas not only augments but absolutely fulfills the other, yet it does not render it superfluous or supplant it. On the contrary, it is only in conjunction with the other — and together with it affirming the same thing — that each can describe the [one divine] Subject, God" (p. 343).

A long and difficult tract of theology lies behind us. From it we may extract especially the following points. Barth is attempting to think through the reality of God in thoroughly trinitarian terms. Three main concepts therefore need to be taken into account and coordinated: God's being *(ousia)*, God's modes of being *(hypostases)*, and God's becoming *(perichoresis)*. God's being correlates with God's Lordship. As the Lord, God is one acting subject — indivisible, sovereign, and singular — the God who is supremely free. God's modes of being correlate with God's internal concrete relatedness. As Father, Son, and Holy Spirit, God is an eternal communion of love. The three divine "persons," each of whom is fully God, coexist simultaneously in mutual self-giving. Finally, God's becoming correlates with God's vitality. As the living God, God's being is in the process of becoming. This life process occurs independently of any relationship that God may have with the world. The triune God does not need the world for the sake of self-actualization, for this God is always already totally actual in the *hypostases* and perfections of his eternal life. Although God's being is simple and not composite, it not only includes various distinctions within itself, but these distinctions coinhere at once simultaneously and dynamically. Each distinction exemplifies the divine being as a whole without losing its particular distinctiveness.[9] No earthly analogy can capture the singularity of this God, whose mystery is best attested in theology by the adoption of a dialectical logic. With these points in mind, we are ready for Barth's conception of eternity.[10]

---

9. My use of the word "exemplify" needs to be taken in context. I use it in the sense of "hypostatize," that is, to render substantially and concretely existent. Here as elsewhere in dogmatic theology Hilary's dictum holds true: *Non sermoni res, sed rei sermo subiectus est* (*De Trinitate* 4). It is not the reality that is subject to the word, but the word to the reality. In other words, the object interprets the terminology, not the terminology the object (cf. Barth, *CD* I/1, p. 354).

10. Barth discusses eternity and time at regular intervals throughout the *Church Dogmatics*. What follows is a critical exposition only of the material on "the eternity of God" found in II/1, pp. 608-40.

Barth's Conception of Eternity:
Its Trinitarian Form and Content

God is eternal, Barth states, both "in himself" and "in all his works" (II/1, p. 608). God's being eternal in and for himself is independent of all his works, and yet also the basis of all his works. The distinction between God's being in and for itself and God's being in relation to the world will be of great importance in understanding Barth's conception of eternity. Unfortunately, Barth does not always keep this distinction clear as his exposition unfolds. Although certain ambiguities and difficulties arise as a result, I do not think they are finally insuperable.

Barth opens his discussion of eternity with a threefold distinction. He distinguishes between "pure duration," "beginning, middle and end," and "simultaneity." Roughly speaking, this distinction corresponds to the trinitarian distinction between being, modes of being, and becoming; or between *ousia, hypostases,* and *perichoresis;* or between freedom, love, and life. This distinction signals that Barth's discussion of eternity will be one long variation on a theme. The theme is the doctrine of the Trinity, now transposed into the key of temporality, but patterned to echo the same intricate trinitarian score.[11] Barth opens with a basic definition: "The being is eternal," he states, "in whose duration beginning, middle and end are not three but one, not separate as a first, a second and a third occasion, but one simultaneous occasion as beginning, middle and end. Eternity is the simultaneity of beginning, middle and end, and to that extent it is pure duration" (p. 608). Eternity, that is to say, is the mutual coinherence of three concrete temporal forms, distinct but not separate, that exemplify one undivided duration, identical with the *ousia* of God. Note that Barth does not mean to imply, by the way, that beginning, middle, and end can be simply equated with Father, Son, and Holy Spirit. There may be a loose correlation here, but it is not strict.[12] The trinitarian parallel is much more nearly formal than substantive. The same theological grammar that gov-

11. In his very severe criticism of Barth's conception, Richard H. Roberts fails almost entirely to take its trinitarian structure into account. "The relative worth of Barth's doctrine of the Trinity . . . is not of prime importance here" (Roberts, "Karl Barth's Doctrine of Time," in *A Theology on Its Way? Essays on Karl Barth* [Edinburgh: T. & T. Clark, 1991], p. 19). Much of Roberts's exasperation can perhaps be traced back to this oversight.

12. Each member of the Trinity, Barth states, is "all at once in his own essence undividedly beginning, succession, and end" (II/1, p. 615).

erns Barth's doctrine of the Trinity is being applied with suitable modifications to his conception of eternity — no more, no less.

The initial definition allows Barth to draw a categorical distinction between eternity and time. The three temporal forms of eternity — beginning, middle, and end — coexist simultaneously "without separation, distance or contradiction" (p. 608). Their mutual unity-in-distinction and distinction-in-unity signify their divine perfection. It is just this perfection that is lacking to time in its created form. "Eternity has and is the duration that is lacking to time," states Barth. "It has and is simultaneity." Eternity for Barth thus correlates with perfection, and created time with imperfection. Eternity is the perfect archetype and prototype of time, but time is merely the imperfect copy of eternity. Time's imperfection is its lack of unity, constancy, and simplicity, therefore its separation, division, or contradiction in its modes of beginning, middle, and end, its tendency toward dissolution and nonbeing. In this sense "time can have nothing to do with God." God's eternal being is not implicated in time's imperfection. "Eternity is not, then, an infinite extension of time both backwards or forwards" (p. 608). Nor is it ensnared in one and the same process of becoming along with the world. Its own unique process of becoming moves from perfection to perfection, from pure duration to pure duration, in the simultaneity of its own eternal forms. Eternity has no tendency toward dissolution and nonbeing just because it is pure duration.

Eternity and freedom, Barth observes, are linked in the scriptural depiction of God. "Whenever Holy Scripture speaks of God as eternal, it stresses his freedom" (p. 609). Eternity and sovereignty mark the ontological divide that distinguishes God from the world. Scripture sets God at the beginning and end of all things. It sets him high above and unfathomably beneath all that is not God. But it does so only to understand God as the one who is "utterly present" to humankind, and who "in his own person" has "complete power" over humankind (p. 609). The ontological otherness of God does not — as is often mistakenly concluded from Barth's famous use of the term "wholly other" — prevent God's immanence in the world. On the contrary, argues Barth, God's presence to the world is so pervasive, multiform, and rich, that it represents "the triumph of God's freedom in immanence" (p. 316). "God can be present to another," Barth writes. "This is his freedom. For he is present to himself. This is his love in its internal and external range. God in himself is not only existent. He is co-existent. And so he can co-exist with another" (p. 463). By contrast to modern processional views of eternity, God's immanence in the world is not an order of ontological necessity, but a decision of free and sovereign grace. God's immanence neither contradicts nor compromises his freedom, but rather exemplifies and expresses it. "To grant co-existence with himself to another," writes Barth, "is no contradiction to his essence. On the contrary it corresponds to it" (p. 463). Eternity thus correlates with the divine freedom to act and prevail in love. "Eternity is the source of deity in God," Barth concludes, "in so far as this consists in his freedom, independence and lordship" (p. 610). The eternal otherness of God is and guarantees this freedom. God is free to be constant in love, just because, being eternal, time has no power over him (p. 609).

Because eternity is the pure duration of God's being in and for himself, and therefore also of his being for the world, it cannot be defined merely as the negation of time. Eternity is rather the unique time of the triune God. It is the time of God's self-identity, self-differentiation, and self-unification, the time of the *perichoresis* of the three *hypostases* in the undivided divine *ousia*, the time of the divine life of divine love in divine freedom. In this sense eternity is not merely "timelessness." It does not merely exist as time's negative in the form of a bipolar opposition. Eternity is rather the positive mode of time unique to the Trinity. The classic definition of Boethius meets with Barth's strong approval, because it so aptly brings out that eternity is a positive rather than negative quality. *Aeternitas est interminabilis vitae tota simul et perfecta possessio*, wrote Boethius (*De consolatione philosophiae* 5.6). "Eternity is the total, simultaneous, and perfect possession of interminable life."

What Barth does with this definition, in effect, is simply to relocate it within an explicit doctrine of the Trinity. Life and simultaneity are, as we have seen, ideas that Barth associates with the trinitarian *perichoresis*. Totality, perfection, and possession are, in turn, ideas that correlate with the simplicity, singularity, and sovereignty of the trinitarian *ousia*. From this standpoint the one strikingly new element in the definition is "interminability." The definition states not merely that the divine life is endless or unlimited, but that it cannot possibly terminate, that it knows no possible dissolution, not only no tendency but no possible tendency toward nonbeing. Therefore the definition of eternity does not depend on the negation of time. "We know eternity primarily and properly," writes Barth, "not by the negation of the concept of time, but by the knowledge of God as the *possessor interminabilis vitae*. It is he who is the *nunc*, the pure present. He would be this even if there were no such thing as time" (p. 611). God is the sovereign possessor of pure self-presence, of interminable trinitarian life, of perfect love in perfect freedom, "before and beyond all time and equally before and beyond all non-temporality" (p. 611).

The ideas of simultaneity and totality, however, seem to imply certain distinctions not found in the Boethian definition. From a trinitarian standpoint, at least as Barth carries it through, they can be taken to imply temporal distinctions that correlate with the trinitarian *hypostases.* They are taken to imply, in other words, the distinctions of beginning, succession, and end. It is beginning, succession, and end that God possesses perfectly, simultaneously, and totally in his interminable trinitarian life. Note, however, that here is where Barth's account, as mentioned earlier, starts to become slippery and ambiguous. Although Barth fails to keep the distinction clearly before us, God's being as it is in itself needs to be more carefully distinguished, though not separated, from God's being in relation to the world than his account quite manages in practice, though it is surely what he intends. More precisely, Barth presupposes but does not always make sufficiently clear that God's trinitarian life includes a form of beginning, middle, and end peculiar to itself. The beginning, middle, and end that God possesses simultaneously and totally are, first of all, peculiar to the trinitarian *perichoresis,* to the eternal process of becoming, in which God moves from perfection to perfection in and for himself. This eternal becoming, in which his own absolute beginning, succession, and end are all present to God simultaneously — that is, his own eternal self-positing of himself as Father, Son, and Holy Spirit — in turn serves as the basis on which all creaturely time can be and is taken up by God and made present to himself in its totality simultaneously. In short, God also makes all creaturely time present to himself in the mode of simultaneity, and this simultaneity does not obliterate but upholds creaturely temporal distinctions. What makes the simultaneity of all creaturely time in God both possible and intelligible, however, is the prior simultaneity of God's own unique time in and for himself.

Barth writes: "God's eternity is itself beginning, succession and end. To this extent it also has them, not conditioned by them but itself conditioning as beginning, succession and end. It has them actively, not passively, not from another being or from time, but from itself and therefore in itself. God is both the prototype and foreordination of all being, and therefore also the prototype and foreordination of time. God has time because and as he has eternity" (p. 611). When Barth states here that eternity is beginning, succession, and end, he cannot be equating eternity with creaturely time. "Beginning, succession and end" can only mean those forms that are peculiar to God's trinitarian life in and for itself. Barth thus goes on to say that eternity has these temporal forms "not from another being or from time, but from itself." Just as God's *ousia* is presumably not conditioned by his *hypostases* but conditions them, so also God's eternity is not conditioned by the temporal forms it possesses but rather conditions them. It conditions them by possessing them simultaneously without losing their distinctions. These temporal forms in eternity are, in turn, the archetypes that serve as prototypes for the creaturely forms of beginning, succession, and end. They are the prototypes through which creaturely time, with its own peculiarities and limitations, is foreordained.

If this interpretation is reasonably correct so far, then it may help us when Barth delivers his zinger: "God has time because and as he has eternity" (p. 611). Recall Barth's previous statement that "time can have nothing to do with God" (p. 608). That one meant that God is not implicated in the imperfections of creaturely time. Taken in context, the new sentence can only mean that God nonetheless has *creaturely* time because and as he has eternity. Whereas the previous statement emphasized God's otherness from time, the new one highlights God's readiness for time. Eternity does not exclude but includes a certain peculiar mode of temporality, its own peculiar forms of beginning, middle, and end. In this mode they lack the instability that belongs to creaturely time as such. On the other hand, these forms are not merely static or frozen, for they coexist in a mode of dynamic simultaneity (p. 611). Because and as eternity has its own forms of beginning, succession, and end, it can and also does have a relationship to the creaturely forms of the same. The creaturely forms "are grounded and made possible and limited" by the eternal forms. Eternity decides, conditions, and controls them. Barth can therefore conclude that eternity "is itself that which begins in all beginnings, continues in all successions and ends in all endings" (p. 610). Eternity grounds time in its basic forms and surrounds it on every side.

In himself as pure eternity, God really has "time," that is, his own special mode of temporality, his own unique forms of beginning, succession, and end. Therefore he can and does have time for us, not just apparently or figuratively. That is, he has a basis in himself for a positive relation to creaturely time, a basis on which he can and does freely enter into time and take time for us. God has time, writes Barth, "and therefore time for us, in virtue of his eternity" (p. 612). The time God has for us is Jesus Christ. He himself is God's time for us. The time God has for us in Jesus Christ is "the time of his patience, our life-time, time for repentance and faith" (p. 612). It is a time uniquely grounded in eternity.

As the mediator between God and humankind, between heaven and earth, Jesus Christ is also the mediator between eternity and time. Eternity and time find their unity and their distinction in him. In him they are one while remaining distinct, and distinct while remaining one. In him eternity and time really have "fellowship" with one another (p. 616). In him, that is, they really coexist in the mode of mutual indwelling, of complete mutual participation and interpenetration, of *koinonia*. This fellowship or mutual indwelling has two vectors, as it were, one from above to below and the other from below to above. Although the two vectors coexist simultaneously, each one, as Barth understands it, describes this fellowship as a whole. Recall Athanasius's famous statement that "God became human in order that humans might become God" (*De incarnatione Verbi* 54). God's becoming human without ceasing to be God represents, so to speak, the downward vector, while humankind's elevation to God without ceasing to be human represents the upward vector. Transposed into a temporal key, we may say that eternity thus becomes time without ceasing to be eternal, and that time, in turn, becomes eternal without ceasing to be temporal.

At this point in the exposition, in other words, the logic of the doctrine of the Trinity intersects with the logic of the doctrine of the incarnation. As if each of these logics were not difficult enough on its own, the difficulties are now compounded. It may help if we think in terms of two different grammatical patterns. The trinitarian pattern, as we have seen, is a pattern of dialectical inclusion. It is a pattern in which three different forms of one indivisible being are perpetually generated and unified. The three forms, each of which represents the one being in its totality, eternally coexist in, with, and for one another simultaneously. They include one another in unity and distinction. The incarnational pattern, in turn, derives from the historic Chalcedonian definition. Formally speaking, it involves two terms and a relationship. The two terms, Christ's deity and his humanity, are related by a pattern of unity, distinction, and asymmetry. They are related, that is, "without separation or division" (unity), "without confusion or change" (distinction), and with a precedence allotted to Christ's deity and a subsequence to his humanity. What this Chalcedonian pattern governs is the fellowship between Christ's deity and his humanity.[13] It governs that fellowship in both its downward vector and its upward vector. It is from the standpoint especially of the upward vector that the point of intersection with the trinitarian pattern emerges most clearly into view.

From this point forward Barth's exposition may be divided into three parts. First, he looks at the downward vector, then at the upward vector, then at the intersection of the incarnational pattern with the trinitarian pattern. The downward vector concerns the entry of eternity into time, the upward vector concerns the elevation of time into eternity, and the intersection concerns the conjunction of simultaneity and sequence in the union of eternity with time.

The Downward Vector: The Entry of Eternity into Time

Along with the Trinity, the incarnation is the basis on which Barth understands the nature of eternity, the nature of time, and the nature of their relationship. He begins with the downward vector in order to show its implications for the nature of eternity.

> The fact that the Word became flesh undoubtedly means that, without ceasing to be eternity, in its very power as eternity, eternity became time. Yes, it became time. What happens in Jesus Christ is not simply that God gives us time, our created time, as the form of our own existence in the world. . . . In Jesus Christ it comes about that God takes time to himself, that he himself, the eternal One, becomes temporal, that he is present for us in the form of our own existence and our own world, not simply embracing our time and ruling it, but submitting himself to it, and permitting created time to become and be the form of his eternity. (p. 616)

The entry of eternity into time carries implications for the nature of eternity itself. It means that God has fashioned the shape of eternity so that, without ceasing to be eternity, it conforms with the shape of time. From

---

13. Note that the pattern is merely a formal device, but that the fellowship is a concrete, substantive reality.

this standpoint the incarnation is the fulfillment of creation. When God humbles himself in Jesus Christ by entering time, he becomes one of us, like us in all things. "In Jesus Christ," writes Barth, "God actually takes time to himself. He raises time to a form of his own eternal being." By conforming the shape of eternity to the shape of time, God does not contradict or diminish his deity. On the contrary, "the true and fullest power of deity is displayed in the fact that it has such power over itself and its creature that it can become one with it without detriment to itself." God is and remains "timeless" in the sense that God does not share in time's imperfections. Yet God is not merely temporal in the sense of being ready for time by virtue of his own special mode of temporality. By entering into time God actually takes time, created time, into himself. He makes it into "his own garment and even his own body." This appropriation of time by eternity is what happens in the downward vector. "This is just what takes place," says Barth, "in Jesus Christ. His name is the refutation of the idea of a God who is only timeless" (p. 616). From this standpoint eternity cannot be understood as "pure timelessness." For when the Word became flesh, eternity became time. "Without ceasing to be the eternal God," Barth writes, "God himself took time and made it his own" (p. 617, revised).

The Upward Vector: The Elevation of Time into Eternity

The entry of eternity into time also carries implications for the nature of time. When eternity enters into time, time does not remain untouched by eternity. Generally speaking, the creation is fulfilled and surpassed. The "positive relation of God to the world established by the creation" is fulfilled by the incarnation (p. 616). For time in particular this fulfillment means healing. It means that time's imperfection is transcended and overcome. In Jesus Christ and in every act of faith in him, "real created time . . . acquires the character and stamp of eternity, and life in it acquires the special characteristics of eternal life." The imperfections of time are healed by their contact with the perfection of eternity. When God enters time in Christ, he does not succumb to it. "He always maintains his superiority to it. When he subjects himself to time, he does freely what he does not have to do. He masters time. He re-creates it and heals its wounds, the fleetingness of the present, the separation of the past and the future from one another, as well as their separation from the present" (p. 617, revised). When God takes our time up into himself, he heals it by contact with the perfection of his love, "lifting it up to be the time of eternal life" (p. 618).

Note that time's healing is distinct from salvation from sin. Time's wounds, as here set forth, are inherent in the good creation. They may be exacerbated and corrupted by sin, but they are not identical with it, nor are they hostile to God. When measured by eternity, they are merely imperfections, not corruptions. Whether God would have become incarnate even if the world had not fallen into sin was, as we know, a question that Aquinas denied and Duns Scotus affirmed. Barth, however, regarded it as speculative and unanswerable when stated in that form. Nevertheless, Barth here approaches the position of Scotus. He affirms that, among other things, the incarnation resolves a plight logically independent of sin, namely, the plight of transitoriness and dissolution into nonbeing. He does so, however, in a remarkably Thomistic way. Although Barth disagreed with the standard Thomistic understanding of nature and grace as applied to sin, he agreed with it as applied to transitoriness. Barth agreed with Aquinas, in other words, that in the work of healing time, grace does not destroy nature, but rather perfects and exceeds it.[14]

Note also that the upward vector depends entirely on the downward vector. The fact, in other words, that eternity includes a potentiality for time does not mean that time includes a potentiality for eternity. Time is not coeternal with God. In itself and as such it does not share at all in the predicates of eternity (p. 614). Nor does time cease to be time even in its healing. Although the creature tastes eternity through its fellowship with God, "it does not on that account itself become God and therefore eternal" (p. 609). Time remains time, only in a healed and eternal form, a form that for now can only surpass our understanding. Time's healing, in any case, comes to time strictly from without as the gift and miracle of grace.

---

14. For an analysis of the disagreement between Barth and Aquinas on nature and grace with respect to sin, see my essay "Baptized into Christ's Death: Karl Barth and the Future of Roman Catholic Theology," in *Disruptive Grace: Studies in the Theology of Karl Barth* (Grand Rapids: Eerdmans, 2000), pp. 253-78. Briefly, with respect to sin Barth held that grace is the *Aufhebung* of nature, thereby incorporating a strong element of negation (the cross) overcome in turn by the negation of the negation (the resurrection).

The Conjunction of Simultaneity and Sequence: The Union of Eternity with Time

Time does not exist, Barth concludes, apart from eternity's embrace. Eternity embraces time on all sides, preceding, accompanying, and fulfilling it. To say that God is eternal means that God is "the One who is and rules before time, in time, and again after time, the One who is not conditioned by time, but conditions it absolutely in his freedom." God does this in three ways. "He precedes [time's] beginning, he accompanies its duration, and he exists after its end." This threefold relation is "the concrete form of eternity as readiness for time" (p. 619). The temporality of eternity is thus distinguished into pretemporality, supratemporality, and posttemporality. These are the three forms of eternity in its relation to time. Like the three divine *hypostases* of the Trinity, each embodies eternity as a whole, and like them each exists in simultaneous coexistence with the others. Finally, in analogy to the trinitarian *perichoresis,* each coinheres with the others dynamically, moving in its own inherent teleology from perfection to perfection, always the same yet ever new.

Each form of eternity's readiness for time will now be taken up in order.

1. God is pretemporal. God's existence precedes human existence and that of all things. "God was in the beginning which precedes all other beginnings. He was in the beginning in which we and all things did not yet exist. He was in the beginning which does not look back on any other beginning presupposed by this beginning itself. God was in himself. He was no less himself, no less perfect, not subject to any lack, superabounding from the very first even without us and the world" (p. 621). God is who he is perfectly in his pretemporal mode of existence. For he is who he is before the world and without it. He is, that is to say, the Holy Trinity. "This pretime is the pure time of the Father and the Son in the fellowship of the Holy Spirit" (p. 622). God's eternal existence as the Holy Trinity precedes his relationship to the world, and everything in his relationship to the world presupposes his eternal existence as the Trinity. The Trinity is therefore the presupposition of creation, reconciliation, and redemption. It is also the presupposition of God's pretemporal decision of election. In this "pure divine time" of perfect trinitarian existence, "there took place," writes Barth, "the appointment of the eternal Son for the temporal world, there occurred the readiness of the Son to do the will of the eternal Father,

and there ruled the peace of the eternal Spirit — the very thing later revealed at the heart of created time in Jesus Christ."

The mysterious coinherence of eternity with time in the incarnation, together with the equally mysterious coinherence of God's pretemporality with God's supratemporality, means, as the New Testament regularly attests, that Jesus Christ existed "before the foundation of the world." "For Jesus Christ is before all time, and therefore eternally the Son and the Word of God, God himself in his turning to the world, the sum and substance of God insofar as God chose to create and give time, to take time to himself, and finally to fix for time its end and goal in his eternal hereafter." Everything temporal is predestined in Jesus Christ. Everything temporal comes from God's free eternal love. Everything temporal is penetrated and ruled by this free love from all eternity. In his pretemporal turning to the world, "and with it to a time distinct from his eternity, this God, Yahweh Sabaoth, is identical with Jesus Christ" (p. 622).

2. God is supratemporal. This term is adopted for lack of a better alternative. It means not only that God is over time, but that God also exists with time and even in time. God not only embraces time on all sides, accompanying it at all points, but also pervades time from within, radiating out in all directions from a center within time itself, namely, from the event of the incarnation. The incarnation is "the concrete form" of eternity in its supratemporal significance.

> God's eternity is so to speak the companion of time, or rather it is itself accompanied by time in such a way that in this occurrence time acquires its hidden center, and therefore both backwards and forwards its significance, its content, its source and its goal, but also continually its significant present. Because, in this occurrence, eternity assumes the form of a temporal present, all time, without ceasing to be time, is no more empty time, or without eternity. It has become new. This means that in and with this present, eternity creates in time real past and real future, distinguishes between them, and is itself the bridge and way from the one to the other. Jesus Christ is this way. (p. 627)

The real future that eternity creates in time is the future of eternal life in communion with God. The real past, in turn, is the past of sin and death as abolished in the cross of Christ. This old reality of sin and death is "continually opposed" by the new reality of eternal life, even as the new reality "comes breaking in triumphantly" again and again (p. 627). Jesus Christ stands between the old reality and the new. "In him the equilibrium between them has been upset and ended. He is the way from the one to the other and the way is irreversible. He is the turning." Therefore "the past is that from which we are set free by him, and the future that for which we are set free by him" (p. 628). "To have time and to live in time means to live in this turning. In this turning we live — not in eternity, but in the real time healed by God, the time whose meaning is immediate to God." Time is not therefore essentially a process of dissolution leading only to nonbeing and death. For "time has acquired its middle point in Jesus Christ, and has therefore been made new" (p. 629).

3. God is posttemporal. This statement completes the idea of eternity as that which embraces time. God is after all time and after each time.

> We move to him as we come from him and may accompany him. We move towards him. . . . He is when time will be no more. For then creation itself, the world as a reality distinct from God, will be no more in its present condition, in everything which now constitutes its existence and being. . . . For everything will have reached its goal and end. Man here and now reconciled to God will be redeemed. . . . The meaning and necessity of all ways and movement are fulfilled and exhausted in it. It is the perfection which remains, so that over and beyond it there is no new horizon. This perfection is God himself in his post-temporality. (p. 629)

God is not only the beginning of all beginnings, but the end of all endings. He is "the Last as he was the First. He is, therefore, the absolute, unsurpassable future of all time and all that is in time." The end of all things will mean final judgment. God will look back and judge everything, deciding "how far it has really been, just as he had already decided when it did not exist." Everything will be gathered up and sifted through. "Corresponding to this judgment, all that has been will be before him what it must be, accepted or rejected, acquitted or condemned, destined for eternal life or eternal death." God will be the fulfillment or the demise of each one.

The end of all things will also mean the final revelation. God's kingdom is real in some strong sense even now, although its reality is concealed from us. "It is only in its revelation that the kingdom of God is posttemporal and therefore lies in the future. . . . God's revelation stands before us as the goal and end of time." At the end of all things we shall no longer believe in God's kingdom. We shall see it. "It will be without the concealment which surrounds it in time and as long as time continues" (p. 630). "We shall then have that for which we must now pray, and which we do really receive in its fullness, but in the veil of hope, so that we must continually pray for it again."

In short, God himself in his posttemporal form is the eternity toward which we move. "To this extent he is the God of hope, the imminent peace which is prepared and promised to his people, into which it has not yet entered but will enter." He is the fulfillment which we await and for which we hope and pray. "God has and is also that which so far we do not have and are not" (p. 631). What God is yet to be at the end, he is already in himself, and has been from the beginning; and what he is yet to disclose to his creatures, he will also finally impart; and what he will finally impart to them will be a share in his own unsurpassable, irreversible, and interminable glory and life.

Barth stresses, finally, that, in analogy to the trinitarian *hypostases* (p. 639), no rivalry can exist between the three forms of eternity (p. 631). Each form needs to be emphasized in its own way. They are not to be played off against one another, as has too often occurred in the history of theology. They coexist together in union with time in a real simultaneity that is also a real sequence. In the beginning, middle, and end, in equal divinity — in the same love and freedom — God is the one and all. "So then," Barth writes, "if we are to love him and know him, we must give him equal attention and seriousness in all three dimensions. . . . We must emphasize this, because when our thinking is by nature systematic, it is so easy to be guilty of some kind of preference, selection or favoritism in this matter, and therefore of the corresponding omissions" (p. 631).

The internal distinctions of eternity reflect the life of the triune God. "Eternity is really beginning, really middle, and really end, because it is really the living God. There really is in it, then, direction, and a direction that is irreversible. . . . There is no uniformity in it. Its forms are not to be exchanged or confused" (p. 639). They coexist simultaneously in a perichoretic unity-in-distinction and distinction-in-unity, moving dynamically in perfection from perfection to perfection, and therefore from their pretemporal beginning through their supratemporal middle to their posttemporal end (p. 640).

Although eternity is surely "a complete mystery," Barth states that it is also "completely simple." It is as mysterious and as simple as the Trinity itself. But in any case, it is the pure temporal essence of the living God. "In the last resort when we think of eternity, we do not have to think in terms of either the point or the line, the surface or space. We have simply to think of God himself, recognizing and adoring and loving the Father, the Son and the Holy Spirit. It is only in this way that we know eternity. For eternity is his essence. He, the living God, is eternity. And it is as well at this point, in relation to the threefold form of eternity, to emphasize the fact that he is the living God" (p. 639).

Mysterium Trinitatis:
Barth's Conception of Eternity

BRIAN LEFTOW

There's a lot to like in Prof. Hunsinger's paper. For instance, he has Barth nailed when he says his treatment of eternity is "the doctrine of the Trinity . . . transposed into the key of temporality." He also puts his finger squarely on what I find to be the most perplexing part of his topic, that for Barth "in some strong sense eternity is timeless [and yet] eternity is a mode of time that is peculiarly God's own. . . . It is as though he were saying: 'God is temporal, and yet God's temporality is unlike any time that we know.'" I think Prof. Hunsinger's point that for Barth the doctrine of God's eternity is "a subtopic in the mystery of the Trinity" can help us resolve the time/ timelessness puzzle. I'll try to show how.

Two Views of Eternity

Western theists agree that God is eternal. They also agree on some things this entails, e.g., that

  i. *God exists forever,* and
 ii. *God existed before the universe did.*

Where they disagree is on how to interpret such claims as (i) and (ii). Some take (i) to assert simply that God exists at all times, i.e., has always existed, exists now, and will always exist. These take (ii) to assert straightforwardly

191

that there was a period of time during which God existed and the universe did not yet exist. These theists hold that God is temporal, or exists "in" time.

Others, for a variety of reasons, think temporal existence does not befit God. One argument that it does not runs this way: Lives in time have parts that are wholly past, parts now going on, and parts yet to come. If part of one's life is wholly past, one can no longer live it. One can only remember it. If part of one's life is yet to come, one cannot yet live it. If one thinks about it at all, one can only anticipate it. Now if one's life has sad, bad, or painful parts, it can be good to have them over, and good not even to think about what may be yet to come. But had God never created a world whose sin and pain might grieve him, or become incarnate to save it, his life would have had no sad, bad, or painful episodes.[1] In this case there would have been nothing in God's life which it would be better to have over with, or to ignore or merely anticipate. Thus it would have been better if God's life had no wholly past or future parts — and so God, as a perfect being, would have had a life "outside" time, i.e., not divided into past, present, and future parts. But whether one lives "in" or "outside" time is a matter of one's nature.[2] And creating the world did not change God's nature. So if God would have been "outside" time had there been no world, he actually is outside time.

Atemporalists must give more complex accounts of (i) and (ii). For atemporalists, (i) asserts only that at every time it is true to say that God exists. But this is not (they say) because God exists *at* these times. If I am here and you are there, it is true here to say that you exist, but not because you are located here. I, here, say that you exist (over there). So too, say atemporalists, when I say truly that God exists, I, here (in time), say truly that God exists (over there, outside time). For an atemporalist, (ii) might say there was a period of time during which the universe did not yet exist and it was true to say that God existed.[3]

---

1. This is a conditional proposition. It does not imply that God's life *does* have any negative episodes, and it is compatible with the truth of *this* conditional: had God created a world whose sin and pain might grieve him, and become incarnate to save it, his life would have had no sad, bad, or painful episodes. In short, I here take no position on whether God is impassible.

2. Some recent philosophers would question this step in my argument. See, e.g., Thomas Senor, "Divine Temporality and Creation Ex Nihilo," *Faith and Philosophy* 10 (1993): 87-89. But I give this argument only as a sample of atemporalist reasoning, and defending it further would take us too far afield.

3. This is not the only or the best atemporalist reading of (ii), but we need not seek a better for this paper's purposes.

The Problem

Debate over what it is for God to be eternal tends to focus on one question: Is God temporal or atemporal, "in" time or "outside" time?[4] Barth's treatment of God's eternality is one of the most perplexing parts of his work. What makes it perplexing is simply this: Barth seems to hold both that God is temporal and that God is atemporal.

Barth begins his treatment of eternity this way:

> The being is eternal in whose duration beginning, succession and end are not three but one, not separate as a first, a second and a third occasion, but one simultaneous occasion as beginning, middle and end. Eternity is the simultaneity of beginning, middle and end, and to that extent it is pure duration. . . . Time is distinguished from eternity by the fact that in it beginning, middle and end are distinct and even opposed as past, present and future. Eternity is just the duration which is lacking to time, as can be seen . . . in the temporal present and in its relationship to the past and the future. Eternity has and is the duration which is lacking to time. It has and is simultaneity. (p. 608)

Two points stand out here. One is that the eternal present *lasts*, rather than passing into the past: "above all, His present does not imply any fleetingness" (p. 640). This is why eternity is "pure duration" and "just the duration which is lacking to time," whose present passes away. The other is that while time consists of the past, the present, and the future, in eternity there is only a present, not a past or future. Were there an eternal past, the eternal present would pass into it, and were there an eternal future, it would take the eternal present's place. If there were either, there would not be a *simultaneity* of beginning, middle, and end in Barthian eternity. Instead, beginning would be past when middle was present, and so on.

Now consisting of past, present, and future is a core, paradigmatic property of time. So if Barthian eternity lacks past and future, it appears not to be a form of time. Barth seems to confirm this: "Eternity is not time. . . . Eternity has and is the duration which is lacking to time. . . . Time can have

---

4. Barth rejects this focus. See Karl Barth, *Church Dogmatics* II/1 (Edinburgh: T. & T. Clark, 1957), pp. 610-11 (hereafter cited in the text). But all the same, he does have a position on this.

nothing to do with God. . . . [E]ternity . . . is in fact non-temporality"
(p. 608). Yet Barth also writes that "God was before we were. . . . His existence precedes ours . . . not . . . only in its own way in correspondence with
its essence and dignity [but] physically as well" (p. 621). Here Barth replies
to Boethius, who wrote that a timeless God preceded the world not by some
amount of time but by the simplicity of his nature — which was supposed
to make it in some way superior to ours.[5] Barth insists: God was in addition
literally, physically, temporally before the world. But time (we think) just is
a tissue of before/after relations. Anything that exists before something else,
we think, is ipso facto in time. So given his insistence that God stands in be-
fore/after relations, it is hardly surprising for Barth to say that "Eternity is
. . . God's time and therefore real time" (p. 613).

It can thus seem that Barth's God is and is not in time, i.e., that Barth
simply contradicts himself. There are also smaller puzzles within this main
puzzle. For if eternity is time, it is not a time with a past and a future: "'before' in Him does not imply 'not yet'; 'after' in Him does not imply 'no
more'" (p. 640). But how can this be? And is this in fact what Barth means?
For he also writes that in eternity there is "peace between . . . present, past
and future, between 'not yet,' 'no' and 'no more'" (p. 612). If there is peace
between these things, one thinks, surely they are *there* to be in peace.

I will not address the smaller puzzle here. But I do think Barth avoids
contradiction in the larger matter. I soon try to show how.

Barth and Boethius

As Hunsinger notes, Barth quotes with approval Boethius's definition of
eternality as *interminabilis vitae tota simul et perfecta possessio* (p. 610).
Boethius simply took this definition over from pagan Neoplatonist philosophers. He did nothing to integrate it with his Christian theology. It occurs, in fact, only in his *Consolation of Philosophy,* a work whose Christian
ties are so minimal that some have doubted that Boethius wrote it. The
definition became standard for medieval Christian theologians. But there
too, there was nothing especially Christian about it. It was simply a bit of
useful philosophy.

Hunsinger tells us that Barth relocates this definition "within an ex-

5. Boethius, *Consolation of Philosophy* V, prose 6, 38-40.

plicit doctrine of the Trinity." He is right. One of Barth's concerns in writing of God's eternality is more fully to Christianize the doctrine. Barth tries to Christianize it both epistemologically and metaphysically. The metaphysical move — not that Barth would so call it! — is what helps with the time/timelessness puzzle. But let me first talk about the epistemological move.

Barth makes his epistemological move when he refuses to let the Platonic treatment of the concept of eternity as simple atemporality dominate his thinking: "Eternity is the *nunc* which is . . . not subject to the distinctions between past, present and future. But again, it is not subject to the abolition of these distinctions. . . . The theological concept of eternity must be set free from the Babylonian captivity of an abstract opposite to the concept of time" (p. 611). Instead of treating eternality as sheer atemporality, Barth picks and chooses among the properties Platonism allots to the temporal and those it allots to the eternal. The doctrines of the Trinity and the incarnation guide his choices. So Barth treats these as epistemically prior to anything he might adopt from pure metaphysics. Barth has a metaphysical reason for doing so (again, not that he'd call it that!). It is that, as he sees it, every property in the Boethian definition has its being as a function of and as determined by the divine life, not vice versa.

Barth makes this point plainest with a set of concepts which do not figure in the Boethian definition: "That . . . eternity . . . does not possess beginning, succession and end is true only to the extent that it is not 'possessed,' qualified, dominated and separated by them as by a general principle of being foreign to itself. Insofar as [eternity] is itself the sovereign God it does also possess beginning, succession and end. . . . It decides and conditions [and] controls them" (p. 610). In other words, God's nature, not some independent nature of time, determines what beginning, middle, and end are.[6] So when he lets trinitarian concepts control temporal concepts rather than vice versa, Barth reflects the true relation between them (as he sees it).

---

6. Barth adds that God's eternity "is itself that which begins in all beginnings, continues in all successions and ends in all endings" and is their "prototype" (p. 611). Here he in effect treats eternity as the Platonic form for beginning, succession, and end, in which temporal beginning, succession, and end imperfectly participate. In this light too ought we (I think) to take Barth's claim that "time . . . has its ultimate and real being in the *simul* of eternity" (p. 613).

Barth's epistemological move has a metaphysical underpinning. But Barth's metaphysical move proper — his metaphysical Christianizing of the concept of eternity — is to fill in the content of Boethius's definition in trinitarian terms. I now set out how Barth does this.

Boethius's definition took being eternal as a way of living. If being eternal is a way of living, God's actually being eternal is his living his life. What is a life? My life begins at birth and is going on now. Birth is its first event, or else something in my mother's womb was. Right now I am living its present event. A life, then, is just a causally connected sequence of events which happen to the same person. Of what events does the life of God consist? Hunsinger tells us that for Barth "God's life is the process by which he posits himself as the Holy Trinity." Barth himself says, "The inner life of God is the life of Father, Son and Spirit. . . . His life resides in this process of generation" (p. 305).[7] A process is just a causally connected set of events. So Barth's answer — I agree with Hunsinger — is that God's life consists of the inner-trinitarian events, the Father's begetting, the Son's being begotten, etc. Thus for Barth, God's being eternal *is* his being the Trinity, i.e., his living the events of begetting, spirating, etc. Eternality is just "the form of the divine being in its triunity" (p. 615) — i.e., just an abstract facet of being triune.

If God's being eternal is just his having a life consisting of the trinitarian events, Boethius's definition, by referring to God's life, implicitly refers to the doctrine of the Trinity.[8] This is Barth's metaphysical Christianizing of Boethius's definition.

Hunsinger notes that for Barth "eternity is . . . the positive mode of time unique to the Trinity." Here he echoes Barth's claim that eternity is "the absolutely unique time of God distinct from all other times, but for that reason true time" (p. 616). Some reasons this is true, I now suggest, are tied closely to Barth's "reduction" of God's eternality to God's being triune.[9]

What is time? Augustine could not answer, but I will. The word "time"

7. George Hunsinger's paper in this volume drew my attention to this text.

8. It is the definition's talk of God's life which particularly appeals to Barth: cf., e.g., II/1, p. 611.

9. Barthian eternity is at least epistemically a form of time. For we have only temporal terms with which to describe eternity. So just because time is eternity's imperfect image, eternity is at least epistemically a form of time: it is something for which temporal terms, appropriately qualified, are the least inadequate description. But Barthian eternity also qualifies as a sort of time objectively.

has at least two main uses. We use "time" to refer to the actual sequence of causally linked events that make up history, in such sentences as "throughout time there have been quarks." It is time in this sense that the incarnation heals, in Barth's account. A variant on this first use takes "time" to refer to the sequence of causally linked events that make up *one item's* history. In this use "time" is a kind of synonym of "life": we can say "his life on earth was short" or "his time on earth was short" with equal good sense.

This simple answer lets us see one reason why Barth calls God's eternity a form of time. For on Barth's view God's being eternal is his living a life, a sequence of causally linked events making up his history. To live a life is to live a time, in one use of "time." So on Barth's view, God's being eternal is his living a time. The events which make up God's "time," for Barth, are begetting, spirating, etc. — those which "posit" the triune persons. So God's life is a time in the present sense, just because it consists of the trinitarian events. This is part of what Barth is getting at, I think, when he writes that in

> the *nunc aeternitatis* . . . is . . . the inner movement of the begetting of the Father, the being begotten of the Son and the procession of the Spirit . . . in it there is order and succession. There is a before and an after. God is once and again and a third time, without dissolving the once-for-allness. . . . If in this triune being . . . of God there is nothing of what we call time, this does not justify us in saying that time is simply excluded in God. . . . On the contrary, *the fact that God has and is Himself time, and the extent to which this is so, is necessarily made clear to us in His essence as the triune God.* (p. 615, emphasis added)

Succession, before, and after are the characteristic relations which make time time; but here they are traits of the inner-trinitarian events. In the Trinity God is "once and again and a third *time*" — i.e., in a first, second, and third event. In this passage God's having and "being" time, though in his being "there is nothing of what we call time," is his having a life consisting of the trinitarian events.

In a second main use, "time" refers to a general form any other possible history would have shared. We see this use in such sentences as "Time has a direction" or "Time consists of past, present, and future." Now Barth, we have seen, also writes that eternity is God's "time, the absolutely real time, the form of the divine being in its triunity" (p. 615). Now for Barth, God is necessarily triune. Being in three persons is of his essence. So for

Barth, just as "time" can refer to a general form any other possible creaturely history would have shared, "eternity" can refer to the general form any other possible divine history would have shared. Barthian eternity is the divine mode of time in this second sense.

God's life is (or is in) a form of time in this sense even if it is not "in" our time, or has few or none of the properties we associate with time in the second use of "time." But in fact, on Barth's account God's eternity has a direction, as time does (p. 639).[10] Time moves from past to present to future. Eternity, as Barth sees it, "moves" from Father to Son to Spirit.[11] (Does this make the Son the privileged center of the Trinity, as the present is the privileged center of time?) But it does not "move" as time "moves." The past is over, the future yet to come. But for Barth nothing in God's life is ever over. The Father eternally begets. The Spirit — the "future" in the Trinity — is as fully present as the Father. This is what Barth means when he insists that God's beginning, middle, and end endure, and are simultaneous. That there is direction in the Trinity's life does not entail that the persons do not exist simultaneously.

As this is so, Barth's talk of "movement" is best taken as a way of indicating a *causal* direction, a set of dependence-relations among events: the Father's begetting *causes* the Son's being begotten, and so eternity "moves" from Father to Son. But this does not entail that Barth's talk of this direction as temporal is mere metaphor. Many theories of time base its direction on that of causality. It would accord well with such theories to take the causal direction of eternity as the foundation for a timelike or temporal direction.

We have an account of how the Trinity is the core of Barth's account of God's eternity. We also have a first step toward unraveling the time/timelessness puzzle, for we see at least some of what Barth means by calling eternity a form of temporality.

Barth's View

I now suggest that Barth does have a view of eternity that is not obviously inconsistent. I make my case for this by providing models or analogies for

10. Barth calls eternity's direction "irreversible" (p. 639), having already said of the direction from Father to Son to Spirit that there is no "possibility of its reversal" (p. 615).

11. So p. 615: "this *principium ordinis* is . . . a *principium temporis* in God Himself."

the various claims Barth makes, and (where appropriate) for their con-junctions. Barthian eternity is a set of event(s) — the events of God's life. Barth, I suggest, makes at least seven claims about these events.

Barth holds that in eternity there is no past or future. We can take this as a claim that

(1) Eternal events do not occur before or after *each other*.

Barth holds that in eternity there is only a present, and that all of eternity is "one simultaneous occasion" (p. 608). We can take this as a claim that

(2) All eternal events occur at once.

Note that (1) does not imply (2). One could hold (1) and also hold that eternal events are not simultaneous either — if one held that no temporal or timelike relation could link eternal events.

To continue, for Barth there is direction and movement in eternity. Per what I said earlier, we can take this as a claim that

(3) Eternal events are *causally* ordered in such a way as to count as begin-ning, middle, and end.

Holding (2) and (3) commits Barth to holding that causes and their effects can occur simultaneously, but while this view is controversial, so is its de-nial. Again, for Barth God is pre-, supra-, and posttemporal (pp. 619, 623-24). We can take this as a claim that

(4) Eternal events all take place literally before, during, and after each temporal event.[12]

This is not controversial on its own. One event A can occur before, during, and after another event B: this happens whenever A begins before B and ends after B, for then A has a part before, a part during, and a part after B. Nor is the conjunction of (2) and (4) strange. For it can happen that two or more events AB begin at once before and end at once after an event C. Then AB, as wholes, stand in before and after relations to C but not to each other. A and B as wholes are then simultaneous with each other, but not with C. This provides at least an analogy with Barth's view, which is that God stands in before/after relations to *us*, but his life does not involve them *internally*. For Barth God's life is *totum simul*. But its events, which

12. For the claim that they literally take place *during*, see p. 623.

are "one simultaneous occasion," are, in their simultaneity, in our past, present, and future. This fact also provides a sense in which the eternal present lasts: for its events are in an everlasting simultaneity. On this reading the lasting of the eternal present involves duration through time. But it does not contradict my reading that Barth writes that "eternity is not an infinite extension of time both backwards and forwards" (p. 608). For it is not this lasting through time that *makes* God eternal.

Barth also asserts that

(5) It is not the case that occurring before something makes an event temporal.

For on his account such events as the Father's begetting the Son occur *before* anything temporal. Yet they are not temporal, but eternal. So for Barth there is some further condition for being temporal which such events as the Father's begetting the Son do not meet. To defend (5) Barth needs to defend a "thick" account of being temporal, one on which being temporal takes more than occurring before or after something. But this sort of account is quite respectable. For instance, the standard four-dimensional interpretation of special relativity: on its account, being temporal requires being before or after something *and* having a position in space.

Given his claim about the Father's begetting, etc., for Barth,

(6) Being nontemporal is compatible with standing in temporal relations, and

(7) Being an event does not require being temporal.

(7) may be about as defensible as a "thick" account of being temporal. For on any "thick" account there may be events which are not temporal. For instance, if we have souls and these think, their thoughts will be mental events which have no location in space, and so flunk the requirements for being temporal which are embedded in special relativity's standard reading. Still, even given (7), one could argue that any genuine event must be able to stand in before/after relations, and so defend (6).

(1)-(7) form a complex picture. But if they are inconsistent or contradictory, they are not *obviously* so. My analogies are reason to think that they are not so at all. So while Barth does have an argumentative burden to shoulder, the critic who would charge him with contradiction has one at least as heavy. This depiction of Barth hinges on the claim that for him eternity is a set of events. So it once more points us to the centrality of the Trinity in Barth's account.[13]

When Hunsinger writes that Barth's treatment of eternity is "as though he were saying: 'God is temporal, and yet God's temporality is unlike any time that we know,'" he resolves the time/timelessness puzzle on the side of saying that Barth's God is temporal. My account agrees with him. As I see it, Barth's God is temporal. What makes him eternal, i.e., differentiates his life from ours, is his enduring through time as the Trinity. I am not sure that I am right in this, for there is a great deal else in Barth's account of eternity of which (1)-(7) take no account. But at the least, I hope, they represent one *strand* of Barth's thinking, and if they do, at least one strand of it may well be consistent.

13. I am indebted to George Hunsinger for pointing out how central trinitarian considerations are to Barth's account.

Epilogue: Barth as a Teacher

JOHN D. GODSEY

The year was 1953. It was summertime when I, with my wife and two children, aged seven and eight, arrived in Basel, Switzerland. Fresh from graduation at the Theological School of Drew University, I was on the verge of fulfilling a dream: to study with Karl Barth at the University of Basel! That spring Paul Lehmann, as a visiting professor from Princeton, had taught a course at Drew entitled "The Theology of Crisis," which enhanced my growing interest in Barth, and my mentor at Drew, Carl Michalson, had urged me on with these words: "If you want to pursue a doctorate in theology, why not do it with the world's most outstanding theologian!" I wrote to Barth of my intentions, and he wrote back that if I came, he would be willing to consider my becoming one of his doctoral candidates.

So here I was in Basel, the city familiar to both Erasmus and Calvin, the city where Oecolampadius led the Reformation in the sixteenth century, the city where Karl Barth was born in 1886, and though he had grown up in Bern, the city where Barth had lived since his ouster from Germany by the Nazis in 1935. Basel, the beautiful, ancient city in the heart of Europe where three countries meet. Basel, an awe-inspiring combination of medieval charm and modern commerce and industry, divided by the Rhine River into Greater Basel and Lesser Basel, two parts connected by lovely bridges and, at strategic points, by small flat-bottomed boats that ferry passengers from one side to the other and are attached to overhead cables and propelled by the strong current of the river. Basel, with its impressive red-sandstone cathedral, the Münster, built on a high bank overlooking the Rhine, and many other fine churches scattered around the city; its Museum of Fine Arts with its Holbein paintings; its Market Place, with the daily colorful display of flowers and produce; its city hall with its sixteenth-century clock facing the square and its seventeenth-century murals in its courtyard; its opera and theaters and hotels and train stations, its buses and streetcars and bicycles. Basel, with its peculiar dialect, which only the natives could understand. And finally, on the hill above the Market Place, the university, built around Peter's Square (Petersplatz), with its gleaming new main building where Barth lectured — as did his well-known colleagues on the theological faculty: Cullmann, Staehelin, Eichrodt, Baumgartner, van Oven, Thurneysen, Reicke, Schmidt, Buess, among others, and on the philosophy faculty, Karl Jaspers and Barth's younger brother Heinrich.

Upon arrival, I joined a wonderful community of Americans, often with spouses, who were either already pursuing or beginning to pursue doctoral studies at the university. Also working with Barth were John Deschner, Shirley Guthrie, Charles Hall, and Paul van Buren. James Wharton was in Old Testament and Gilbert Thiel in church history. Coming later but overlapping with me were Jack Bailey, James Cox, Neill Hamilton, and John Yoder. Others who studied in Basel but were not doctoral candidates were Paul (Bud) and Betty Achtemeier, Harold Nebelsick, and Calvin Seerveld, and English speakers from other countries included David Torrance from Scotland, Emilio Castro from Uruguay, and David Bosch and Johannes Lombard from South Africa. Many others on sabbatical leave or studying in other European universities came for short periods of time to hear Barth. And a German student whom you at Princeton know very well was in Basel taking his doctorate under Cullmann while I was there: Karlfried Froehlich!

The big attraction in Basel for all of us, of course, was Karl Barth himself. In 1953 he was sixty-seven years old, but in good health and quite vigorous and productive. Behind him were his tumultuous years in Germany: his teaching at Göttingen, Münster, and Bonn, and his leadership in the Church Struggle during the Nazi period. Behind him was the Second World War, when he did military patrol along the Rhine; it had been over for eight years. Behind him was his address at the founding of the World Council of Churches at Amsterdam five years previously, and the subsequent debate with Reinhold Niebuhr. We were now in a new era. On the theological scene, Barth was dealing with Bultmann's proposal to demythologize the New Testament; politically he was criticizing the West's attitude toward Russia and its conduct of the cold war. Barth may have mellowed some with age, but he had lost none of his critical powers. Nor had he lost any of the vital interest in his family or in his parishioners at the Basel jail. And of course, his lecturing and writing continued apace, as did the smoking of his pipe. Regarding the latter, you may recall Martin Niemöller's saying about theologians: if you were a liberal, you smoked cigarettes; if you were conservative, you smoked cigars; but if you were a Barthian, you smoked a pipe!

That fall I began attending Barth's lectures on dogmatics. What was he like as a lecturer? I don't think I can improve on a description given by Marie Fuerth Sulzbach in a 1954 article in the *Christian Century* entitled "Karl Barth — a Portrait." Here is what she wrote:

> Four times a week, at four o'clock in the afternoon, some 160 students gather in Dr. Barth's big, ultramodern classroom at the university. About a quarter past four they begin to stamp their feet on the floor — their traditional method of applause. Walking slowly up to the lecture desk is a big rumpled bear of a man with tousled gray hair and glittering spectacles. Carefully he puts down his worn briefcase, extracts a sheaf of paper and arranges it before him. Carefully he takes off his spectacles and exchanges them for a blacker and heavier pair. Then he begins: "Meine Damen und Herrn . . ."
>
> For the next hour and a half the students listen to a new section of the great *Dogmatics*. They are the first in the world to hear it, for Dr. Barth's lectures are the "growing end" of his work. Each has been dictated to his secretary only that day or the day before. He makes corrections on his manuscript as he lectures, and later, after further corrections, the lecture and its companions are sent to the printer. It takes about three semesters of lectures to make up one volume of the *Dogmatics*.

This account of Barth's lectures accords with my memory, except at two points: first, I remember applause being the banging of your knuckles on your desk, the scraping of feet on the floor being a sign of disapproval of something that had been said; and second, I recall the lectures as lasting one hour rather than an hour and a half. But otherwise, Sulzbach's description is right on target. During my three years at Basel, from the winter semester of 1953 through the summer semester of 1956, Barth was lecturing on what became volume IV, part 2 of the *Church Dogmatics,* that is, that part of the doctrine of reconciliation entitled "Jesus Christ, the Servant as Lord," and it was obvious that he enjoyed working on this section dealing with sanctification, a doctrine dear to the hearts of theologians in the Reformed tradition. At times Barth spoke with such passion that you thought you were hearing a sermon, and he used facial expressions and gestures to emphasize important points. On a hot day he would take a handkerchief from his pocket and frequently mop his brow. He was in no sense an unapproachable, aloof professor, but one who was outgoing and open to students. He possessed a powerful mind, enormous energy, a sharp wit, and a fine sense of humor. But he seemed not to think too highly of himself. After all, how could he — and still be a disciple of a crucified Lord?

Barth's weekly teaching schedule was very demanding. In addition to the four lectures on dogmatics, he held a so-called Sozietät for German-speaking students only; a systematics seminar, which was limited to about thirty regular participants but open to many more students who sat behind the others and could simply listen and observe; and finally a colloquium, held on alternate weeks for English-speaking and French-speaking students. Barth was at his best in these smaller settings: probing, challenging, correcting, and inspiring. He loved the give and take, the argument and debate. But he would abide no nonsense. A German student in a seminar on Schleiermacher tried to curry favor by using Barth's own arguments against Schleiermacher's theological position, and Barth cut him off, declaring: "Your first obligation is to read Schleiermacher himself and come to understand him from the inside; only then do you have a right to criticize him."

Barth's systematic seminars were held not on the main university campus but in the theological seminar building overlooking the Rhine River. The room he used was adorned with a marble bust of Schleiermacher, so that one could hardly fail to connect the two theologians. Barth conducted his seminars by having one student present a so-called Protokoll, a running account of what had taken place at the previous session, and then another student would present a précis of the reading assignment for the day. After that the discussion would begin. During my six semesters the subject matter of the seminars was as follows: (1) Luther's writings of 1520; (2) the Christian hope (the theme of the Evanston Assembly of the World Council of Churches held in the summer of 1954); (3) Luther and the "Schwärmer" ("Enthusiasts" or "Fanatics"); (4) Schleier-macher's *Speeches on Religion* ("Reden"); (5) Schleiermacher's shorter theological writings ("Monologen," "Weihnachtsfeier," and "Kurze Dar-stellung des theologischen Studiums"); and (6) the Roman Catholic doc-trine of the church.

The English-speaking colloquium held every other Tuesday evening was a special delight because of the intimacy and the language spoken. What began with a few students sitting around the dining room table at Barth's home on Pilgerstrasse, a few blocks from the university, soon had to be relocated because of the growing number of students, first to the Theological Seminar Building and then, when Barth had to move from Pilgerstrasse and bought a house a few miles from the university on Bruderholzallee, to a private room in the nearby Bruderholz Restaurant. The new location, high on a hill overlooking the city, was easily accessible by streetcar, and the proprietor of the restaurant allowed Barth to hold the colloquium there so long as everyone bought something to drink: coffee, tea, soft drinks — and on a cold night Barth might have *Glühwein*.

The subject matter of the colloquium was Barth's own writings. Dur-ing my years of participation we covered volume I, part 1 of the *Church Dogmatics*, as well as four significant monographs: *Church and State, The Christian Community and the Civil Community, The Teaching of the Church regarding Baptism,* and *The Christian Understanding of Revelation.* One student would prepare a précis of the assigned reading for the session, ending with a few questions to stimulate dialogue. Barth would deal with these questions and then entertain questions from others. If you are inter-ested in the questions and answers, I invite you to read the book *Karl Barth's Table Talk,* which was published by John Knox Press in 1963. I will give you one example. A student asked about human freedom. Does free-dom mean you can say yes and no to God? Barth answered:

> The decisive point is whether freedom in the Christian sense is identi-cal with the freedom of Hercules: choice between two ways at a cross-road. This is a heathen notion of freedom. Is it freedom to decide for the devil? The only freedom that means something is freedom to be myself as I was created by God. God did not create a neutral creature, but His creature. He placed him in a garden that he might build it up; his freedom is to do that. When man began to discern good and evil, this knowledge was the beginning of sin. Man should not have asked

this question about good and evil, but should have remained in true created freedom. We are confused by the political idea of freedom. What is the light in the Statue of Liberty? Freedom to choose good and evil? What light that would be! Light is light and not darkness. If it shines, *darkness is done away with,* not proposed for choice. Being a slave of Christ means being free. (p. 37)

Barth's English was not the best, but he managed to communicate well. He had never studied the language in school but had learned it when middle-aged with the help of President John Mackay of Princeton, who on a visit had instructed him in the basics and urged him to practice by reading British mystery novels. His favorite mystery writer was Dorothy Sayers, and when he had to move from Pilgerstrasse he took from his attic a large box of mysteries and offered them to those of us who spoke English as "a gift from above"!

Barth's new house on Bruderholzallee was more spacious and inviting. When you knocked on the door, you would usually be met by Frau Nelly Barth, a small, soft-spoken woman who would usher you up the stairway, at the top of which on the left was the doorway leading to Barth's office. On the wall as you ascended were hung sizable pictures of many of the theologians one finds in Barth's *Protestant Theology in the Nineteenth Century,* and just inside on the wall of his office were pictures of Calvin and Mozart hung side by side at the same height. Over his desk was Matthias Grünewald's painting of the crucifixion, with John the Baptist standing below the cross on one side, pointing his bony finger toward the tortured body of Jesus and saying, "He must increase, I must decrease." Alongside his desk was a record player and many records, mostly of Mozart's music, which he played morning and evening. It reminded him of the joy of God's creation.

Barth's office was lined with books from top to bottom, and in an adjacent office, likewise lined with books, sat Fräulein Charlotte von Kirschbaum, Barth's research assistant, secretary, and theological companion — the woman who typed almost all of the *Church Dogmatics!* She had lived in the Barth household since 1929. A warm and friendly and competent woman, she was, in a sense, Barth's alter ego, an indispensable confidant, adviser, and friend. She accompanied him to every lecture, seminar, and colloquium, but sat quietly and never entered into any discussion. She was particularly helpful to students by making appointments, providing bibliographical information, and sometimes sitting in on discussions about dissertations. Since Barth did not own a car, she and he rode the streetcar to his classes and used the garage in the basement of the house for storage of more books and files. Some of those books, by the way, were about the American Civil War, about which Barth had an intense interest, not only because since a boy he liked to study military strategy and maneuvers, but because he believed the Civil War was the decisive event for understanding America, especially its problem of racism. As he once put it, "The South was never pacified."

As a doctoral candidate I had several meetings with Barth. Mainly we would discuss matters of my dissertation topic, namely, the theology of Dietrich Bonhoeffer, but sometimes we would talk about incidents in his own life or his views about this or that. I will give you two examples. The first concerns a meeting with Bonhoeffer. Barth had had no contact with Bonhoeffer for several years when in 1931 Bonhoeffer appeared at the Swiss border at Basel and was stopped by the border guards. Bearing a Nazi-endorsed pass, he was headed for Geneva to use his church contacts on behalf of the conspirators against Hitler who were trying to eliminate him and bring the war to an end. Bonhoeffer had become a civilian employee of the Abwehr, the German Military Intelligence Agency in which the conspiracy was centered. Because of their suspicions, the Swiss police would not let Bonhoeffer enter without someone to vouch for him. So Bonhoeffer called Barth and asked him to do so. Barth agreed to vouch for him, but only on the condition that Bonhoeffer visit him on his way back to Germany and explain what he was up to. On his return Bonhoeffer stopped at Barth's house and told him all about the resistance movement and the plans to overthrow Hitler and make peace with the Allies. Barth told Bonhoeffer that he was not at all happy with the leadership of the military officers in the resistance plan, because he was afraid that if the coup succeeded, the military might not be willing to relinquish power and set up a democratic government. In that case the situation might be no better than before. But Bonhoeffer felt that the chance was worth taking. Their frank discussion meant that any doubts Barth had about his friend Bonhoeffer were totally allayed.

On another occasion I asked Barth how much of the Barmen Declaration he wrote, and he said he wrote all of it except nineteen words added by Hans Asmussen. And then he told me this story. When members of the Lutheran, Reformed, and United churches who were opposed to the

Nazification of the church in Germany decided to come together in Barmen on May 29-31, 1934, they appointed three persons to work on a common theological declaration for the meeting. These were Thomas Breit, a Lutheran from Bavaria; Hans Asmussen, a Lutheran from the Old Prussian Union; and Karl Barth, a representative of the Reformed. Breit wrote the other two to meet him at a hotel in Frankfurt, where they could work out the declaration together. This they did, and during the morning they outlined the six points they wanted to make and decided on their plan of action. They would eat lunch at the hotel, then each go to his room and work out his own statement concerning the six areas, beginning at two and ending at five o'clock. Then they would come together at five, compare what each had written, and work out a common statement based on their three contributions.

Lunch arrived, and it was a fairly heavy one, served with wine, and afterward there was coffee and liqueur and big black cigars. Then they went to their separate rooms. Barth ordered more coffee to be sent to his room and set to work, writing the whole declaration as it now stands, Bible quotations and all, between two and five (all, that is, except for the nineteen words noted above). At five o'clock there was a knock at the door. Asmussen entered and sheepishly explained that he had fallen asleep and slept the whole time. A bit later Breit came and exclaimed, "Oh! Ich habe geschlaffen!" (Oh, I went to sleep!). Both the Germans had lain down for their afternoon nap, a custom in Germany, had overslept, probably because of the wine and liqueur, and came with blank sheets of paper, whereas Barth, not accustomed to the nap, had written the Barmen Declaration! The other two men readily accepted his work, and thus it was that this Swiss Reformed theologian ended up writing the declaration or confession for the most important synod during the Church Struggle. Sometime later Asmussen made a special trip to Bonn to ask Barth if he could make a small addition to point 2, and Barth said, "Sure!" The words, as translated into English, are these: "Through him (Christ) befalls us a joyful deliverance from the godless fetters of this world for a free, grateful service to his creatures." Barth's comment on the whole affair was the following: "Church history is probably full of queer incidents like this!"

Three events in 1956 linger in my memory. The first was Barth's memorial address celebrating the 200th anniversary of the birth of Wolfgang Amadeus Mozart on January 27, 1756. Tickets went on sale on January 18, and the event took place at 10:45 A.M., January 29, in the Great Auditorium in the Stadtcasino in downtown Basel. A string quartet playing Mozart's music entertained an overflowing crowd, and Barth gave a spirited address. His enthusiasm for his subject was evident, and also his delight at being asked to speak on this auspicious occasion. He, a mere theologian, was paying tribute to this world-renowned composer before hundreds of music lovers! Barth submitted the text of his address for inclusion in the Paul Tillich Festschrift, *Religion and Culture: Essays in Honor of Paul Tillich.* As he commented later, "the golden sounds and melodies of Mozart's music have from early times spoken to me not as gospel but as parables of the realm of God's free grace as revealed in the gospel — and they do so again and again with great spontaneity and directness. Without such music I could not think of that which concerns me personally in both theology and politics" (*How I Changed My Mind,* p. 72).

The second event occurred not long after the birth of my daughter Gretchen on the first of February. Barth and Frl. von Kirschbaum paid a visit to our apartment to see this latest addition to our family. Gretchen was lying peacefully in her crib. Barth leaned over and looked at her, then turned to me with a twinkle in his eye and asked: "Do you think she has original sin?!"

The third event was the great seventieth birthday celebration for Barth, which was held in the university's student affairs house at 7:30 P.M. on May 11, one day after the actual date of his birthday. In attendance were not only Basel faculty and students, but prominent theological colleagues, former students, and friends from all over Europe. The music of Mozart was played, and a large portrait of Barth was ceremoniously unveiled near the entrance on the first floor of the building. After Barth spoke words of appreciation, the crowd proceeded to the bottom floor, which had been turned into a huge banquet hall. Following dinner, several tributes were paid to Barth and a large Festschrift entitled *Antwort (Response)* was presented. It contained seventy responses to Barth's theological work. Believe it or not, Barth suspended his lectures on dogmatics during the upcoming summer semester so that he could write each contributor a personal letter of thanks! We American students wanted to do something typically "American" to mark the occasion, so my wife baked a large cake, which we decorated with seventy candles. At the right moment, we lit the candles and one of us proceeded cautiously up to the head table where Barth was sitting. I have a picture of him blowing out the candles as we sang "Happy Birthday" to an amused Karl Barth! All in all, it was an unforgettable evening!

I have already spoken of Barth's keen wit and humor, but now let me give you a few examples, some of which were supplied to me by friends.

1. A graduate student asked Barth: "What is the role of reason in your theology?" Barth answered: "I use it."

2. A man on the street who was introduced to Barth asked him if he knew the great theologian. "Know him?" Barth replied. "I shave him every morning!"

3. After the service in a parish church where Barth had been preaching one Sunday, he was met at the door by a man who greeted him with these words: "Professor Barth, thank you for your sermon. I'm an astronomer, you know, and as far as I am concerned, the whole of Christianity can be summed up by saying 'Do unto others as you would have others do unto you.'" Barth replied: "Well, I am just a humble theologian, and as far as I am concerned, the whole of astronomy can be summed up by saying 'Twinkle, twinkle, little star, how I wonder what you are.'"

4. Asked about his view on temperance, Barth quipped: "One may be a non-smoker, abstainer, and vegetarian, yet be called Adolf Hitler!"

5. A theological professor from Scandinavia who visited Barth spoke a great deal about sin and the devil. Had Barth sufficiently taken these powers into consideration? After a long discussion, Barth asserted that the matter could be summarized thusly: "We are united in Christ, but not united in the devil."

6. When an American doctoral candidate in Old Testament told Barth that Professor Baumgartner had proposed that he write a dissertation on "the place of animals in the Old Testament," Barth said, "I hope you find something nice to say about pigs." When asked "Why?" Barth replied: "Because I love pork chops!" When the student had finished his research, he told Barth that he was sorry, but he really couldn't find anything nice to say about pigs. Barth replied: "Schade, aber nicht zu schlimm. (It's a pity, but not too bad.) My doctor has forbidden me to eat pork any more."

7. Sometime before Barth's seventieth birthday celebration, Frl. von Kirschbaum showed me the picture of Barth that was to be used in the Festschrift *Antwort*. I asked her if I could have a copy, and she said yes. On hearing this, Barth turned to me and said, "I just want to

remind you of one thing, Herr Godsey: remember the second commandment!"

8. Paul Tillich had been to Bethlehem and stopped off in Basel on the way home to visit his old friend Karl Barth. With great excitement he told Barth of his visit to the Church of the Nativity. He recounted going down into the crypt where there was a silver star, marking the birthplace of Christ. "Karl," he said, "on that star there is an inscription 'Hic verbum Dei caro factum est,' 'Here the Word of God was made flesh.' You know, Karl, that sums up the whole of my theology — all except for that 'hic'!" "Ah, Paul," Barth replied, "that 'hic' sums up the whole difference between your theology and mine."

9. Finally, Barth could joke about his own work, while at the same time making an important point. "The angels laugh at old Karl," he wrote. "They laugh at him because he tries to grasp the truth about God in a book of Dogmatics. They laugh at the fact that volume follows volume, and each is thicker than the previous one. As they laugh, they say to one another, 'Look! Here he comes now with his little pushcart full of volumes of the Dogmatics!' — and they laugh about the persons who write so much about Karl Barth instead of writing about the things he is trying to write about. Truly, the angels laugh."

Karl Barth — he was truly a remarkable human being! As Bonhoeffer observed after visiting him in Bonn in 1931, "Barth in person is even better than his books." After my departure from Basel in 1956, I saw him on four more occasions. In June of 1958, with dissertation complete and accepted, I returned to Basel for my oral examinations with Cullmann, Staehelin, and Barth. After these were over, Barth invited me to lunch at his home. We had a delightful luncheon and celebrated the fact that I had passed the exams. Moreover, we were joined by Frau Barth, Frl. von Kirschbaum, and Barth's theological assistant Hinrich Stoevesant, which made the time even more special. The second time I saw Barth was in Princeton in 1962, when he was on his American tour. I heard his lectures in the Princeton University Chapel, and some of us who had been his students in Basel had an opportunity to visit with him and Frl. von Kirschbaum. Finally, when I was on sabbatical leave in Göttingen during the school year of 1964-65, I visited Barth twice: first in September of 1964, when I found him ill and in the hospital, and then on June 9, 1965, when I spent over two hours with him alone in his study. He had recovered his health, and we had a wonderful conversation about many things.

In speaking of his illness the previous fall, he reported that his successor at Basel, Heinrich Ott, had had an audience with Pope Paul VI while attending a meeting in Rome, and when learning of Barth's hospitalization, the pope said he would pray for him. "Believe it or not," said Barth, "the next day I was better!" He also reported that he had received a letter from Albert Schweitzer, who had heard of his illness and had sent his condolences — a letter he said touched him deeply. Also, he said that none of his doctors had forbidden him to smoke his pipe, and he was grateful! "Die Pfeife brennt noch immer!" he quipped — "The pipe burns as always!"

Now that he was feeling well again, Barth said he was enjoying reading the works of some of the younger theologians: Jüngel, Moltmann, Pannenberg, and others. He was also eagerly awaiting the third volume of Bruce Catton's history of the American Civil War. In relation to the Civil War, he recounted this story. On July 2, 1963, he had participated in the oral examinations of an American doctoral candidate at the university. Because of the date, he couldn't resist the temptation to test the student's knowledge of his own heritage. "Do you know what happened in your country 100 years ago today?" he asked. When the student admitted that he didn't know, Barth said, "Shame on you. It was the second day of the Battle of Gettysburg!"

Barth asked if I noticed anything different about his office, and I observed that he had a new desk and chair. He beamed and asked if I knew the whereabouts of the old ones. I said no, and he then told me they were now on display in the library of Pittsburgh Theological Seminary! It seems that Donald G. Miller, president of Pittsburgh Seminary, had visited him in Basel and had asked if his seminary might have the desk and chair Barth had used while writing the *Church Dogmatics,* explaining that in exchange he would receive new ones. Barth snapped up what he considered to be a good bargain. After showing me the file drawers in the desk and the rollers on his comfortable chair, he said, "These are so much more beautiful than my old ones. I feel like a bank president! Perhaps one could say of me, 'In his old days he has become modern.'"

I asked Barth if he would write any more volumes of the *Church Dogmatics,* and he said: "Probably not. After all, I have already written enough for people to read. When people ask me about a thirteenth volume, I am inclined to ask if they had finished the first twelve!" He compared his unfinished work to the Strasbourg Cathedral, which has only one tower although the plan called for two. "There is a certain merit," he said, "to an unfinished dogmatics; it points to the eschatological character of theology!"

I left Barth that day, the last time I saw him, with those words on my mind: "the eschatological character of theology." I could close these reminiscences on the same note, but instead I choose to end with some words of Barth about the doctrine of election: two passages from Robert McAfee Brown's fine introduction to his English translation of Georges Casalis's *Portrait of Karl Barth:*

> Barth asserts that God deals with human beings "not with a natural Therefore, but with a miraculous Nevertheless." (CD II/2, 315) The sequence is not "humans are unworthy, *therefore* God rejects them," but rather "Humans are unworthy, *nevertheless* God elects them." That is why humans can hope, why they can believe, why they can trust in God. (p. 18, translation altered)

And finally, this:

> The gospel is not the mystery of incomprehensible darkness (as it has often been for the orthodox) but the mystery of incomprehensible light. It is not that we see so little of what God has done that we are puzzled, but that in the light of God's revelation in Christ we see so much of what God has done that we are dazzled. (p. 18)

Karl Barth — a man dazzled by the gospel, dazzling as a witness! A man whose guiding light was the Word of God, who followed the light of that Word with faithfulness and integrity throughout his adult life, and who found his journey as a disciple of Jesus Christ to be sustained by the joyful and comforting presence of God's grace-filled Spirit. The world is not likely to see another like him!